Marketplace Trade and West African Urban Development

Krys Ochia

Marketplace Trade and West African Urban Development

A Paradox

Krys Ochia
Gainesville, FL, USA

ISBN 978-3-030-87558-9   ISBN 978-3-030-87556-5   (eBook)
https://doi.org/10.1007/978-3-030-87556-5

This Palgrave Macmillan imprint is published by the registered company Springer Nature Switzerland AG
The registered company address is: Gewerbestrasse 11, 6330 Cham, Switzerland

CONTENTS

ABBREVIATIONS

ACET   African Center for Economic Transformation
AMATAS   Amalgamated Market Traders Association of Anambra State
CBD   Central Business District
DMaT   Department of Marketplaces and Traders
EASI   Enable, Avoid, Shift, Improve
GDP   Gross Domestic Product
IMF   International Monetary Fund
IMT   Intermediate Means of Transport
MMI   Mobility Misery Index
MODEST   Marketplace-oriented Development Strategy
OECD   Organization for Economic Co-operation and Development
OMATA   Onitsha Market Traders Association
ONA   Onitsha-Nnewi-Awka
P3   Public-Private Partnership
SAR   Special Administrative Region (Hong Kong)
SBA   Small Business Administration
SCORE   Service Corps of Retired Executives (Founded 1964)
SNA   Social Network Analysis
SSATP   Sub-Saharan Africa Transport Program
TNC   Transportation Network Companies
TOD   Transit Oriented Development
TSP   Traffic Signal Priority
TWG   Technical Working Group
TZS   Tanzania Shilling
UMDD   Urban Marketplace Development District
UMDDC   Urban Marketplace Development District Committee

UN	United Nations
UTP	Urban Transportation Planning
VAT	Value Added Tax

LIST OF FIGURES

LIST OF TABLES

CHAPTER 1

Introduction

Researchers, planners, development practitioners, and policy makers are encouraged to refocus attention on large urban marketplaces and traders that dominate the economy of cities in (West) Africa because of their linkages to urban transport. As the urban population increases, it will expand the size of the informal economy in these areas, in the absence of a strong formal economy. As a result, this book is framed around the following themes to evaluate the linkages and address the existing gap in urban development in (West) Africa:

- The sociology of complex marketplace relationships forces traders to engage in non-discretionary out-of-stall business contacts during business hours. These contacts are necessary for sustaining the financial viability of the stall, family, and ultimately the urban economy.
- These contacts are unexplored and largely unknown, but they have unintended negative impacts on urban transport. Despite the undeniable linkage between large urban marketplaces and transport, planners, development experts and policy makers have neglected to consider the marketplace institution in urban development through policy and project planning and that has created a paradox in (West) African urban development.
- To contextualize the neglect, Onitsha market-stall traders dump between 10.2 and 14.7 million mean annual trips on the urban road

© The Author(s), under exclusive license to Springer Nature Switzerland AG 2022
K. Ochia, *Marketplace Trade and West African Urban Development*, https://doi.org/10.1007/978-3-030-87556-5_1

1

system; therefore, planners should consider reimagining the urban transportation planning process to repurpose trader travel data to reflect, integrate, and underscore the marriage between marketplace trade and urban traffic conditions to address The Paradox.

- From its strategic command post of the urban economy, the marketplace institution continues to contribute to reduce urban unemployment and income inequality. Because of their daily numerical strength, structural economic power, and complex internal community activities, a large urban marketplace functions as and should be recognized as a (business) city within a (general) city.
- Consequently, the Urban Transportation Planning process should rely on the travel behavior of traders for core data source in a meaningful UTP process in these areas. The travel behavior reflects the differently-structured social and unstructured economic frameworks in motion that is reinforced by low motorizations levels and narrow urban road system. Adopting a universal UTP process that relies on data from households and driver behavior is improper for useful urban transport planning in (West) Africa.
- Existing large (West) African marketplaces should be recognized and administered as growth poles within an Urban Marketplace Development District, UMDD, with ¼ mile radius around the district prioritized for urban improvements. Constructing new marketplaces or modernizing existing large urban markets with the necessary infrastructures will create backward linkages to address urban traffic problems; and,
- (West) African governments should consider institutionalizing marketplace development design standards and creating a Department of Marketplaces and Traders, DMaT, like the creation of Ministry of Women's Affairs that elevated gender discrimination issues. Relevant stakeholders should be represented in an Urban Marketplace Development District Committee, UMDDC, to collaborate in future urban development projects that prioritize the marketplace institution in the urban economic space.

As the power struggle between formal and informal economy rages on and more traders become middle-class earners, while some critics push for formalization of the informal economy, how do urban development regimes recognize and integrate a reimagined and repurposed planning process and marketplace-centered policies to promote urban development in (West) Africa? Is de-marketizing Africa the answer, or should (West) African countries nurture, embrace, elevate, and sustain large urban marketplaces for continued urban economic growth within a non-formal (formerly known as informal) economic framework that should be a co-equal of the formal economy? These crucial questions facing humanities in the (West) Africa region deserve globally-structured answers from relevant stakeholders.

Presently, in (West) African cities, traders and the marketplace institution dominate the local economy and large urban marketplaces constitute unofficial cities during business hours. This work considers these unofficial cities as business cities within general cities. A World Bank Group publication observes that being an African reduces the probability that an individual is an entrepreneur in the manufacturing sector by more than 95% (World Bank, 2003: 167). Upon analyses of the urban informal economy in Dakar, Senegal; Cotonou, Benin; and Ouagadougou, Burkina Faso, Benjamin and Mbaye (World Bank, 2012) affirmed the aphorism that in West Africa, a dynamic informal economy dominates the stagnant formal economy, instead of the reverse. These will contribute to explain why there are books and research materials mainly on formal and informal economies, microenterprises and entrepreneurs, small and medium size enterprises, street vendors, and female rural/urban market traders, but there is limited knowledge of men and women who occupy permanent stalls in large urban marketplaces who constitute the major actors in the urban informal economy. In addition, there is lack of knowledge about out-of-stall business contacts made by these traders that result from maintaining complex social and economic relationships around which their traditional business management and operational structure revolve. More importantly, these contacts are generally unexplored and largely unknown, but they exert significant unintended and unaccounted consequences on the urban mobility system; therefore, there is the need to rethink urban transport planning processes in these areas, as these contacts are mainly concentrated during non-peak travel times. Researchers, planners, development practitioners, and policy makers have not focused their attention and considered the impacts created by the urban economic powerhouse, the marketplace, and its daily trader residents, and developed appropriate evidence-based policies and plans for framing meaningful urban development in these areas, and that is the paradox surrounding marketplace trade and urban development in West Africa.

The urban travel behavior of dominant informal economy stall traders has a linkage to the condition of urban traffic in developing areas. We posit that addressing trader marketplace needs will contribute to addressing urban mobility problems. There is a need to stop relying on peak-hour home-based driver travel information for transportation planning and urban development, because to do otherwise will tantamount to purposefully neglecting the differences between the Global South and North in economic structure and socio-cultural characteristics that yield differing travel behaviors. Neglecting the travel behavior framed around a dominant and persistent informal economy in the South that is spatially and characteristically different from the travel behavior structured around efficiently moving individuals during peak hour from their residences to work and school in a highly motorized formal Western economy is simply unrealistic. There will be a pushback for this paradigm shift from those who are committed to maintaining the status quo in transport planning and development ethos, the glaring differences notwithstanding. They must reconsider it as a part of on-going global renaissance on social justice through introspection that encourages challenging long-held biases in order to yield the desirable culture change. This must be the appropriate time to revisit the insistence that home-based peak-hour travel behavior of drivers stay the international gold standard for conducting urban transportation planning. Consider the recommendation (Smart City, December 26, 2017) for a smart transport system in developing nations: In order to reduce infrastructure investment in additional roads and metros, the writers recommend that (African) cities shift trips to non-peak hours. For cities with large urban marketplaces, the economic structure has made non-peak travel 'routine,' and it is already contributing to all-day traffic congestion. Meanwhile, the International Labor Organization is seriously at work to develop a social construct that recognizes the significant contribution of informal economy entrepreneurs in sustaining the urban economy in developing areas—and that is a step in the right direction.

Because of their economic lifestyle, traders place a higher value on essential stall-based business contacts over commuting trips. Given the significance of large marketplaces and traders in the urban economy, best practices require relying more on these contacts for prioritizing urban development needs in (West) Africa and for that matter in the developing areas. To contextualize this phenomenon, in Onitsha, Nigeria, empirical evidence suggests that marketplace stall traders generate about 10.2–14.7

million mean trips annually (adjusted for 10% under-reporting) implying that peak-hour work and school trips from residences commonly relied on in the West for transportation planning may not serve the needs of large informal economy entrepreneurs and cities in the developing areas. Residing daily in these large urban marketplaces, traders constitute large economic communities whose trips affect the urban mobility system; therefore, their travel behavior should be of great importance and significance in urban development circles in (West) Africa. As an increasing number of traders are becoming visible middle-income earners, even as academic debates around the struggle for power between formal and the informal economies rage on, traders are demonstrating that the informal economy can and is establishing its propensity and resiliency in promoting economic development and growth. That provides an additional justification to conduct serious in-depth exploration of the inner workings of the marketplace institution to understand how and why traders continue to structure their business operation in a particular manner, their evolving ascendency into the middle class notwithstanding. Based on their business success, on a social welfare spectrum, stall traders will be placed toward the most privileged end of the spectrum, while pavement capitalist street vendors and hawkers will occupy the opposite end of the spectrum—the least privileged end of the spectrum. That adds to the reasons why stall traders in large urban marketplaces deserve proper presence in the urban development space.

As the pace of urbanization picks up, and as (West) African countries continue to export unprocessed strategic raw materials that dampen job creation in the formal economy, together with the growing importation of consumer goods mainly for urbanites, it is believed that traders will continue to operate from and occupy their current strategic command post in the urban economy. Urban economic development experts would also agree that such dominance will justify the need to recognize the importance of traders and assist them, as they continue to contribute to urban income mobility. Stakeholders can deploy evidentiary information and work with public policy makers to design and build new urban marketplaces or modernize existing ones with input from international development agencies to manage trader activity to complement the urban transport system. Empirical evidence can also be used to dissuade practitioners from "planning without indigenous facts," a common practice prevalent in several developing countries. After all, "The economic and financial sustainability of cities is inextricably linked with the viability of the city's transportation system (Ibitayo, 2012)."

Stall traders have permanent places of business—lockup market stalls—typically constructed on public lands but are often lumped together with curbside sellers who are so visible on the streets. These pavement capitalists, together with rural non-agricultural and (African) agricultural informal economy small-scale traders, have garnered a large body of research. A cynic may argue that this is a deliberate attempt to reassure the public that the informal economy continues to be a drag on countries and all efforts should be directed at revitalizing formal economy activities, such as manufacturing. Traders in rural agriculture-related informal economy and urban street sellers have also attracted more attention from researchers who appear to be interested in rural (village) and unstructured (urban pavement capitalist) African economy than successful stall traders in the informal economy; therefore, street-level vendors, the pavement capitalists, and other informal traders, who also occupy the least privileged spectrum of the social welfare continuum of urban market trade, are not considered in this book. This is the group that Allison Brown identifies as operators fighting for space in "rebel streets." Shopkeepers, including the relative few in shopping plazas, who are more spatially distributed and are unconstrained by government space allocation schemes and occupy relatively larger business spaces based on their ability to pay, and neighborhood front yard sellers, are also excluded from this work. This is because of differences in the organization and structure of their businesses when compared to those of marketplace stall traders in large urban marketplaces.

Women traders in the informal economy have also received some relative attention. In her work *Women and the Informal Economy*, Kinyanjui (2014) laments that even though women dominate urban markets in Nairobi, Lagos, and Accra, there is limited analysis of their role as urban marketplace traders in African city dynamism, as they conduct their daily trading activities. We surmise that those "activities" would include business-induced out-of-stall contacts covered in this work. Contrast the absence of large urban marketplace-stall-trader empirical information to the plethora of data and research analyses on the travel behavior that allow practitioners in the West to estimate trips for new shopping centers, mixed uses, and office complexes to allow them to gauge what the existing roadway capacity could support in order to propose needed improvements commensurate with the impact of a new development, and the need becomes clear. In order to advance to that stage in (West) Africa and other developing areas, there is first a need to understand what statistical variables contribute to induce non-peak-hour business travels of traders. The availability of such information will enhance policy making and promote intelligent urban development planning.

The professional informal–formal male and female marketplace stall traders in large urban markets evaluated in this book run relatively complex business operations. They have relatively large inventory, provide employment to those who could otherwise engage in non-productive underground informal activities (about 20% of African population are youngsters, with 40% in the workforce and 60% of them unemployed), and together with other business owners, tend to own a disproportionate amount of urban real estate. Moreover, their economic activity has local, national, and international linkages. With these characteristics, it is certainly acceptable to state that they deserve the attention of researchers when trading constitutes a significant portion of the urban labor force. Focusing on Onitsha, Nigeria, where trading constitutes 58% of the urban labor force, and those who conduct their business from sheds or market stalls comprise about 80% of the trader population, it is wise to explore their relationships within the urban space. This includes understanding and documenting their travel behavior as this constitutes the first step in re-examining the current urban planning process in order to develop the proper methodology for minimizing their impact on the urban transport space. To address this, for example, any new large urban market or a refurbished market could emphasize selecting a proper location, an accommodating stall design, and distributing sellers by commodity group to improve their financial welfare. There also could be a policy to educate traders on how they could contribute to sustain the marketplace institution by making different stall operational choices. And for policy makers, they need to rely on data that show a linkage between traditional marketplace stall operation and the urban environment to allow them to contextualize the benefits of designating marketplaces as new urban growth poles. Collectively, this strategy is what we describe as MODEST, or Marketplace-oriented Development Strategy. The sustainability of the urban marketplace and market traders is dependent upon how effective and decisive planners and policy makers are in integrating the impact of business contacts of traders and their needs into planning and managing urban infrastructure in (West) African countries.

Over one thousand years before Christopher Columbus set foot in the New World, West African market traders residing in the southern fringes of the Sahara in Ghana, Mali, and Songhai empires were exchanging goods with Arab traders from across the Sahara. Other empires in Oyo and Benin, like their expired counterparts, expanded and wielded similar economic power because of capital accumulated through trading. Those small business owners were simply known as 'traders,' and the same label was applied to many generations thereafter until the International Labor Organization formalized the "formal and informal" sector labels. It was an attempt to differentiate this service sector activity from perhaps similar "modern" small business activities in the West. Ultimately, it has been realized that an 'informal' sector business has no universal yardstick. Meanwhile, in *The Urban African and His World*, Bascom (1963: 177) notes that markets in non-industrial Yoruba cities of the early twentieth century did "not involve a simple exchange of goods between the producer and the consumer,... but was carried on by middlemen whose role and motivations are similar to those in our own (*read* European) society." Irrespective of the similarity in role and motivation, the label stuck and an underclass of business owners was born. As a result, we suggest the use of the term *non-formal economy* to differentiate traders and others in the group from the *formal economy* segmentation. Consider that pick-pockets, purse snatchers, and small-time drug dealers in the underground economy are often classified as operators in the *informal* (underground) economy; so, the new typology will contribute to eliminate the confusion. Participants in the non-formal economic sector are legitimate *albeit* small-scale entrepreneurs.

Hewing to that arbitrary dichotomy, the latest work by Ghana Urbanization Think Tank (2019) *Cities as a Guidelines for Ghana's National Urban Strategic Resource: Policy Revision* failed to devote space and time to the informal economy, even as traders in large urban (West) African markets are climbing the economic ladder into the middle class and are contributing to reduce urban unemployment. The failure to recognize the productive capacity of the informal economy would contribute to explain why the goods and services produced in the sector fail to routinely enter the calculation of the gross national products of many developing countries. The document produced by the Ghana Urbanization Think Tank would be considered progressive-issue oriented, and rightfully so, as there are discussions on finance, safety, security, climate change, industrialization, and light and low-skilled (formal) manufacturing—areas the group believes will push Ghanaian cities to transition from a political convenience to a strategic reserve, the authors concluded. But, Winnie Mitullah, a Senior Research Fellow at the Institute of Development Studies at the University of Nairobi, has warned that the neglect of the micro and small traders must be reversed, if African countries are to change existing poverty trends (Pambazuka News, June 1, 2006). Taken together, it is encouraging to learn that the same ILO has vowed that whether you call it unorganized sector, or informal economy, or something else, the organization will continue to work on the sector because it is still central to ILO's mandate of social justice, according to Werner Sengenberger, of the Employment Sector Office. Others (Chukwuemeka et al., 2017: 55), however, would argue that the formal–informal economy is succeeding as a viable economic activity, and there are bases to reconsider the stigmatization, because after all, they remind readers, "there is informality in the upper echelons of the society from financial capital to political relationships" and those are not generating any corresponding friction, debate, or similar dichotomization and stigmatization. The Organization for Economic Co-operation and Development, OECD (1998) on the other hand, previously had preferred the term "popular economy," or "domestic economy," apparently as an attempt to douse the fire on labeling.

Elsewhere, some international bodies and local developers are collaborating with some African governments to initiate the formalization of the informal economy, including the construction of modern shopping malls/plazas for sellers, even when the World Bank (2014) reports that most businesses may not even gain from formalization. Constructing Western-style enclosed malls to formalize trading will assist trader activities by creating a safe space, but it will de-marketize the unique African marketplace experience if it does not include design standards, openness, and features that encourage solidarity among traders, provide opportunities to attract and bring together sellers and buyers from all economic backgrounds, and foster that interpersonal relationship between traders and customers that is helping traders to build wealth and climb the economic ladder. The familiar marketplace personal and human-scale ambience will be replaced with the unfamiliar (the impersonal mall environment), should the mall-construction scheme expand. The concept of a mall connotes establishments inhabited by sellers who may not cater to all consumers and may be considered marginally an elitist institution and antithetical to traditional marketplace trading. This is because the unaffordable rents attract relatively high-end sellers who consider themselves "Westernized business women/men" and not traders who tend to stock specialized high-end merchandise but not the type of goods, including foodstuffs that are regularly found in familiar marketplaces where the poor that constitutes more than a majority of (West) Africans shop. Indeed, these malls comprise an aggregation of modern specialized shops and locals know who typically shop in those establishments—urban elites and yuppies.

It is well known that the International Labour Organization, ILO (2014), is encouraging the transition from informality to formality through the creation of social security benefits and the creation of employee unions and other methods to give voice to informal economy workers. For a sector that is already overburdened with rules, this merely could be another ploy at subtle attempts to suppress and slow down the progress in a prospering informal sector economy with new rules and regulations. In continuation of the thrust, in *Women and Men in the Informal Economy: A Statistical Picture* (ILO, 2018), the organization supports the fulfillment of UN Target 8.3, 2030 Agenda for Sustainable Development that promotes development-oriented policies that support *productive* (emphasis added) activities, formalization and growth of micro-, small- and medium-sized enterprises, which is not clear if it includes traders given the word "productive" in the text. It allows workers to have adequate social security protection, and organization and voice at work, when traders, for example, appear more interested in diversifying their activities by venturing into low level informal manufacturing than formalizing their business. The African apprentice system is the traditional educational training program for reproducing the workforce and could suffer some shock, as imposing those work rules on traders could create misunderstanding among stall traders and stall owners/masters, should the 2030 Agenda rules become universally accepted without adjustments to accommodate local conditions. For example, Bascom (1963: 180) observes that "Yoruba society is pecuniary and highly competitive, and economic failure can lead to frustration, aggression, or suicide, but not to starvation because one can count on the support of his lineage," an enduring social security system not accounted for in the Agenda. The apprenticeship system, for example, is an indigenous job training and employment program for individuals who are interested in professions that are not covered in the public school system and/or for individuals who are financially-locked out or incapable of engaging in regular classroom instruction. Providing social security to relatives and family members may be expanding anyway, as the cost of interpersonal communication and cash transfer has steadily declined, as the use of technology for financial transactions has increased. In other words, a different type of social network support system exists in some societies that may differ from those in the West, but it does not invalidate its functionality and success in stabilizing a family in time of crisis. To traders, diversification serves as a cushion against economic fluctuations and an investment strategy to shield income from taxation, a universal strategy of capitalists. Revenues from (in)formal manufacturing are transferred to trading income to disguise poor performance of the manufacturing activity because they realize that taxing manufacturing income is much easier for government than taxing trading income due to poor or non-existent record keeping—but it does not necessarily make trading a non-productive activity. Meanwhile, Tanzania has introduced the use of Electronic Fiscal Devices for direct transaction to extract VAT from traders with over 20 million TZS annual sales (US$10,000) which was met with trader resentment, according to the *Sunday Mail* (August 2, 2015).

According to ILO (2018), most of the employment in Africa (85.8%) is informal which suggests viewing it as a co-equal of the formal sector. Excluding agriculture, Africa's informal employment is 71.9%, with 70.2% in Services which includes traders. In West Africa, informal employment is 92.4%, and excluding agriculture, it is 87% and about 38% are in the service sector. In Nigeria, however, informal employment is about 73%, and excluding agriculture, it is between 50 and 65% with about 25% specifically in trading and 9.6% in manufacturing. These are potential small businesses who could be affected by formalization, a process that could potentially increase antagonism and distrust of government. The African Development Bank in *West Africa Economic Outlook* (2018) also notes that the service sector's share in West African economy is the largest in most countries, and manufacturing's share is the smallest in all of them. So, trading has become a very popular career in the informal economy of cities (Ogeah & Omofonmwan, 2013) in Nigeria, and other (West) African countries. In fact, in Onitsha, for example, as originally construed, the phrase *onye nazu afia* or "trader" is someone who has a stall and is engaged in distributive trade in the (Main) Market. Other individuals engaged in distributive trade would typically classify themselves with reference to what commodity they sell, and spatially at what urban market. Following that line of classification, to qualify for an elective position in today's statewide traders' union, the individual is, therefore, required to own and operate a stall in the market that they plan to represent. That is how significant the stall-trading label is in this premiere commercial center in West Africa.

In conclusion, there must be a realignment in research, planning, policy making, and development in (West) African countries that recognizes the contribution and impacts of these key participants in the urban economy. The new social construct by the ILO that elevates the significance of informal sector (including traders) should include a commitment to also understand the nexus between operational and management activities of market-stall traders, and the inadvertent stress they place on the urban transport system. This would help to broaden the understanding about the existing, even though neglected, and discounted, linkage between marketplaces and urban transport, an understanding that is expected to act as an incentive to reframe and restructure urban development and transport management processes in these areas. It is hoped that planners, development practitioners, and policy makers will develop and deploy a 21st Century vision that acknowledges and recognizes the unique importance of the marketplace institution in meaningful urban development. The new focus will allow for reimagining transportation planning and urban development processes to advantage traders within a marketplace growth pole to help create the expected positive externalities on urban transport, a strategy that is collectively known as MODEST. It is similar to urban land development strategy that encourages and is directed to increased use of transit that is popularly referred to as TOD, or Transit Oriented Development after all, the struggles and successes of urban market traders are contributing to reshape and strengthen the informal economy and the urban economy in (West) Africa and elsewhere.

Organization of the Rest of the Book

Chapter 2 examines urban market traders as entrepreneurs in an ever-growing Third World city with poor urban mobility infrastructure and a labor force that lacks relevant job skills. It discusses the need to understand and document trader travel behavior and establish the linkage between marketplace activities and the urban transport system. Chapter 3 provides the background on Onitsha, Nigeria. It describes its historical development to attain the label of the largest market town in Nigeria and one of the largest in West Africa. The chapter includes discussion on the organization of marketplace trade and how that organization informs daily stall operational and management activities. Chapter 4 examines the challenges, organized into three themes, facing urban market traders and explores their coping mechanisms while Chapter 5 theorizes about selected stall attributes that will induce and control stall business contacts to support the enterprise. It includes information on data collection, data specification, and stratification to assist in analyses of the travel behavior. In Chapter 6, the focus is on the geography of contacts made by traders in a large urban marketplace. There is a discussion of the contributory power of identified stall attributes to induce business-related out-of-stall contacts. There is also a discussion of the why and who makes trips and constraints facing traders in making contacts in a typical Third World (West) African city with documented transport and technological challenges. In Chapter 7, the issue is the sustainability of the marketplace institution and traders in (West) Africa, given the impacts of traders on the urban mobility space. It also evaluates whether large urban business cities formed by traders should qualify as core sources of travel data for transport planning in the developing areas. Chapter 8 is an outline of planning and policy development strategies to sustain urban marketplace trade and address the paradox of marketplace trade and West African urban development.

There is an Appendix that shows coefficients of regression for attributes. References are assembled at the end of each chapter.

References

Bascom, W. (1963). *The urban African and his world*. Etudes et Essais.

Benjamin, N., & Mbaye, A. A. (2012). *The informal economy in francophone Africa: Firm size, productivity, and institutions*. World Bank and Agence Française de Développement. © World Bank. https://openknowledge.worldb ank.org/handle/10986/9364 License: CC BY 3.0 IGO.

Biggs, T., & Shah, M. (2003). The problem of African entrepreneurial development. In G. S. Fields & G. S. Pfeffermann (Eds.), *Pathways out of poverty: Private firms and economic mobility in developing countries*. The World Bank/Kluwer Academic Publishers, World Bank, Washington, DC © World Bank. https://openknowledge.worldbank.org/handle/10986/25896 License: CC BY 3.0 IGO.

Bonnet, F., Vanek, J., & Chen, M. A. (2018). *Women and men in the informal economy: A statistical brief*. WIEGO and ILO.

Brown, A. (Ed.). (2018). *Rebel streets and the informal economy*. Routledge.

Chukwuemeka, C. V., Scheerlinck, K., & Schoonjans, Y. (2017). Collective spaces of informal and formal markets as drivers of self-organization processes of urban growth in emerging cities: Learning from Onitsha, Nigeria. *EU Human Cities*, 51–72

Fields, G. S., & Pfeffermann, G. (Eds.) (2003). *Pathways out of poverty: Private firms and economic mobility in developing countries*. The World Bank/Kluwer Academic Publishers, World Bank, Washington, DC © World Bank. https://openknowledge.worldbank.org/handle/10986/25896 License: CC BY 3.0 IGO.

Ghana Urbanization Think Tank. (2019). *Cities as a strategic resource: Guidelines for Ghana's national urban policy revision*. Washington, DC.

Ibitayo, O. O. (2012). Towards effective urban transportation systems in Lagos, Nigeria: Commuters' opinions and experiences. *Transport Policy*, 24(November), 141–147

International Labour Organization. (2014). *Transitioning from the informal to formal economy*. Geneva

Kinyanjui, M. (2014). *Women and the informal economy*. Zed Books.

McKenzie, D., & Woodruff, C. (2014). What are we learning from business training and entrepreneurship evaluation around the developing world? *World Bank Research Observer*, 29(1), 48–82. https://doi.org/10.1093/wbro/lkt007

Mitullah, W. (2006, June 1). Street vendors and informal trading: Struggling for the right to trader. *Pambazuka News*.

OECD/Club du Sahel. (1998). *Preparing for the future: A vision of West Africa in the year 2020*.

Ogeah, F. N., & Omofonmwan, S. I. (2013). Urban Markets as a source of employment generation in Benin City, Nigeria. *African Journal of Social Sciences*, 3(4), 62–78.

Smart City. (2017, December 26). *Smart transport for developing nations*. Smart City.

The African Development Bank. (2018). *West Africa economic outlook, macroeconomic development and poverty, inequality, and employment*. AFDB, Abidjan, Cote d'Ivoire

Yikoniko, S. (2015, August 2). Kariakoo market: Where Africa meets. *Sunday Mail*.

CHAPTER 2

Marketplace Entrepreneurs, Mobility Infrastructure, and Linkages

As every capitalist entrepreneur understands, the goal is to maximize profit by aggregating the means of production—land, labor, and capital. What the trader produces is service to consumers, and this service has societal and economic value. Land, as usual, has a fixed location and capital has acquisition cost associated with it. Labor is a fungible resource to be exploited in the production process. To minimize the cost of capital, the trader mainly depends on personal savings to start a business but must pay an annual (fixed) rent and fees (for land which the trader has no control over its input price) to the government for business use of market-place trading space, locally known as the shed or market stall. As we will later learn, the trader-entrepreneur cannot control the input price of the 'raw material,' that is goods sold in the stall, but the trader has developed alternative strategies to minimize that cost in order to maximize profit. The same principles apply to controlling the cost of labor—the entrepreneur trader relies on apprentices who are most often family members or other relatives who work in the stall. The apprenticeship system is the indigenous formal educational career training and certification program for traders, blacksmiths, brick layers, and other artisans. In the end, the trader-entrepreneur reproduces future traders by stocking a new stall with goods for the apprentice after several years of what is considered free labor (even though traders indirectly pay by providing clothing, living accommodation, and nourishment for the apprentice who

15

K. Ochia, *Marketplace Trade and West African Urban Development*, https://doi.org/10.1007/978-3-030-87556-5_2

is accepted as a bona fide family member). As an entrepreneur, the trader ensures that the cost of goods for the new stall does not exceed the assumed total cost of labor extracted from the apprentice. Based on long experience and tradition in the marketplace, traders have developed a rule of thumb for determining the number of years for apprenticeship for different lines of goods, meaning that traders (and apprentices) are on the aggregate, familiar with the number of years of apprenticeship that are suitable for different types of goods sold in the marketplace. Potential apprentices, through their sponsors, and their mentors may negotiate the terms, but each party already has a general knowledge of the length of the apprenticeship program and commensurate compensation, again a method of controlling capital, as traders directly contribute to reduce urban income inequality. This provides a background of this group of capitalists under study and the knowledge will guide the rest of the discussion as we evaluate the urban space within which these entrepreneurs operate their business. The synopsis creates a boundary for assessment and understanding of business mobility choices made by traders, as they manage capital and labor available to the stall, choices that link the marketplace to urban transport.

Traders have developed and maintain complex social and economic relationships as part of market-stall business operation. These relationships induce out-of-stall contacts. There is a need to understand the inter-relationships between market-stall operation and the non-home-based business contacts by traders because it will contribute to clarify our understanding of the inner workings of the marketplace institution. Continuing to ignore the inter-relationship between stall operation and non-home-based business trips and failing to take planning actions to adjust the behavior of traders will prove detrimental to the future growth of (West) African urban economies, especially in those countries with large urban marketplaces. We are specifically focused on stall traders instead of lumping them together with street sellers and vendors (McDade & Spring, 2005) to better understand their impact on the urban economy and transport. Notice that micro and small-scale enterprises contribute 40–60% of non-agricultural GDP in several African countries, and 38% of all West African non-agricultural employment (87%) is in the service sector where we find traders. The term 'non-home-based' means that the contacts are characterized by not having their origin or destination at the place of residence of the traveler. Basing this work on the experience of traders in Onitsha with the largest market in Nigeria and one of the largest in the West African sub-region provides the opportunity to offer researchers and other development practitioners a better understanding of how the traditional operation and management of a modern market stall contribute to induce non-discretionary contacts that have unintended but unexplored environmental impacts on the urban mobility infrastructure. These contacts are necessary and are completed to support the economic and financial health of the business, and ultimately the urban economy. The work, therefore, fills a void in the literature and provides a framework for evaluating other (West) African market centers with the goal of maximizing the effectiveness of investments in marketplace-focused urban development projects that are expected to reduce the impacts of large urban marketplaces on urban transport. After all the OECD (2016) has projected that by 2050, about 56% of Africans are expected to live in cities and warns that well-functioning cities don't just happen; they are created to function well, the Organization reminds all stakeholders creating well-functioning cities requires the intervention of policy makers, development practitioners, and planners. In an edited book by Burdett and Sudjic (2010), several authors evaluate large cities of today and provide ideas on how to manage the cities of tomorrow to accommodate people, businesses, and the environment to allow them to continue as a positive force for growth, as more people will be living in them by 2050. Managing trader activities is one way of contributing to this global futurism of making cities more livable through sustainable transportation which is quite familiar to those living in the Global South. But yes, (West) African cities must also function well. The International Finance Corporation, an arm of the World Bank Group, has published a study that finds that the mere fact that an individual is an African reduces the probability that the same individual is an entrepreneur in the manufacturing sector by 95%, implying affinity of locals to participating in non-manufacturing activities such as trading. So, we know that in Africa, it is informal–formal trade and distributive service, not manufacturing, that dominate urban employment, even though small-scale manufacturing, not major manufacturing, is typically promoted by many development experts and researchers, probably because it might trigger the need for technology transfer which would affect unemployment in the transferring nations.

Researchers on markets and distributive trade in the developing areas have provided useful studies interested in the organization and operation of markets (Asante, 2019; Brycerson, 2011; Hill, 1970; Kinyanjui, 2014; Lyon, 2003) but have paid little attention to the nexus between market-stall business operation and travels, and their impacts on the urban mobility space. Even though P.T Baker observed in 1965 that market traders control the cash in the (Nigerian) economy, there is still a lack of knowledge concerning how traders in Onitsha and, for that matter, other cities in the developing countries utilize and therefore affect the conditions of urban transport, as result of marketplace inter-relationships that are supportive of the financial health of the business. There is a long-standing assumption that (urban) market-stall traders do not leave their stalls after they arrive in the stall to allow them to maximize profit and accumulate capital because researchers will have us believe that "Typically... (a fulltime urban market female trader in Harare, Zambia and elsewhere) arrives at the market between 4:00 AM and 6:00 AM and leaves between 5:00 PM and 6:00 PM (Chamlee-Wright, 2002: 990)" which tends to reinforce the misconception. In the marketplace, entrepreneur traders take actions to externalize their business cost irrespective of whether there is a public social cost associated with their action. Externalizing their cost includes impairing the travel opportunity of other road users by increasing the access cost for those users, including consumers who patronize traders. Taken at its face value, this may not appear to be creating any urban travel problems, but it does—it increases traffic congestion with concomitant increases in travel time.

Given the misconception about trader behavior, there appears to be no existing body of knowledge upon which we can base theoretical statements about the daily non-home-based travel behavior of traders and their urban impacts that policy makers, planners, and development practitioners could consider in proffering remedies for urban development improvements that will concurrently generate benefits for the transport system. For example, we do not understand the relationship between the number and frequency of business contacts made by traders and the size of the trader's stall, or for that matter the location of the stall—attributes which inform traders' trip-making behavior. It is then not surprising that some governments in Africa have built or support the construction of new markets, refurbished existing markets, or erected new shopping malls with limited knowledge of how, for example, the location of the market, the size of the stall, gender of stall occupants, or the presence or absence of a personal means of transportation would affect how traders manage and operate the stall vis-à-vis interact with the urban mobility system. There may be a lot of opinions, but there are limited facts. Urban marketplace trading is a personal family business that is still structured around infor-mality and its success depends on continuously building, maintaining, and strengthening social ties and relationships within and outside the marketplace institution during business hours.

The concept of an urban shopping mall with enclosed air-conditioned spaces will be an added incentive for shopping, but it will de-marketize the unique and familiar African shopping experience provided by the market-place institution. A modernized large open air marketplace shopping area (with skylight and air-conditioning) is probably a better substitute. Realize that existing large (West) African urban marketplaces are serving similar one-stop shopping function like Walmart and Amazon in the West, or Jumia (in Africa) and Takealot (in South Africa), but without similar technologies, supply chain, and price control guarantees from manufac-turers and suppliers, or even a robust public policy support often today's mall shopping in (West) Africa is typically associated with processed food, expensive clothing, and shoes that are out reach for many shoppers. As in the West, it also serves as gathering places for young adults with or without children, but that is probably not the main business goal of mall developers—it is to attract paying tenants who attract paying shoppers. These shopping malls have another characteristic—there is no haggling over price because economic Darwinism allows only selected sellers who can afford the relatively high rent to sell to selected shop-pers who can afford the relatively higher tag prices. In the mall, items for sale are tagged with visible selling prices that allow customers to 'pick and pay.' The growing trend of modern shopping malls in Africa also could be an economic ruse for the gradual elimination of that unique traditional and social exchange institution—the marketplace—that socially and culturally bind the trader to her customers and continues to attract and intrigue foreign tourists for its vibrancy and resilience in the face of multi-national corporatization that is taking over urban shopping experi-ences and encouraging mall sellers to view themselves as modern business men and women, and not traders—a form of social distancing from the marketplace institution. There is also a school of thought that argues that the bias toward formalization is an effort to 'de-marketize' the African indigenous economy, as speculation abounds that the key beneficiaries will be urban land speculators, developers, government taxing authorities, and tax collection agents. This feature is creating urban conflicts between these groups and informal economy operators. Meanwhile, the Wash-ington University Global Studies Law Review reports that for informal businesses in the Cameroon, for example, formalization laws can be disruptive to the ability of entrepreneurs to sustain themselves (Dickerson, 2014). The fate of the traditional (urban) marketplace as a unifying informal social institution for renewing social ties and relationships, organizing (for community development), socializing and, as an efficient center of information collection and distribution, in addition to serving as an economic exchange institution for all classes of buyers and sellers, may be hanging in the balance. The push to formalize and undermine the marketplace appears to be a strategy to diminish the emerging ascendancy of the institution as an avenue for many traders to climb the ladder of social and economic prosperity, in defiance of formal economy enthusiasts.

In Ecuador, Lanjouw (1999: 94) found that the linkage of non-agricultural sector to agriculture suggests that a vibrant non-agricultural (informal) sector can provide an avenue out of poverty. Elsewhere, in a World Bank publication, Fields and Pfefferman (2003) are pushing the notion that it is (formal) manufacturing and private firm employment that offer the pathway out of poverty. This power struggle debate between formal and informal economy provides additional basis for researchers and planners to immerse themselves or at least invest some time into understanding the inner workings or dynamics of the marketplace to allow for expanded evaluation of how and why traders continue to frame their business operation in the traditional manner, their ascendency into the middle class notwithstanding. Meanwhile, there is unequal power relation or conflict between informal economy traders and government that is instructive but inconsequential. For example, some (West) African government are powerless in enforcing regulations against large urban marketplace traders to any degree that there is no incentive for market—stall traders to modify their marketplace behavior. This is because there are no punitive measures to force traders to modify their operational and management behavior that harms the urban mobility environment.

There appears to be a cadre of formal economy originalists who believe that the path to prosperity mainly passes through employment in the leading (small and medium) manufacturing sector, but it is certainly becoming a challenging proposition to defend as traders are upending that paradigm by breaking the proverbial glass ceiling of economic prosperity through informal service activity. It is, therefore, befitting to understand the business needs of urban marketplace stall traders and to develop new urban policies that, for example, recognize large urban marketplaces as new growth poles. And, with proper improvements that attend to the operational business needs of traders, these entrepreneurs will spend more time in their places of business and release more urban travel space for shoppers and other road users. This will offer traders an enhanced opportunity for capital accumulation that will continue to strengthen their capacity to spur economic growth in (West) African cities, even as West Africa urbanizes. Chamlee-Wright (2002) describes the relationship and sisterhood sorority culture among Accra, Kumasi, and Madina traders in Ghana as these traders have ingeniously organized themselves into close-knit groupings or clusters in the marketplace to promote their financial success. The connections developed within the sorority provide vital economic function and mutual support. Chamlee-Wright observes that even direct competitors will sell for one another in the case of sickness, or when the seller is making out-of-stall business contact, we will add. The researcher reminds us that the casual chats, gossips, and in-depth discussions involve traders in one another's lives and serves a social function in the market—associational bonding that may be relinquished to modernity in a shopping mall setting. So, with all these have planners and researchers expressed sensitivity to the operational needs of trader-entrepreneurs in planning, organizing, or managing urban development to minimize the impacts of traders on the urban mobility space?

URBAN MOBILITY SPACE

Diandas (1984: 197–210) has reminded scholars interested in conducting urban transportation studies in the developing areas that a useful study would be the careful assembly of facts about cities and the travel in them supported by discussion and diagnosis of problems aimed at seeking suitable combination of remedies to strengthen (urban) economic activities. For those cities, we must consider and include the study of non-discretionary business travels made by a differentiated trader group, and available and suitable combination of remedies that will include providing adequate facilities and amenities for the group that will contribute to extend the half-life of urban transport infrastructures. Other researchers (Dissancyake & Morikawa, 2002; Koushki, 1988; Ramakrishnan et al., 2020; Starkey & Hine, 2014; Tonelli & Dalglish, 2012) have directly responded to the challenge posed by Diandas but have focused on familiar and traditional transportation planning and development ethos of intra-urban journey to work and school trips. As standard Western travel behavior studies of households, they do not contribute to our understanding of non-home-based travel behavior in the developing areas, as most trip makers are informal economy workers whose travel preferences support their business; neither do they specifically contribute to our knowledge of business-related out-of-stall travels made by marketplace traders in the Global South. The knowledge is significant as the urban economy is controlled by traders in (West) African countries, and as their population continues to enlarge, as rapid urbanization becomes an existential threat to reducing urban poverty. In these areas, the different socio-economic and cultural arrangements make these traditional transportation planning studies irrelevant because entrepreneur traders place higher value on contacts completed from the stall to support the financial health of the business and the family over routine home to stall (work) trips. In the Global South, the economic culture is dominated by informal economy with multiplicity of self-employed entrepreneurs arriving at or leaving the business premises at will, uncontrolled by the rhythm of the day (clock face) but by the collective needs of their customers, it is certainly appropriate for planners to engage in an alternative transportation planning and urban development processes to reflect these differences. A revised planning framework should start with recognizing the detrimental environmental effects of daily intra-urban travels by stall marketplace traders. The peak-hour travel to work and school of households still forms the backbone of universal transportation planning. This transferred bias hurts urban societies and economies in the Global South with different economic and cultural characteristics, and the self-imposed bias is rife for re-evaluation. The traditional home-to-work trip standard cannot justifiably continue to serve as the international gold standard for transportation planning. For example, traders in the marketplace that dominate the urban economy should begin to serve as major source of transportation planning data. Planners have not realized that ignoring the travel behavior of small-scale operators scattered throughout the city in developing countries is one thing, but ignoring trips made by a large critical mass of entrepreneurs in a city, the marketplace, within the official city is a totally different and professionaly an indefensible planning mistake. This is because there are practical implications of traders' business travels from their daily unofficial city on overall urban environment. As a result of the traditional neglect of these trip makers, there are limited evidentiary data to assist us in addressing the collective impacts on society of these out-of-stall business contacts. Meanwhile, the OECD (2016) has observed that Africa is urbanizing at historically rapid pace in tandem with unprecedented changes in the demographic structure. It observes that the population living in cities doubled to 472 million between 1995 and 2015, and by 2050, fifty-six percent of Africans are expected to live in cities. Accordingly, the population of traders (and their urban transport impacts) will also be expected to worsen, if actions are not taken to manage them. These are the cities that Pedersen and McCormick (1999) note are already suffering from the effects of economic dualism where parastatal, foreign-dominated formal, and indigenous informal economies are poorly integrated, largely as a result of the (weak) institutional environment (or capacity) in which they have developed. The dualism has created an environment in which locals tend to populate the informal economy with limited opportunities to join the formal economic sector. This has resulted in the emergence of a disproportionately large informal economy operators, including those in marketplace trade, that have not gained traction with policy makers and planners. The limited employment opportunities in the formal sector also means that a substantial proportion of migrants from rural areas who choose trading as a career, and when they own stalls in the marketplace, will also fall into the 'forgotten' column by policy makers, and their impacts on urban transport will also be 'forgotten' or remain unrecognized. Ultimately, the linkage between large urban markets and transport will continue to remain majorly unknown and largely unexplored. Assisting traders to minimize the amount of time spent interacting with the mobility system will increase their rate of transition into middle income and improve urban economic growth. By continuing to frame transportation planning and urban development, and policy concerns around traditional contacts by households, planners, researchers, and policy makers risk jeopardizing the economic prosperity of cities and traders who dominate the economy of (West) African urban centers.

Stopher et al. (1984) have argued that the justification for focusing on home-based trips is primarily based on the importance of work and school trips in Western economies. In the West, we know, for example, that generally about 80% of all trips have their origin or destination at the family residence, while about 30–40% of all those trips are work-related and about 10% are individual trips made in the course of work and to and from school. As a result, numerous data collected on travel and traffic have enabled the development of theories related to household trip-making behavior. Such theories, for example, relate trip making to variables such as age, the size of the household, family income, the number of automobiles available, and the number of licensed drivers. Similar theories have also been developed to relate individual non-work trip-making behavior and shopping and recreational activities. The plethora of data and research in those inter-relationships have allowed planners and practitioners in the West to estimate trips for new subdivisions, shopping centers, multifamily developments, office complexes, and other developments that allow planners and engineers to gauge what the existing urban mobility infrastructure could support and to propose and require additional improvements commensurate with the impact of the new development. For (West) African planners, practitioners, and policy makers, by understanding how the type of good sold, the spatial location of the trader, gender, the number of individuals in the stall, and the availability of a personal automobile affect why traders engage in necessary out-of-stall business contacts, they will begin to theorize about how to manage them to promote sustainable urban economic growth. Furthermore, it will serve an additional purpose—weaning planners off that common problem prevalent in the developing areas, and that is planning without indigenous facts, to paraphrase Wolfang Stolper, when they plan, design, and locate new markets or modernize existing markets. Policy makers also need facts about linkages between traditional marketplace stall operation and the urban transport as they formulate policies regarding the location of new markets, and more important, as they refocus attention on the place of marketplaces in the urban development architecture. The sustainability of urban marketplace and market trade is dependent upon how effective and decisive planners and policy makers are in integrating the needs of traders into policies and management of the urban infrastructure space. This is why other researchers (Akad et al., 2001; Rosenbloom & Plesis-Fraissard, 2011) have warned against using imported data for transportation planning in the developing countries because adopting them will not yield the desired results because of differences in social and economic culture. Using locally-derived scientific knowledge and empirical data will certainly foster proper urban development planning decisions, and as D.N.M Starkie puts it, thought also could be given to balancing traffic with available road network, with aid from technology, instead of endeavoring to increase road network in step with traffic in resource-starved (West) African countries.

As we know, a significant proportion of those who find employment in the urban informal economy in the developing countries engage in the buying and selling of goods. For example, Astrop et al. (1996: 216) observes that market trading is a major source of employment for women in India, and in Ghana, we learn that traders form a robust entrepreneurial class (Chamlee-Wright, 2002: 979). As we pointed out earlier, as the population of cities in the developing countries continue to grow, it is reasonable to assume that the number of traders will continue to increase. This is particularly important as urban centers in the developing countries continue to play an important role in overall economic development as they serve as centers of commerce. It is certainly unreasonable to continue to ignore the significance of the intersection of trader activities and the health and condition of urban transport. According to UN Habitat (2009) between 1991 and 2006, Onitsha grew at an average population rate of 2.6%, and the typical daytime population of the commercial center reached between 1.5 and 2.0 million people. It is conceivable that some of the day time visitors patronized traders, and it is also conceivable that the population growth contributed individuals who engaged in commerce to keep pace with increasing number of shoppers. To put this in perspective, Table 2.1 illustrates the importance of commerce in the informal economy, measured by percent in labor force, in selected urban centers and countries. In Kenya, up to 34% of the labor force are in commerce and, in Nigeria, almost one-third of the labor force are engaged in commerce. Consequently, a UN Habitat Plan, completed in collaboration with state and local Nigerian governments, intends to reinforce the vision of Onitsha as the foremost commercial nerve center of national and international repute. Because professional traders make up about 58% of the urban labor force and those who conduct their business

Table 2.1 Percentage of labor force in commerce (selected cities and countries)

Urban Center	Percent	Country	Percent
Freetown	65.5	Sierra Leone	31.3
Mombasa	40.7	Kenya	34.1
Lima	27.5	Peru	26.3
Hiniara	22.8	Solomon Island	21.1
Dagupan	22.0	Philippines	19.1
Onitsha	57.5	Nigeria	28.9
Cotonu	42.5	Benin	27.3

Source Various published documents, including CIA Fact Books from sheds or market stall comprise about 80% of the trader population, it is reasonable that researchers document the propensity of these entrepreneurs to make out-of-stall contacts to understand their impacts on the urban transport system.

The economic life of a market stall revolves around the business contacts completed by stall members while the characteristics of the stall inform choices to make out-of-stall contacts, and these contacts affect the character of urban transport. These unique inter-relationships have not resonated with and properly recognized, considered, or documented by urban development experts and planners in developing areas. The knowledge will be useful in establishing proper development strategies and intelligent plans that will incorporate stall attributes and associated travel behavior of traders into the design and location of markets to modify trader impacts. As the marketplace institution is demonstrating that it has the capacity to support the building of wealth, more individuals will be drawn into informal trading which requires the need for knowledge of the marketplace so that the new entrants do not exacerbate existing transport and traffic problems attributed to the marketplace institution.

Some skeptics might suggest that traders in Onitsha or elsewhere in developing countries may not generate an appreciable number of out-of-stall business contacts that will play any role in the condition of traffic in cities, but those are opinions, not facts. In fact, trading operations and stall management present characteristics to make us believe that the opposite is true. For example, in analyzing the daily commuting (AM-PM travel) behavior in Lagos, Nigeria, Olayemi (1977) found that intra-urban movement is dominated by journey to work and school trips (73.3%) while business (commuting) trips constitute only 9% of total urban trips in that primate (one-time) capital city. More importantly, however, Olayemi emphasizes that while petty traders make only two trips daily (to and from the market) other professional or market-stall traders[1] often make many

---

[1] We are not interested in traders who do not have permanent stalls or those who have shops along city streets because market-stall traders are in the middle of that continuum of the most advantaged (lockup shop owners who rent shop and storage space based on their financial ability to pay) and the least advantaged (street sellers who cannot afford permanent location for their business) entrepreneurs in this social space. In her study of traders in Ghana (Accra, Kumasi, and Madina), Chamlee-Wright allowed a similar typology and placed traders into three categories—Hawkers (street vendors), Market Stalls, and Lock-up Shop owners. However, McDade and Spring (2005) lumped street traders with

trips during the day that it no doubt contributes to the heavy traffic characteristic of Lagos during off-peak travel hours. If that is the situation in a city dominated by formal employment in manufacturing, financial, and government sectors, then for cities where the marketplace and traders are in the majority, such impacts must be of value to development experts and planners. We argue that there is an unmistakable need for a close examination of traders' travel behavior in urban areas of Nigeria, and by extension other commercial centers in other developing nations, to obtain empirical data for better organizing, planning, and delivery of overall urban infrastructure needs.

MARKETPLACE BUSINESS OPERATION AND NEED FOR ACCESS

What are the operational characteristics of marketplace stall trade that predispose urban market traders to making multiple business contacts after they arrive at the stall at the beginning of the business day? The key contributing factor is the push to maintain that complex sociology of internal inter-relationships developed within the marketplace institution to foster economic survival, sustenance, and business growth. According to Bauer (1965: 26), the activities of the trader represent the substitution of labor for capital, and the population growth mentioned above illustrates how more labor will be needed and added to the marketplace. Even though some traders may have modern (low level) technology to assist them with the operation of the stall, there are still stall-related operational activities that cannot be conducted over the Internet or the cell phone. Traders can engage in electronic bank transactions, including making payments, placing orders over the phone, but paying for the order the trader prefers face-to-face meeting because of built-in mistrust of business partners. Fafchamps et al. (2004) found that only 3% of traders in Benin, Malawi, and Madagascar have a telephone in a study of market efficiency and profits. In their study of African food markets, Clare and Romanik (2008) found that this would explain the high cost of personal travel to enforce contract agreements. Furthermore, attending to family needs, paying for personal expenditures and social outings requires withdrawing

stall traders in their study of male and female entrepreneurs in a study of 10 African countries.

funds from the bank by physically visiting bank premises. As part of customer service, it is not unusual to accompany a bulk buyer to an inter-urban bus station (Motor Park) and assist her in securing and paying for a seat on the bus and ensuring that the bus driver and his assistants do not overcharge her for her load. When goods arrive, they must be warehoused or brought to the stall and that needs the physical presence of the trader or another stall member to inspect and properly store the goods. Eating meals, visiting the doctor, or going to school on behalf of the children, for example, must be completed in person. There are also family emergen-cies. To better manage capital (flow), many traders will appear in person to conduct business with suppliers or those with the capacity to stock-pile especially if they are buying with supplier credit, contrary to Hawkins (1965: 23) and Hodder and Lee (1974: 145) who believe that African traders cannot be classified as retailers or wholesalers. Small-scale traders who buy from other traders for resale in the market are retailers, and this class of traders are unlikely to have climbed or are climbing the economic ladder at the same rate as other traders who buy in bulk or directly from manufacturers, or from middle men who import goods for sale in the marketplace. In fact, Fafchamps et al. (2004) found that in Benin, Malawi, and Madagascar large traders tend to source their supplies from more distant markets and those with insufficient working capital tend to buy from large traders to resell locally in smaller quantities. Following Clare and Romanik (2008: 28), African traders who travel to meet producers to ensure that products are delivered as specified could be doing this from the marketplace as part of non-discretionary business interactions that also contribute to renew relationships and reconfirm trust.

Many African consumers have affinity to shop brand names, as a result of extended positive experience with the product; therefore, a typical stall would maintain a relatively large labor force, perhaps controlled by the physical size of the stall or the financial capability of the stall owner to share responsibilities to meet vagaries in consumer taste. For traders who have storage locations outside the market, accessing those locations will also add to the propensity of stall members to make trips, if the bene-fits outweigh the cost, that is, if there is money to be made. Remember, urban market trading is highly competitive as zoning gives buyers the exposure to many sellers who stock the same type of merchandise within the zone. This arrangement forces sellers to engage in quick turnaround, even if it means low profit margins. Even though the un-differentiation of goods within a zone contributes to lower profit margin, it works in favor of the consumer. To make goods readily available to customers, the intervening factor is the location of the market and whether there is an available stall member to bring the good from the 'warehouse' to the store. In the alternative, the trader must redirect the customer to a neighbor and that singular action will eat into the trader's profit even though there is reciprocity—the reciprocity has more to do with building relationships and enhancing inter-dependency among traders than giving business to a competitor. For example, traders who occupy a line—sellers of the same goods in the same market zone—tend to support each other during times of loss or emergencies. As a result, some traders are often selected, if they fail to volunteer, to attend to those grieving or attend to those in the hospital and those activities add to total trips generated from the stall during business hours. This is one of the results of comingling the personal (private) with the public (business). Making out-of-stall business contacts is usually challenging for traders, but in the face of potential negative financial consequence, the trader is compelled to make the contact. Those who make out-of-stall contacts must depend on a mobility system that was not built around the needs of marketplace traders who eventually have come to dominate the urban economy. The following is an assessment of how there is disconnect between the business contacts needs of traders and the structure and condition of urban mobility infrastructure.

Planned urban mobility systems tend to characterize cities of developed economies. Moreover, advanced technologies (transit system priority, TSP) have been applied in providing enhanced mobility services such as queue jump and synchronized timing at street intersections. In contrast, most urban centers in the developing countries, especially in Africa, grew as a result of their unique positions as centers of colonial administration. But colonial attitude toward (urban) development was oriented to resource-based extraction and exploitation, as illustrated by a statement attributed to Sidney Cain, the Under Secretary, Economic Development Division of the (British) Colonial Office, namely that "there was nobody (at each colonial administrative office) whose particular business was to be a 'development chaser' in each territorial government (Lee, 1967: 140)" which in today's world would be considered classical form of social injustice and act of structural discrimination, as urban roads were also constructed without traffic lights as a result, investment in the development of urban mobility infrastructure was not a priority. A few miles of urban paved roads were sufficient to meet the intra-urban travel needs of colonial administrators. That was how the foundation was laid for uncoordinated and haphazard mobility development framework in these areas. The framework failed to consider or include the needs of eventual key economic actors, urban market traders. One of the results is the absence of efficient relationship between land use, such as the location of urban marketplaces, and transport, even as cities continued to grow. Perhaps, the feeling from the beginning was that the few automobiles plying the streets did not justify investing in a planned-out expansive urban mobility architecture that will accommodate future travel needs. Those few automobiles that were plying the few paved roads belonged to colonial administrators and their lieutenants. To justify the dis-interest in coordinated urban infrastructure development, colonial subjects, or locals, as they were typically referred to, who were used to sustainable transportation—walking and occasional bicycling—did not need more than narrow streets to complete their daily chores in town, the argument went. It was shortsighted negligence and cities are still burdened with the inadequate foundation laid several decades ago, as many governments layer over roadway improvements onto an inadequate framework. Commenting on urban development and the British colonial administration in Port-Harcourt, Nigeria, Wolpe (1974: 64) observes that "the official (colonial) and (local) mercantile interests were not always coterminous. The colonial office had to concern itself with a wide range of problems that often had little to do with the requirements of the (local) business community" which would have included building suitable marketplace infrastructure that would meet the needs of traders or the mercantile interests, developing an efficient system for moving people and goods, and paying attention to accessibility issues near and around indigenous marketplaces. So, most of the population centers in the colonies grew without adequate provision of urban infrastructures that would have prepared cities for future expansion, as the urban economy further differentiated and grew. Consequently, there is maddening congestion on city streets with houses placed adjacent to the edge of the pavement and often located within what would ordinarily constitute legal public right of way. Today, pedestrians and automobiles continue to share and jockey for space on narrow city streets. Traders who leave their stalls to respond to business and personal needs during business hours tend to compound the problem. Research shows that less than 10% of land area is devoted to roads in many African, South Asian, and SE Asian cities such as Nairobi, Kenya, Kolkata, India, and Jakarta, Indonesia (Cervero,

2014: 12). Starkey and Hine (2014: 38) observe that with about ten percent of land devoted to transport, cities are destined to not properly handle urban traffic congestion and this is exacerbated in (African) cities with large urban marketplaces. In general, the authors note that in developing countries, roads are reported to account for between 5 and 15% compared to about between 20 and 25% for most European cities and about 35% for US cities where the mobility system received and continue to receive appropriate planning and maintenance attention.

Studies have shown that there is a positive correlation between the development and maintenance of an effective mobility system and improvement in local and regional economic systems. In ex-colonial territories, the earliest phase of transport development was between ports and the centers of economic resources in the hinterland. It was argued that such port-hinterland linkage was a precursor to total economic development in the areas, but this policy missed the inclusion or even consideration of the needs of the locals in planning and implementation of a supportive mobility system to benefit local (urban) economies. A similar strategy was applied by Le Corbusier in developing and implementing the master plan for the capital city of Punjab, India, that excluded the major local population from legal housing and employment (Sarin, 2019). The author laments how the designer applied Western planning concepts to a new city in Third World India. What you find is the creation of dual social and spatial structures resulting from the poor process in implementing the master plan. What resulted from the process was unmistakable formation of dual employment and social housing conditions that manifested itself in the emergence of a large informal economy and the establishment of squatter settlements in the new capital city, contrary to the expectations of planners. Similarly, for ex-colonial cities, the preferred colonial development strategy resulted in a dual system that today most residents still find themselves in an informal economy within that dualistic economic system. This also is the economy that confronts migrants upon arrival from the hinterland to the city. In the end, all participants in the urban economic system, including traders, are forced to muddle through an economic system relying upon available albeit inadequate transport infrastructure. A foundation that was laid down many years ago has taken root and incremental tinkering at the edges by post-colonial administrators, aided by a poor maintenance ideology, has contributed to existing conditions. A useful lesson is that urban infrastructure development should always consider and involve local beneficiary stakeholders, and for our purposes, marketplace stall traders in these large urban market centers. Besides, involving traders could raise their sense of civic responsibility.

Post-colonial administrations are not by any means held harmless for the condition of today's urban infrastructure in (West) African urban areas. Clare and Romanik (2008) reminds us that African governments tend not to incorporate the needs and interests of traders into policy making and marketplace improvement. Starkey and Hine (2014: 45) report how planners and government agencies (in Africa) tend to continue to focus infrastructure development on those with automobiles—a Western bent—to the detriment of the carless and the poor. They report the case of planning a mega-highway project in Kenya—the Thika Highway Improvement Project—that deliberately ignored the access and business needs of market traders in Githurai Market, a well-known large regional market, in a zeal to appease drivers and project sponsors. The construction dislocated traders, and when questioned in parliament, the Assistant Transport Minister was quoted as responding that his Ministry is not responsible for securing alternative land for use by traders, a demonstration of the disconnect between an understanding of the roles and responsibilities of public servants and community interests and the populace they are supposed to serve. These market traders do not matter because planners and development experts have not recognized and therefore elevated their significance and contribution to economic well-being of society. Accordingly, ignoring the input of beneficiary traders in any re-design, remodel, or construction of new urban markets in (West) Africa should be discouraged.

Economists and development practitioners have since recognized the difficulties involved with gathering data in the developing areas to support sound planning processes and practices. Srinivasan and Rogers (2005) lament that data on travel behavior in developing countries, such as India, are minimal. According to Iheanacho (2014), one of the challenges of development planning implementation in Nigeria is the absence of relevant data. He reiterates that (successful) development planning principally depends on availability of data. Its absence in Nigeria, the researcher observes, is due to inadequacies or weak capacity embedded within the Federal Office of Statistics and unwillingness of Nigerians to reveal information. The fear of providing personal information to strangers conducting a research survey is rooted in the distrust established between citizens and colonial governments that has been passed down through generations in many ex-colonial territories as many replacement post-colonial administrators continue to act as colonialists, especially in the last three decades; so, it is not an exclusive Nigerian problem. In general, according to Josse (2020), one of the major problems in planning and managing cities in Africa is the lack of information about the city and its inhabitants, meaning that without data "policy-making can only be very hit-and-miss" as it becomes difficult to detect and assess what people need. During the field study for this book, many traders could not comprehend why this author would travel "all the way" from the United States just to find out how market traders were managing their stalls and interacting with the transport system, as a result of their operational and management styles. They were curiously suspicious about the motive(s); so, education is part of the answer to eliciting useful personal information from informants. Collaborating with the leadership of the traders' organization, for example, to explain the purpose of gathering marketplace data is a plus, and if the researcher publishes a newspaper article explaining the goal of the survey, the likely questions, and benefits of the survey prior to the commencement of the field survey, it will contribute to minimize antagonism and the level and intensity of distrust by respondents, as union leaders could explain the purpose of a study to mid-level leaders who would share the information with other resident traders. Besides, the assistance from other traders who have participated in the survey could contribute to allay any fears. Collecting and analyzing such data constitute the first steps in understanding and then improving the internal mobility problems of traders.

In the absence of useful statistics, practitioners have tended to plan without indigenous facts, a phenomenon other authors (Godbless et al., 2019: 8) have alternatively described as planning with "lack of comprehensive statistics" or "planning with manipulated data" (Iheanacho, 2014). The argument in the literature is that in making local urban development decisions, development advocates and managers should involve beneficiaries who possess detailed knowledge of local conditions and will potentially benefit from the project (Akad et al., 2001; Conley & Tafulene, 2015; Rosenbloom & Pleisis-Fraissard, 2011; Starkey & Hine, 2014). The empirical data provided in this book will serve as a proper tool for formulating evidence-based wise local plans by arming stakeholders with invaluable community-generated information on the relationship between stall operation and management, and the choice to make out-of-stall contacts. We theorize that should practitioners understand the significant attributes responsible for inducing non-discretionary, out-of-stall business contacts, they can apply and manage the values of the attributes in designing and developing new marketplaces or in refurbishing existing markets. This indirectly enhances the ability of (West) African governments in managing overall urban mobility system. To accomplish this goal, planners and policy makers, for example, could regulate the size of stalls and chose the location of new markets to minimize the impact of marketplace operation on the urban environment. In the alternative, the empirical data could be used to calibrate or simulate additional data that could be applied to future urban development planning. After all in discussing the role of men and women in the informal economy, the International Labor Organization (2018) stresses the need and prerequisite of using accurate data and information for planning in order to achieve the 2030 Agenda for Sustainable Development. Accurate data and access to it are discussed throughout this work.

For proper design of marketplaces and management of marketplace activities, there must be an understanding of how the magnitude of business contacts is a function of stall attributes. This will assist in future land use decisions related to marketplaces. Furthermore, it is anticipated that facts presented here would be useful in educating traders and their leadership about how the traditional operation of the stall contributes to local urban traffic problems that present access challenges to their customers. Accordingly, traders could be persuaded to contribute to support the upkeep of urban roads even though research (Dike, 1982; Hanna & Hanna, 1977; Kilby, 1969) has shown that the concept of "improvement" to the African urban dweller is often interpreted to mean improving the individual's hometown or place of origin, even though the urban area provides the individual with their source of family livelihood. But, Geschiere and Gugler (1988) have observed some attitudinal changes as some migrants who are trapped in the city are revisiting the "collective connections" developed with their relatives in rural areas. This is validated by the work of Trager (2001). In her study in western Nigeria, she found that urban residents share the concept of multilocality that allows individuals to maintain multiple connections at the same time, and for those engaged in international migration, there is transnationalism. In that world, the urban dweller is cognizant of their obligation to their urban place of residence without necessarily giving up their obligations to their hometown. Sharing a personal anecdotal experience may be in order. In Portland, Oregon, Africans in the diaspora formed an African organization in the late 1990s when we became concerned about how the local media was portraying Africa in the mass media. It was always famine, civil war, mayhem, or animals—just classic stereotypical stories about Africa in the local media. On January 1, 2000, the largest newspaper in the state, The Oregonian, ran a story about how the world welcomed the New Millennium (*The Oregonian*, January 2, 2000). It showed a 12-year-old boy reading from the Koran in Baghdad, a couple wearing prayer shawls and singing at a Franciscan Center in Beaverton, Oregon, a 22-year-old man selling betel nuts in Taipei, Taiwan, a farmer ferrying bales of hay in a tractor in Kentucky, USA, a Chinese man practicing tai chi in Shanghai, China, and for Africa all the paper could print was a Turkana woman in loin cloth bare-breasted while breastfeeding her baby. The picture story was the tipping point for diaspora Africans in the area. Dubbed the Turkana Effect, we viewed the pictorial depictions as an excellent teachable moment to engage in a conversation with the editors of The Oregonian newspaper who had weaponized the pages of the newspaper against the interests of modern-day Africa. An existing diaspora organization, Africa in the Mass Media, formerly working to help various African communities, started to dialog with the publishers of The Oregonian newspaper on improving Africa's public image through continuing community awareness programs regarding the African continent. The newspaper re-invented itself and started to feature positive stories about the continent with assistance from the group. This type of local involvement did not distract members from obligations to families and groups in the African continent. Perhaps, traders could be convinced to participate in the upkeep of the mobility system, should they realize that the integrity of the system is directly tied to the financial health of their business and their ability to support relatives back in the homeland.

Since 1975, the World Bank and other international organizations such as UN Habitat and OECD have been arguing and urging policy makers in the developing countries to maximize the use of existing urban mobility infrastructure rather than building new capital-intensive projects, as an option for addressing local urban transport problems. The concept has morphed into what is currently known as sustainable development that allows for proper and respectable co-existence of different modes between the curb and those in the sidewalk. But, in order to explore the merits of any policy option, there is the need to assemble data on current urban movement characteristics of beneficiaries, no matter what triggered the intra-urban contact. This is where this work could serve a common purpose for stakeholders interested in urban economic development in (West) Africa, because so far the informal economy in sub-Sahara Africa remains among the largest in the world with informality ranging from the lows of 20–25% in the Mauritius, South Africa, and Namibia to a high of 50–65% in Benin, Tanzania, and Nigeria (ILO, 2018: 19). Therefore, data gatherers need to pay attention to the significant portion of actors who are active in the informal economy. The argument is that since the cumulative quantitative and qualitative out-of-stall business contacts constitute the core predictor of business success or failure, all other factor remaining equal, planners need to be sensitive to the benefits of those contacts which, in the aggregate, are shoring up the economic importance of marketplace trade. The assembly and maintenance of such database will reduce the temptation to use manipulated data and/or imported data that may prove less valuable in the developing areas. It will also reduce the temptation to continue to plan without facts. To amplify this point, we paraphrase Peter Hart (1970) who, in teasing out the missing link for growing small-scale entrepreneurs, observed that the most urgent requirement in developing countries is for sociological and economic research into business operations and for marketplace traders, to understand factors that are instrumental in allowing them to dominate the urban economy while negatively impacting the urban mobility environment. The author continues, researchers should evaluate how to incorporate the findings into development planning. This is a powerful and insightful admonition that is taking years to fruition. Now, the next section is an excursion into how the marketplace trader is linked to local, national, and international producers, in both the formal and the informal economy to further demonstrate the necessity of redirecting attention to the marketplace institution in the urban development ecosystem.

Urban Market Traders and Linkages to Local, National, and International Economy

In this work, urban marketplace traders are not just treated as workers or participants in the 'informal' economy, they are also being given a voice in recognition of their role as significant actors in maintaining a strong urban economy. (West) African governments are implored to use facts to work with those who continue to ignore the facts and refuse to address existing linkages between the marketplace and urban travel systems. Failure to address this linkage is inimical to stable urban economic growth. This is especially important when urban economic growth is a function of the rate of capital formation by traders through price advantages gained through linkages to formal and informal economies at the local, national, and international levels. Anthropological work in Kumasi, Ghana (Clark, 2010), demonstrates how Ghanaian market women are deeply integrated into local and global economies in a country where 80% of women are engaged in trading. Meagher (2013) has completed an exhaustive literature review of linkages between the informal and formal economy. The review shows that from the 1990s' the largest linkages are related to how labor, information, and resources are structured, with additional mapping for national or sectoral inter-firm linkages. The author shows that there are labor market and financial linkages and other linkages between global value chains which happen to form the body of work completed earlier by Carr and Chen (2002). Meagher (2013) quotes a UN (1996) study that recognizes the complexities of linkages and identified linkage categories exemplified as technological, consumption, and financial at international and local levels for different group of workers.

The categories defined by Meagher do not, on a face value, appear to provide us with relief about where to place urban market traders, but the UN study's inclusion of the word "consumption" provides a clue. We theorize that in describing these global linkages, the discourse is premised on the existence and ubiquitousness of formal economic system in the Global North. This discussion is, however, focused on linkages that exist in the supply of products and therefore linkages that exist with providers of labor and capital. The report demonstrates how abundant labor is deployed in the Global South to make products and highlights the associated financial arrangements to ensure an uninterrupted flow of products to consumers in Global North. In addition to the UN document cited by Meagher, Carr and Chen also have an antidote that will assist our discussion on linkages involving urban market traders. The authors provide useful typologies for informal economy employees and workers. They identify employers as owners and owner operators, and the self-employed as owner account workers, head of family business and unpaid family workers. Then for wage workers, the authors state that there are three schools of thought that will explain informal and formal economy linkages, thus: the dualists, the structuralists, and the legalists. According to the authors, the International Labour Organization appears to be the key proponent of the dualist school that sees a clear separation between the two economies. The informal economy persists because economic growth or industrial (formal economy) expansion has failed, to date, to absorb current informal economy employees who are mainly poor and are operating on the margins of the economy. To structuralists, the informal economy is subordinate to the formal economy as privileged capitalists erode employment relations and subordinate and exploit the informal economy to reduce their labor cost and increase competition through enhanced capital accumulation. The legalists view informal work environment as a rational response to onerous government regulation of unregistered businesses. For them, these operators are focused on increasing their own wealth through reduced costs by avoiding regulations or roadblocks for starting and running their business. To Carr and Chen, however, it is all about power relationships, viz, few, if any (dualists), dominant (structuralists) and exercise of own power (legalists). They agree that a more comprehensive framework is needed to explain the array of power relationships. For example, the power relationship and linkages between informal and formal economy, and informal economy and the public sector are different based on which informal economy actor is being discussed, such as street vendors versus garment workers, or, of course stall market traders. Carr and Chen focus their analysis on home-based women workers, but their observations are educational and illustrative for our purposes. The authors show how the production work of these women workers is linked to the global commodity chain that links labor, production, and distribution processes. The products of these women are typically distributed to European and North American markets while the workers are in Turkey, Morocco, Mexico, and Guatemala. Incidentally, African (garment) workers are not included in the list because apparently, they do not produce for those markets. But African marketplace traders are known to import those same goods through established supply chains (linkages) for distribution and consumption by Africans, and that is where the existence of an African linkage is exposed.

(West) African traders in large urban markets may be constrained by government regulations, but not to the degree that the existing power relationship models will make us believe, suggesting that there is an entirely different but symbiotic power relationship between urban market-stall traders and government. Traders have developed known linkages, in line with linkage typologies developed by the work of Meagher, and the linkages are based on the distribution and consumption of finished products. The reluctance of government (formal sector) to exert substantive power over traders, especially those in formal–informal trade, demonstrates the inter-dependence between government and formal–informal traders within the urban economic space. As we will find out in the next chapter, the major trader association in the Nigerian state where data were collected for this book, for example, has been responsible for electing state governors, and some members of the political elite class started their career as urban market traders. Realize that West African traders had carved out and occupied a unique economic position before the arrival of the formal economy as documented by earliest West African Trading Empires of Ghana, Mali, and Songhai between 800 and 1500s when a robust trade in copper, gold, kola nuts, and palm oil from the south of the Sahara were exchanged for salt, ceramics, glass, and oil lamps from the north. The economic strength of the traders defined the economic power and reach of the Empires. And that tradition has endured. The arrival of the traditional formal economy with colonialism and attempts to suppress or subjugate the informal economy, no matter how subtle, such as through taxation was met with unified opposition. The Aba Women's Riot of 1929 (November–December) was organized by women in southeastern Nigeria when the British attempted to impose special taxation on market women traders who dominated the food supply business to urbanizing cities of Calabar, Owerri, and beyond. Not only did the colonial administrators rescind the tax (think Modi Government and small-scale farmers in India and agricultural law crisis, circa 2020–21), women were appointed to positions of power in the judicial system thereby expanding the power of informal trading. In recognition of the position of the informal economy in these areas, there is a large school of thought within the Global South that supports the conclusion reached by Carr and Chen (2002: 7), namely that "the informal economy, long considered incompatible with economic growth and industrialization, (is)... expanding in both developed and developing countries." Given this evolving growth, there is, therefore, reluctance by governments to be heavy-handed in confronting urban market-stall traders, as government is cognizant of the economic power amassed by the sector through its own power struggle with the formal sector. With such pivotal economic position, how are the activities of urban market-stall traders in Onitsha, or for that matter, in other West African countries, linked to formal and informal economies at local, national, and international levels?

We take our frame of reference from the work of Teltscher (1994: 167–187) in Quito, Ecuador. We find the work compellingly appealing because it theorizes that focusing on production (manufacturing) and labor will not assist in explaining trader linkages; rather, there is a need to look at products and distribution services through the supply chain. In Quito's Calle Ipiales, access to products and access to capital are crucial variables that define the inter-relationship between informal commerce and other sectors of the urban, national, and international (formal and informal) economy, the author opines. By understanding how products are sourced and distributed, we will begin to conceptualize how formal–informal traders are linked to the formal and informal production and distribution processes locally, nationally, and internationally. Formal–informal traders who are differentiated from small informal competitors in the marketplace are more likely to cross the country's border to source their supply because of their placement in the most privileged band of the social welfare spectrum, and when they import, they purchase large quantities and are most likely to use their contacts to their advantage, including capital support. Other small operators who are differently positioned can source their supplies locally or buy from large importers and that affects their rate of capital accumulation. In other words, traders who are most privileged are most likely to have direct linkage with (in)formal production and distribution processes while less privileged traders may have direct linkage with local informal suppliers and indirect linkage with national and international formal economy. The most privileged sellers or traders tend to stock large quantities of high-end, intermediate, and low-priced merchandise to meet the consumption needs of diverse consumers in urban and rural areas. For example, market traders in Quito could buy from local producers or national producers in Guayaquil, or they can cross the border or buy from formal producers in Peru or Columbia or import directly from Europe, USA, or China. Urban marketplace traders, therefore, constitute part of a complex distribution system linking urban informal vendors operating at local, national, and international levels. Producers can and do bring their products to the markets in Quito which reduces the search cost (traveling, stress, border problems, absence from family and for single mothers that could be challenging), but buyers may have to offer higher prices for such goods. Elsewhere, we learn from Chamlee-Wright (2002: 996) that Harare urban market women traders are known to make buying trips to Mozambique, Zambia, and South Africa to buy from formal and informal producers.

In West Africa, Walther (2016) has applied the emerging science of Social Network Analysis (SNA) to map 136 large urban marketplace traders who deal in building materials, cereals, textiles, and used clothes to connect traders from Nigeria, Niger, and Benin, who rely on their social contacts or gatekeepers to the markets in the Dendi region of Niger Republic. These traders use their social ties to source goods from the formal economy that other traders have imported from international producers. Again, not only have these traders established product linkage, the gatekeepers, who act as bridges for buyers, often provide capital support for established customers. Walther observes that "the most successful traders are those who can simultaneously bridge several markets and be strongly embedded in a cohesive group of close business associates." Trust is the basis for successful embeddedness. It takes several satisfactory cash transactions before a gatekeeper would even consider offering marginal credit opportunity to a customer, and, if successful, before engaging in relatively substantial capital support that could qualify as real capital linkage with the formal economy. But it typically happens because these relationships are established for the long haul.

In their evaluation of the subject in West Africa, the OECD (2019) found that Nana Benzees—wealthy women traders who usually drive Mercedes Benz private automobiles—in Togo (and Ghana) have gained prominence by relying on exclusive resale rights negotiated with European commercial houses. The report notes that today, the West African market is flooded with cheap wax prints from China and the Nana Benzees have been supplanted by other business women who deal directly with Chinese manufacturers. Moreover, market women traders in Mauritania and Senegal have opened similar new trade routes to Paris, the Arabian Peninsula, China, and Brazil. These traders have realized that buying directly from formal producers increase their profits and rate of capital accumulation without realizing how their informal trading activity is linked to their supplier's formal manufacturing (and employment) activity outside of the West African zone.

Golub and Lewis have examined Mourides market traders in Senegal/Gambia and Yoruba in Benin and Nigeria and they write "The Mouride Islamic Brotherhood plays a major role in the informal economy in Senegal and The Gambia and has developed an extensive global trading network spanning West Africa, Europe and the United States (World Bank, 2012: 174. see also Diouf, 2000)." These groundnut farmer-turned urban marketplace traders operate out of Sandaga Market in Dakar (Senegal) and Okass Market in Touba (Senegal) and control a vast distribution network and sale of various local and imported products. Experienced traders travel to New York, Jeddah, Hong Kong SAR (Special Administrative Region), and China to purchase large quantities of electronic and cosmetic products for resale in Senegal and other countries. Yoruba traders have played a similar role, the researchers observe, and "remain at the center of a large informal economy's international trade group in West Africa, facilitated by kinship ties, varied market tactics, and hierarchical organizational structure (World Bank, 2012: 186)." Kinship ties functionally approximate Western legal business contracts that bind strangers together for reciprocity in social and financial transactions. But kinship ties are much deeper because there are no written documents to back it up, but it is orally transmitted through the ages, as part of inherited traditional privileges which in this case bestow economic advantages. In addition, the same Yoruba market traders import goods from various West African countries, China, and Europe to reduce total acquisition cost and boost sales revenue.

Onitsha Marketplace Traders have developed similar structural arrangements to source saleable goods from local, national, and international formal and informal producers to maximize profit. Based on consumer tastes and demand, Onitsha marketplace has been forced into the quest to develop enlarged national and international product connectivity and capital linkages. Chukwuemaka et al. (2017) of Urban Projects, Belgium, have written a seminal essay on the spatial extension of Onitsha Market to the renowned Alaba International Market, Lagos, an idea that was originally presented on TED Talk as a model for internally creating wealth in the face of adversity and government failures to provide necessary infrastructure (water, roads, and electricity) to facilitate financial support for economic development. The authors reveal that Onitsha was starved of access to road and marine transportation in retaliation for the demise of the Republic of Biafra in 1970. The Niger Bridge, connecting Onitsha and the rest of western Nigeria, especially Lagos, was destroyed during the war and not immediately repaired following the cessation of hostilities. The federal government of Nigeria also shut down marine access to Onitsha and other cities from southern functioning wharfs on the Bight of Biafra (currently the Bight of Bonny). As a result, the only functioning wharfs open to the importation of commodities and exportation of local products were only available from Lagos from 1970 till date.[2] In response, resourceful traders in Onitsha determined that the best way to continue doing business was to extend their market-stall operation to Lagos where the port of Lagos was open for business to allow for uninterrupted movement of goods to Onitsha Market. The Alaba Market has grown into a regional force in Nigeria's commercial sector and with a direct (and undisclosed) link with Onitsha Markets. What this illustrates is the indisputable linkage between Onitsha formal–informal market operators and the global formal economy. The distributive power of Onitsha Market traders is not only creating jobs in Lagos and southeast Nigeria, it is also contributing to job creation in countries shipping containers of manufactured products to Nigeria.

Whatever products traders' source and from where they source the goods is a determinant of profit margin and capital accumulation rates, meaning that (local and regional) intermediaries who buy from these traders are less likely to profit as much as those traders who buy directly from foreign producers. For example, Onitsha traders purchase large quantities of shoes locally from Aba, Nigeria, or they can purchase internationally from Italy, Switzerland, Austria, or Spain. The same goes for fabric where some traders also get supplies from Senegal. Fresh food sellers typically have producers bring the goods to Onitsha for quick sales, except that non-perishable food sellers such as garri, rice, dried fish, onions, and beans may prefer to travel out of town to villages where they could buy in bulk at lower prices from informal agricultural sector producers such as those in the Niger Delta areas. At each level of the transaction, the trader can pay cash or buy on credit at a higher price if trust has been established over time. Locally-manufactured goods with low capital input are cheaper than imported often relatively better quality and high-priced goods. This has created the need for brand shopping which creates opportunities for unscrupulous traders to take advantage of unsuspecting consumers, who are ill-prepared to differentiate between original and knockoff brands. In this business, the greater the number

[2] The River Port of Onitsha received its first barge with containers from Onne Port in Rivers State in October 2020, as a test run for operationalizing Onitsha Port in the first Quarter of 2021, according to the Nigerian Inland Waterways. There might have to be some dredging of River Niger down river to the Atlantic Ocean before ships with containers from Lagos will start servicing the new port after 42 years of inactivity, according to Vincent U. V. & Nwaiwu, C. (2020, October 10). Excitement as Onitsha River Port Comes alive. *Vanguard.*

of intermediaries, the higher the price of the merchandise which is why some traders will pool resources to place bulk orders to reduce costs and relatively increase their profit margin.

So we learn that Onitsha Market traders serve as distributors of local produce and national and international manufactured goods. Their product and capital linkages suggest a continuum of traders who only sell retail to those who make purchases from Lagos or foreign manufacturers and distributors in the informal and formal economy. Whenever possible, they will enter exclusive rights or "lock-down" distributorship which creates a monopoly over quantities bought and sold in the marketplace to increase profits, and over time, the trader may be tempted to open a factory to manufacture and sell the same products previously purchased from a foreign manufacturer, a pointer to why traders might be opposed to formalization of marketplace trade—it acts as an economic bridge to prosperity. The trader will prosper only if the quality is maintained but if other traders, as is the custom, expand into the same production activity and worse, churn out inferior knockoffs, then quality and profits will decline. In the end, there exists a different but unique classes of marketplace (stall) traders who may travel overseas to purchase saleable goods, buy locally, and/or acquire goods from national producers and manufacturers. The complex inter-relationships and the ability of marketplace traders to build and maintain a resilient commercial (marketplace) institution in the face of challenges posed by a global capitalistic system are a plus. The resilience has allowed traders to dominate (West) African urban economies, and continuing to ignore the impact of their activities and failing to address their internal needs is no more a viable or constructive development strategy.

References

Akad, E., Evren, G., & Akad, M. (2001). Transportation planning problems in developing countries. *JOUR*(January).

Asante, A. L. (2019). Urban governance and its implications for the microgeographies of market trading in Ghana: A case of the Kotokuraba Market Project in Cape Coast. *GeoJournal*(May).

Astrop, P. C., Maunder, D., & Babu, D. M. (1996). The urban travel behaviour of low-income households and females in Pune, India. *Center for Transportation Research*. Crowthorne, Berkshire, UK.

Baker, R. W. (1965). Marketing in Nigeria. *Journal of Marketing, 29*, 40–48.

Bauer, P. T. (1965). *West African trade*. A study of competition, oligopoly and monopoly in a changing economy. Routledge and Kegan.

Brycerson, D. F. (2011). Birth of a market town in Tanzania: Towards narrative studies of urban Africa. *Journal of East African Studies, 5*(2), 274–293.

Burdett, R., & Sudjic, D. (2010). *The endless city: The urban age project by the London school of economics and Deutsche Bank's Alfred Herrhausen society*. Phaidon.

Carr, M., & Chen, M. A. (2002). *Globalisation and the informal economy: How global trade and investment impact on the working poor*. ILO.

Cervero, R. (2014). Linking urban transport and land use in developing countries. *The Journal of Transport and Land Use, 6*(1), 7–24.

Chamlee-Wright, E. (2002). Savings and accumulation strategies of urban market women in Harare, Zimbabwe, *Economic Development and Cultural Change, 50*(4), 979–1006.

Chukwuemeka, C. V., Scheerlinck, K., & Schoonjans, Y. (2017). Collective spaces of informal and formal markets as drivers of self-organization processes of urban growth in emerging cities: Learning from Onitsha, Nigeria. *EU Human Cities*, 51–72.

Clare, T., & Romanik, C. T. (2008). *An urban-rural focus on food markets in Africa*. The Urban Institute.

Clark, G. (2010). *African market women: Seven life stories from Ghana*. Indiana University Press.

Conley, C., & Tafulene, A. (2015). Empowering market traders in Warwick Junction, Durban, South Africa. *WIEGO Inclusive Cities Project*

Diandas, J. (1984). Alternative approaches to transport in third world cities: Issues in equity and accessibility. *Ekistics, 306*, 197–210.

Dickerson, C. M. (2014). Bringing formal business laws to Cameroon's informal sector: Lessons and connections from the tax law example. *Washington University Global Studies Law Review, 13*(2).

Dike, A. A. (1982). Urban migrants and rural development. *African Studies Review, XXV*, 85–94.

Diouf, M. (2000). The Senegalese Murid trade Diaspora and the making of a Vernacular cosmopolitanism. *Public Culture, 12*(3), 679–702.

Dissancyake, D., & Morikawa, T. (2002). Household travel behavior in developing countries: Nested logit model of vehicle ownership, mode choice and trip chaining. *Transportation Research Record: Journal of the Transportation Research Board, 1805*(1), 45–52.

Fafchamps, M., Gabre-Madhin. E., & Minten, B. (2004). *Increasing market returns and market efficiency in agricultural trade*. Markets, Trade, and Institutions Division. Discussion Paper 60. International Food Policy Research Institute, Washington, DC.

Fields, G. S., & Pfeffermann. G. (Eds.). (2003). *Pathways out of poverty: Private firms and economic mobility in developing countries.* The World Bank/Kluwer Academic Publishers, World Bank, Washington, DC © World Bank. https://openknowledge.worldbank.org/handle/10986/25896 License: CC BY 3.0 IGO.

Geschiere, P., & Gugler, J. (1988). The urban-rural connection: Changing issues of belonging and identification. *Journal of the International African Institute, 68*(3), 309–319.

Golub, S. S., & Hansen-Lewis, J. (2012). Informal trading networks in West Africa: The Mourides of Senegal/The Gambia and the Yoruba of Benin/Nigeria. In S. Golub & J. H. Lewis (Eds.), *The informal sector in Francophone Africa.* The World Bank, Washington, DC https://openknowledge.worldbank.org/handle/10986/9364 License: CC BY 3.0 IGO.

Godbless, D. D., Ikechukwu, A. C., & Emeto, J. O. (2019). Nigeria development plans and its challenges: The way onward. *International Journal of Advanced Academic Research/social and Management Studies, 5*(12), 1–12.

Hanna, W. J., & Hanna, J. L. (1977). *Urban dynamics in Black Africa.* Aldine-Atherton.

Hart, K. (1970). Small-scale entrepreneurs in Ghana and development planning. *Journal of Development Studies, 6*(4), 104–120.

Hawkins, H. C. G. (1965). *Wholesale and retail trader in Tanganyika.* Frederick A Praeger.

Hill, P. (1970). *Studies in rural capitalism in West Africa.* Cambridge at the University Press.

Hodder, B. W., & Lee, R. (1974). *Economic geography.* St. Martin's Press.

Iheanacho, E. N. (2014). National development planning in Nigeria: An endless search for appropriate development strategy. *International Journal of Economic Research and Development, 5*(2), 49–60.

ILO. (2018). *Women and men in the informal economy: A statistical picture.* Geneva.

Josse, G. (2020). Planning and managing Africa's cities: What place for technology innovations? *Field Actions Science Reports,* Special Issue 22, 52–57.

Kilby, P. (1969). *Industrialisation in an open economy: Nigeria 1945–1966.* Cambridge at the University Press.

Kinyanjui, M. N. (2014). *Women and the informal economy in urban Africa: From the margins to the center.* Zed Books.

Koushki, P. A. (1988). The effect of socio-economic development on household travel behaviour in Saudi Arabia. *Socio-Economic Planning Sciences, 22*(2), 131–136.

Lanjouw, P. (1999). Rural nonagricultural employment and poverty in Ecuador. *Economic Development and Cultural Change, 48*(1), 91–122.

Lee, J. M. (1967). *Colonial development and good government: A study of the ideas expressed by the British Class in planning decolonization, 1933–1964.* Clarendon Press.

Lyon, F. (2003). Trader associations and urban food systems in Ghana: Institutionalist approaches to understanding urban collective actions. *International Journal of Urban and Regional Research, 27*(1), 11–23.

McDade, B. E., & Spring, A. (2005). The new generation of African entrepreneurs: Networking to change the climate for business and private sector-led development. *Entrepreneurship and Regional Development, 17*(January), 17–42.

Meagher, K. (2013). *Unlocking the informal economy: A literature review on linkages between formal and informal economies in developing countries* (WIEGO Working Paper No. 27), April.

OECD. (2016). Where cities can take Africa? 307 (Q 3) *OECD Observer.*

OECD. (2019). *Women and trade networks in West Africa.* Paris.

Olayemi, O. A. (1977). Intra-city travel in metropolitan Lagos: A study of commuting in the fast-growing capital in a developing country. *Geoforum, 8.*

Pedersen, P. O., & McCormick, D. (1999). African business systems in a globalizing world. *The Journal of Modern African Studies, 37*(1), 109–135.

Ramakrishnan, G. A., Srinivasan, K. K., & Pynda, S. P. (2020). Joint models for consideration of public transit and mode choice for work commute. *Transportation Developing Economies, 6*(12).

Rosenbloom, S., & Plesis-Fraissard, M. (2011). *Women's travel in developed and developing countries: Two versions of the same story?* In National Academy of Sciences. Women's Issues is transportation. Summary of the 4th International Conference, Vol. 1. Conference overview and plenary papers. National Academic Press.

Sarin, M. (2019). *Urban planning in the third world: The Chandigarh experience.* Routledge.

Srinivasan, S., & Rogers, P. (2005). Travel behavior of low-income residents: Studying two contrasting locations in Chenai India. *Journal of Transport Geography, 13*(3), 265–274.

Starkey, P., & Hine, J. (2014). *Poverty and sustainable transport: How transport policy affects the poor with policy implications for poverty reduction.* UN Habitat.

Stopher, P. R., & Ohstrom, E. C. et al. (1984). *Logit mode choice models for non-work trips. Transportation Research Record 891.* TRB, Washington, DC.

Teltscher, T. (1994). Small trade and the world economy: Informal vendors in Quito Ecuador. *Economic Geography, 70*(2), 167–187.

The Oregonian. (2000, January 2). The millennium around the world. *The Oregonian,* Portland, Oregon.

Tonelli, M., & Dalglish, C. (2012). *The role of transport infrastructure in facilitating the survival and growth of micro-enterprises in developing economies.* In the Joint ACERE-DIANA International Entrepreneurship Conference 31 January-3 February. University of Notre Dame, Fremantle, WA.

Trager, L. (2001). *Yoruba hometowns: Community, identity, and development in Nigeria.* Boulder, CO.

UN Habitat. (2009). *Structure plans for Awka, Onitsha and Nnewi and Environs 2009–2027.* Nairobi, Kenya.

UN. (1996). *Informal Sector Development in Africa,* NY.

Walther, O. J. (2016). Mapping West African trade networks. In *Brookings, Africa Focus.* Washington, DC.

Wolpe, H. (1974). *Urban politics in Nigeria.* University of California Press.

CHAPTER 3

Onitsha: The Largest Market in Nigeria—One of the Largest in West Africa

Onitsha is a key commercial town in Nigeria, and for that matter, one of the largest in the West African region. That is why it makes a great sample city to study traders. The discussion will focus on the development and rise of the town to its commercial prominence, how trading is organized, the character of the land use system that support urban commercial activities, and an evaluation of the mobility infrastructure relied upon by traders to conduct their daily business. The unmistakable economic prominence of this commercial center will contribute to explain why the state government, in collaboration with the UN Habitat for Humanity, have developed an urban development plan to "regenerate and revitalize" the city, to borrow from the governor, and make it the foremost commercial nerve center of Anambra State, the nation (Nigeria) and the West Africa Sub-Region (UN Habitat, 2009: 51).

THE DEVELOPMENT OF COMMERCE IN ONITSHA

Onitsha is situated approximately 150 miles from the Atlantic Ocean. It is located on the bank of the River Niger, at approximately 6^0 N and 7^0 E. It was founded in the seventeenth century by immigrants from Bini to the west of the River Niger. Onitsha has grown to merge with its surrounding settlements to form a sprawling urban corridor in what is today known as the ONA (Onitsha-Nnewi-Awka) Industrial Axis (UN Habitat, 2009:

© The Author(s), under exclusive license to Springer Nature Switzerland AG 2022
K. Ochia, *Marketplace Trade and West African Urban Development*,
https://doi.org/10.1007/978-3-030-87556-5_3

12). According to Hodder and Ukwu (1969: 234), the original settlement was at Ndende on a low river terrace, standing 30 feet above the
river flood or 100–150 feet above the sea level. According to Floyd
(1969: 284), originally Onitsha had acted as an entrepôt port between
the Delta ports along the Atlantic Ocean and the other trading stations
on the upper Niger and Benue rivers in the interior. It has also acted as
a collection and bulking center for all towns along the lower Niger in
today's Anambra, Delta and River states.[1] During the high flood season,
also known as the rainy season (originally between July and October),
the River Niger is navigable from the Delta ports past Lokoja to Baro,
but during the low water season, also known as the dry season (originally January–June), Onitsha comes into its own, as an entrepôt when
bulk cargo from the Delta ports and produce from northern Nigeria are
transshipped to Onitsha. The completion of irrigation dams up the rivers
has relatively diminished the amount of water flow in the lower Niger
until climate change also increased the amount of rain in the upper Niger
area and, the unlocking of dams often cause high floods in the lower
Niger south of Onitsha (2012 saw the first and worst climate change-
induced flooding, then there were other floods in 2018, 2019, and 2020)
because of its low elevation. Figure 3.1 shows the location of Onitsha in
Nigeria.

Onitsha became a British trading post in the eighteenth century. The
dominance of Onitsha as a commercial center began after European
merchants established their factories in 1857. Prior to that date, the
market in Onitsha was a typical periodic market that allowed Onitsha
to have reciprocal trade relations with various towns in the hinterland.
On a typical trading day, there were about 500 people in the market
(Crowther, 1966). Today, the market town attracts as much as 1.5 million
people daily. Prior to the mid-nineteenth century era, slave trading was
the dominant trading activity in these areas. European Mission Traders,
who arrived in 1857, brought with them Western education, Christianity,
and the copper coins that replaced cowries as the medium of exchange
(Crowther, 1966). The establishment of European factories hastened the

---

[1] For an excellent anthropological background on the collection, bulking and commercial relationship between Onitsha and the other trading posts, see Richard N Henderson
and Helen K Henderson, *Onitsha History, Kinship and Changing Cultures*, 1962,
amightytree.org/otu-onitsha-waterside-1960–1962.

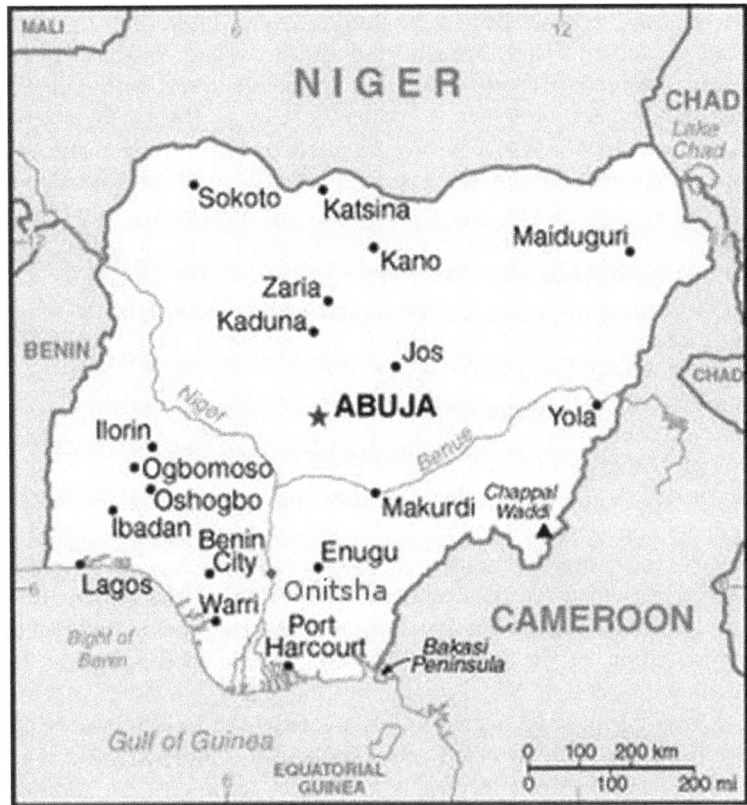

Fig. 3.1 Map of Nigeria showing the location of Onitsha

replacement of slave trading with palm produce trade, according to Elizabeth Isichei. As a result, several local traders switched from trading fish, pottery, potash, and beads to bulking palm produce for overseas markets. With the expanding commercial influence and trading activities, the market moved from its original location at Ndende to the Otu Okwodu site which today forms part of the inner central business district. The 2009 UN Habitat Plan for Onitsha plans to re-develop the Central Business District (CBD) to enhance its commercial prominence and accommodate small, medium, and large-scale commercial activities.

Meanwhile, several British (including John Holt and the United African Company) and French trading firms had established factories and engaged in both retail and wholesale trade with indigenous traders acting as middlemen (Hodder & Ukwu, 1969). Pedersen and McCormick (1999: 114) have commented on this arrangement and its impact on overall African development. "Very often the formal private sector is dominated by enterprises owned by non-indigenous groups." They continue: "The subsystem of non-indigenous business has... developed into an integrated system comprising trade and services, as well as manufacturing industries, and often controlling important parts of the import–export and wholesale trade." This structure of a large informal trade sector and a small formal (manufacturing, financial) sector still characterize the urban economy.

Several other factors contributed to the growth of the commercial town of Onitsha. One of the factors was that "by 1911 the Resident British Administrator for Onitsha Province laid out Onitsha and gave it its first look as an urban settlement (Onyemelukwe, 1974: 51)" that included plans for construction of modern roads. The structural improvement enhanced the commercial attributes of the center. Another important factor was the introduction of municipal services, following the implementation of the Nigerian Township Ordinance passed in 1917. According to Akin L Mabogunje, the 2nd Class Township of Onitsha had a hospital in 1917, water supply by 1929, and electricity by 1950. These urban services attracted migrants to the center who ended up in the burgeoning informal economy, especially commerce. In addition to these improvements, the local governing authorities erected permanent market stalls by 1928 at the site of today's Main Market (in the CBD) in order to create order in the marketplace (Hodder & Ukwu, 1969: 238). The development centralized urban marketplace trade and served as an incentive for growth, as it assured traders of protected space for conducting business.

The introduction of the lorry in the 1920s and its proliferation in the 1930s reduced mobility cost in terms of travel time, fare, and inconvenience. Hodder and Ukwu (1969: 236) report that "records show that the journey from Agwu (Enugu State) to Onitsha (for instance), in 1927 took the greater part of two days, and (that) old traders in Bende (in today's Abia State) Division report that it took three days from there." However, "With motor transport this was cut down to between three and five hours, and no part of Eastern Provinces (now Anambra,

Enugu, Imo, Abia, Akwa Ibom, Cross River and Rivers, Taraba, Benue states and parts of Kogi state) was more than ten hours away, the rather slow speed – 20–30 mph – and the frequent stoppages of the vehicles notwithstanding." The arriving immigrants successfully transferred the concept of the traditional village mini open-market system to the urban area. These urban villagers have transformed the look of the town and its style of commercial activities. For example, the mini-markets became the forerunner to the multiplication in the number of market sites in Onitsha, as government attempted to enforce land use laws, but has been continuously overwhelmed by limited staff and poor training or lack of capacity, and as many of these urban villagers legitimize their brand of land use—everything everywhere—to support their livelihood.

Other developments that benefitted the growth of commerce in Onitsha were the eventual construction of the Main Market and the Niger Bridge. The construction of a modern Main Market by 1955 and the subsequent allocation of stalls to relatively small traders and only to those lines (goods) which most needed to be in the market, on the advice of indigenous traders themselves, was an important development. Perhaps, the preponderance of relatively small traders and the desire to exclude the usually large foreign distributors, who were also in retail trade and, therefore, competitors with traders in the Main Market, provide a demonstration of the early political muscle of traders in local politics. As a rule, the bigger traders stayed out of the Main Market and carried out their businesses in lockup shops located along adjacent streets (Hodder & Ukwu, 1969: 239). To reduce the search cost for goods, the market was divided into zones—the grouping of kindred sellers in a defined area of the market that created the unintended consequence of fierce competition among sellers. Staple food stuff sellers, for example, are located next to the river to make it easier for foodstuffs from up and down the River Niger to unload and sell their products at the market. Typically, buyers congregate at the waterside to consummate deals and pay laborers to off-load the purchase. Conducting the transaction where the water or marine (transport) meets the land (human transport) minimizes cost to both sellers and buyers by taking advantage of this intermodal transfer opportunity.

The intense competition in the marketplace reduces the profit margin, and to retain customers, sellers must develop sharp marketing skills and occasionally dubious customer service—the birth of the apprentice system in the marketplace to assist with customer service. Some traders cut corner by baiting and switching—exchange adulterated copy of a merchandise after settling on a price using the genuine merchandise as a prop. This is how it works. The apprentice under the watchful eye of the stall owner or master haggles and agrees on a price for the article after the buyer is convinced that it is the 'real deal.' Meanwhile, the owner places an imitation or knockoff of the merchandise in the back of the stall for the apprentice. After they agree on the price, as the apprentice walks back into the stall to wrap or bag the merchandise, the apprentice quickly retrieves the knockoff, wraps, and gives it to the buyer. The unsuspecting buyer is completely unaware of what has just transpired. Of course, the buyer is stonewalled if they attempted to return the merchandise. These days the Market Master will intervene on behalf of the customer, especially if the traders' union is involved with the complaint. The Market Master and the union are collaborating to maintain the integrity and reputation of the commercial behemoth.

Despite the intense competition, there is also intense cooperation between traders as a coping mechanism. The cooperation allows one trader to sell the other's merchandise under the guise of owning their stall. This is how this ruse is accomplished. A customer arrives with a request to buy a given quantity of merchandise or a brand that the seller does not stock. The seller will pretend that he has the merchandise in 'the other stall.' As the seller walks down the line with the uninitiated buyer, the seller will scan stalls to identify who has the merchandise or the brand and when he identifies a seller, as they both enter that stall, the trader will quickly assume the persona of the owner of that 'other stall' where he has spotted the merchandise for sale. He will address the occupants by made up names and ordering them to get a chair or cold water for the customer. The stall occupants will play along, as this imposter takes temporary ownership of the stall. In control, he will ask for the invoice of the merchandise. This is the 'invoice' traders maintain and appropriately deploy to persuade customers about what they allegedly 'paid for' the merchandise for which they are willing to take a loss but must make the sale—this is the 'good' for you but 'bad' for me charade. The imposter will share that price information with the customer and haggles over a sale price convincing the buyer that he will lose money, but it is alright to be nice to a customer who has come all this way to buy merchandise. After they agree at an equilibrium price, the customer gets the quantity or the brand he/she wants. The imposter orders one of the stall occupants to assist the customer with the merchandise to the motor park (intercity bus station) for his/her return trip home. Later that day, the imposter returns to that stall and splits the profit with the real stall owner—a win–win-win for all stakeholders, but quite a clever ruse.

The other development that contributed to the growth of Onitsha was the construction of the Niger Bridge (1966) which linked Onitsha town in the east-end of the bridge with the west (including Lagos) directly by road for the first time. Prior to that, traffic across the Niger was handled by motorized ferries and a primitive but more efficient canoe ferry services for travelers without bulky load or personal automobile. With the improved overland transport system, the direct importation of European and locally-manufactured goods was handled more efficiently because total travel time and inconvenience were significantly reduced; for example, loaded lorries took about 40 minutes to cross the Niger, and without breaking bulk (Udo, 1970) and that ferry time was saved from the entire trip. According to Udo, ferrying involved a significant waste of time with cars delayed over 12 hours and lorries for five (5) days at the Asaba end, opposite Onitsha. But the protracted bridge construction contributed to the creation and consolidation of the Nwadimpka evening sauce market[2] located close to the head bridge in the eastside. So, on the eve of the Nigerian Civil War (1967), Onitsha had a large (Main Market/Ose Okwodu consortium) and medium-sized (Ochanja) markets and several sauce markets—Nwadimpka, Ndende, Awka Rd, and Atani Rd. Moreover, it had become a central place and a specialized commercial center serving as a break-in-bulk for both hinterland and distant markets. It had also become a cultural, social, and administrative center in southern Nigeria. As Onuorah Nzekwu would describe it, above all, Onitsha had become "just one great market" town.

With the cessation of hostilities (1970), Onitsha has recaptured and even surpassed its pre-war pedigree—and the berthing of barges and talks by government to make the town an international inland shipping port by allowing ships to berth and directly load/off-load cargo is a great improvement.[3] Since the 1980s, the significantly improved intercity

[2] A sauce market provides basic cooking ingredients and raw indigenous food supplies and mainly serves neighborhood residents. Some Marketers sell prepared food (to construction workers and others).

[3] The federal government is rebuilding the bridge (south of the existing bridge) because it has exceeded its useful life. Because of the diminished integrity of the structural frame, when the traffic is heavy such as the holiday season, travel is limited to one lane each way on the bridge to reduce stress on the frame. See Agbodo, J.A. (2020). Anambra APC

road system, combined with aggressively expanding trucking businesses, such as the Dangote Transport Company, tremendously reduced the demand for river transport facilities and services as the major supply system, as trucks deliver foodstuffs from northern Nigeria and from the other food-producing areas in the hinterland at record levels and time and manufactured goods from Lagos and other ocean ports and other foreign countries (Oxford Business Group, 2012), a demonstration of the existing linkage with local, national, and international formal and informal sectors. According to UN Habitat (2009: 12) since the mid-1990s, Onitsha has grown to merge with surrounding settlements to form a sprawling urban corridor. Table 3.1 shows the population and projected growth rate of Onitsha from 1991 to 2030. The center had about 256,000 inhabitants in 1991 and it is estimated to reach a population of over one million by 2030. About 20% of the workforce are engaged in industry and manufacturing, while 80% are engaged in sales and distribution. The surge in population growth must have contributed to the evolution of new markets and structural changes to older markets, as more urban residents are easily absorbed by the sector. For example, the Ochanja Market was relocated to Upper Iweka Rd with a vestige of original market sellers along adjacent streets with scantily-stocked sheds, while the Nwadimpka Market has been absorbed by an enlarged Head

Table 3.1   Population and population growth rate, Onitsha, Nigeria

Local Govt	1991	2006	2010	2015	2020	2025	2030
Onitsha N	121,157	124,942	210,000	295,000	395,000	425,000	500,000
Onitsha S	135,290	136,662	200,000	300,000	400,000	475,000	525,000
Total	256,447	261,604	410,000	595,000	795,000	900,000	1,025,000
Growth Rate Percent	NA	2.02%	56.73%	45.12%	33.61%	13.21%	13.89%

Source UN Habitat: Structure Plan for Awka, Onitsha, and Nnewi and Environs 2009–2027, March 2009

lauds Buhari on 2nd Niger Bridge, Enugu-Onitsha expressway, others in South-East, *Sun News online,* August, 13.

Bridge Market. The two express road markets (Ochanja and Nwadimpka) are much larger in size than the original markets they replaced. Moreover, the Atani Road Market has been absorbed by the Head Bridge Market, although a vestige of the market also remains and is now attached to a motor park mainly serving the Ogbaru Local Government area south of Onitsha. The original market site and some of the adjacent properties have been developed into hotels, gas stations, and light manufacturing and distribution in an area commonly referred to as the Head Bridge Development Layout (Izueke & Eme, 2013). So, from an early trading outpost, to improvements in motorization and travel, increased accessibility, the continuing population growth, and a unique exchange system in the marketplace have allowed Onitsha the ability to absorb new arrivals to cement its lead as a commercial powerhouse in Nigeria, albeit, in West Africa.

West Africa Urbanizing and Impacts on Urban Marketplace Trade

Table 3.2 shows that population numbers are trending upwards and fast, especially for the primate capital cities—Abidjan, Accra, Lomé, Lagos, and Doula—that house most of each country's infrastructure, administrative, and economic activities. Therefore, it is understandable why a World Bank (2017) document authored by Lall, Henderson and Venables notes that the population density of African cities is like that of many other cities elsewhere. However, what is holding (the non-capital?) African cities back, the authors note, is their low economic density, that is, the lack of

Table 3.2 Population of selected West Africa cities

City	Population	
	2010 (000)	2020 (000)
Abidjan	2,837	3,677
Accra	2,342	4,200
Conakry	1,518	1,938
Lomé	837	1,828
Kano	3,395	3,999
Lagos	10,578	14,368
Freetown	905	1,202
Douala	2,125	3,663

Source Various

thriving urban markets that depend on adequate infrastructure and convenient connection to clusters of residential and commercial structures. Consequently, (economic) growth is not keeping pace with population growth, the authors conclude, and that makes African cities closed to the world. A critic may argue that these cities are not really "closed" to the world by choice or as part of a deliberate, thoughtful, and calibrated development plan; rather, their conditions are the consequence of the continuation of a development tradition bequeathed to the colonies that tied the economic development frameworks of these countries to the interests (aka trading relationships or partnerships) of ex-colonial masters (for example, presently France requires its colonies to deposit 50%, previously 100% which was later reduced to 65%, of their foreign exchange CFA franc reserve in a designated bank in France—a system that benefits the French economy). These arrangements have survived into post-independent and contemporary African economic history. It was principally a development strategy and economic inter-relationship that was based on extracting and exporting raw materials from the colonies for processing overseas. As such, economic development was and is still based on the export of unprocessed strategic raw materials such as oil, bauxite, iron ore, cocoa, columbite, uranium, cobalt, and coltan and the import of relatively expensive finished goods. Consider that at a granular or local level, during the colonial era, in some African countries (for example, British colonies) those involved with the production and distribution of local alcoholic drinks typical in the rural areas where the raw material was plentiful, for example, were subject to arrest and jail time. It was dubbed 'illicit gin' even though African markets were being flooded with foreign brand alcoholic drinks such as Gordon's Gin that squeezed the size of the market for local producers and eventually drove the manufacturing and sale underground. Labeling it illicit provided a legal cover to eliminate the beverage to provide a substitute product. Consider this. The binding trading relationships with the colonizers meant, for example, that as commodity prices were set to fall in 2019, according to the IMF (Oct 2019), the income of raw-material exporting (African) countries would also suffer a decline, and we will add, based on commodity prices set in Brussels or other commodity trading spots elsewhere—illustrating the continued impact of unequal (free) trade relationships (or pacts signed on the eve of de-colonization) and potential capital shortages to African countries to invest to open the door of cities.

For the African-cities-closed-to-the-world argument, enthusiasts should consider a counter explanation provided by Lewellen (1995: 62). "Oil (for example) is a natural product that can be put on a ship for export for little or no processing. The extraction of oil provides relatively few jobs, requires little research, and needs no domestic auxiliary companies to support it. The spin-off effects of production are, thus, minimal." Andy Rooney, an illustrious television commentator in the US once derisively challenged his audience if anyone had ever gone to a gas (petrol) station and asked to buy a barrel or two of oil. He was merely trying to elevate the level of the conversation regarding the enduring free-trade inequity and inequality based on exploitation and the resulting unequal power or trade relationships between raw-material producing and raw-material processing countries. There is no productive agglomeration from raw material-shipping process, neither are there any tangible spin-off effects from the actual export thereof. A spin-off would have included the creation of large formal sector employment in manufacturing of consumer goods (plastic bags, furniture, household goods), industrial goods (rubber for industrial use, asphalt, jet fuel, automobile gas, heating oil), and the creation of highly skilled labor (chemical analysts, chemical engineers, pharmaceutical engineers, agro-chemical industrialists) if crude oil, for example, were processed in African countries. The social spin-off effect is that these manufacturing-related activities would have created an educated middle-class managers and professionals who can articulate societal needs, including the injustice of corruption, and place demand on leaders who otherwise have traditionally dealt with an impoverished population, a majority of who are surviving on $1.25/day and have no time to devote to the pursuit of processes linked to production and distribution of public/social goods. These goods include roads, clean water, electricity, disposal of sewerage, and a healthy education system. The availability of these production inputs will in turn spur more manufacturing activities and an enlarged formal sector employment that produces consumers (markets) with the income to spend on value-added goods and services. In that way, African cities will become open with clusters of producers connected to local and international consumer clusters (markets). Another way to look at this argument is that African countries are providing the engines of economic prosperity for all countries that import African strategic raw materials unprocessed, more poignant when the United Nations Environment Program reminds us that Africa still holds 30% of world's mineral reserves, 8% of its natural gas, 12% of oil reserves, 40% of its gold reserves, and up to 90% of its chromium and platinum. African traditional organic rice farmers, for example, have borne the brunt of imported rice that is advertised and sold as 'better quality' rice to locals who confuse marketing with facts. What these farmers need is modern machines and equipment to allow them to harvest and properly process their product to remove debris and tiny limestone in the rice that necessitate 'picking the rice' (removing debris/little stones) before cooking—a painstaking manual labor that deters buyer and instill the belief that imported rice is better than organically-grown local rice. In that way, their product will be competitive with imported rice.

What we have in African countries, instead, is an economic and development structure that has always depended on the export of unprocessed raw materials to derive national revenues, and with money from the export exchanged to import consumer goods from the same actors. Governments buy social peace by ensuring that there are plentiful consumables, especially for those residing in urban areas that serve as potential hotbeds for civil unrest. The abundance of consumer goods in cities, together with relatively more modern amenities, and the expectation of employment lead to continuing rural–urban migration. Migrants arrive without a promise of a job but with the expectation that there are job opportunities in town, based on observed consumption lifestyle of urban residents. In the absence of jobs in the formal sector, the informal economy is positioned to absorb the excess labor force of new and existing residents. The informal economy has opportunities that allow easy entry, and with weak enforcement of government regulations, some individuals may find refuge and solace in underground informal economy, when everything else fails.

Commenting on spin-off effects when there is manufacturing, Lewellen (1995: 62) opines "Producing tractors... involves great amounts of labor, high levels of education for researchers and scientists, considerable job specialization, numerous auxiliary producers and suppliers and a strong infrastructure of roads and railroads." This is what the processing of iron ore and allied minerals would provide if tractors were built in these areas. A local manufacturing base using local (African) raw materials will contribute to economic growth in cities that will keep pace with population growth. In the absence of these scenarios, market traders and the marketplace will continue to dominate the economies of African cities, and as such, they deserve the attention of researchers and policy makers. Table 3.3 shows 2018 export and import data for sub-Saharan Africa.

Table 3.3 Sub-Saharan Africa export and import of product goods

Product Group	Export Product share %	Import Product share %
Raw materials	52.49	11.92
Intermediate goods	24.55	21.06
Consumer goods	16.35	37.88
Capital goods	6.25	25.92

Source WITS, Sub-Saharan Africa Trade (2018)

From these data, assuming that African countries can responsibly account for the real volume or quantity of raw materials they export, it appears that sub-Saharan African countries export half of their manufacturing jobs through the export of raw materials that, if locally processed, would have had the most visible impact on the manufacturing sector. Aside from being weakened by exporting raw materials, sub-Saharan Africa imports almost 40% of their consumer goods. Put differently, sub-Saharan African countries are continuously creating formal sector jobs elsewhere—both in processing raw materials and manufacturing consumer goods—while weakening the creation of similar job opportunities in their own countries, even as fast-paced urbanization continues. As one highly placed government official put it to me, we are so poor and that is why they are so rich, she bemoaned, reflecting the prevailing (and entrenched) unequal exchange system. What is left is the agricultural sector with associated low-skill manufacturing such as beer brewing, tomato paste canning, and production of fruit juice. If (West) African countries continue on this treadmill, as urbanization continues unabated, it will be difficult to establish that strong wage sector that will absorb the (un)skilled labor; therefore, marketplace trading will continue to play a dominant role in the economies of African cities because traders are responsible for selling consumer goods in Africa's consumption cities. Cities will continue to practice internal colonialism by indirectly benefitting from enclave economies of mining and extraction of raw materials in rural areas for export. Taken together, the complete story is that African cities may not have closed their doors, as cities are urbanizing, but with relative availability of large quantities of finished consumer products in urban areas, together with relatively more urban services and employment opportunities, cities will continue to act as magnets for migrants from the hinterland (as some older adults retire and move back to the hinterland) that add to the urban population, at a faster rate than cities can efficiently absorb. This results in the continuing expansion of the informal economy (see Kennedy, 1988; Rapley, 2002) similar to the 1870–1910 US urbanization period when approximately 50% of urban employment was in the service sector—a condition that contributes to make African cities appear as if they have closed their doors to the world.

Cities are crowded, disconnected, and costly, the World Bank authors observe, and we will argue that it is because of the established and entrenched dependency (fortified by globalization) economy. To address this problem, they offer that (West) African cities become economically dense and not merely crowded, and one way to achieve that goal is to draw firms and skilled workers to a more affordable and livable urban environment in cities, but therein lies the conundrum, as we just explained above. Should African countries start to process those raw material in Africa and produce more consumer goods, cities already have a cadre of unemployed and under-employed workers who are willing to avail themselves of employment opportunities in the formal economy; otherwise, according to Teltscher (1994: 171), as most workers in the less developed countries are already employed in the service sector, the prediction that an increasing number will continue to be employed in trading activities will continue to be realized, a valid prediction made based on her work in Latin America. A reversal of such trend would make African cities economically dense, as the World Bank authors surmise, but by assisting (West) African countries to expand and strengthen their manufacturing base to produce regionally and globally-traded goods and services, instead of maximizing the manufacture of tradable goods for the local market. Assistance could come in the form of providing a renegotiated structural framework of support that indigenizes the processing of a large proportion of major raw materials locally and exporting finished products. A substantive support would include a willingness to transfer the technology, as raw materials and labor are already in abundance in the Africa. Pursuing this strategy would contribute to improve the economic density of African cities, we will argue.

As shown in Table 3.4, the urbanization rate in sub-Saharan Africa in 2013 was at par with Latin America and the Caribbean of 1950, but her per capita GDP was only at 54.73%. The low levels of GDP would suggest that sub-Sahara Africa had unsophisticated economy like the Latin American/Caribbean Zone had in the 1950s, and that is a consumption-based economy; therefore, it is anticipated that commerce

Table 3.4 Comparing Sub-Saharan urbanization

Units of Measure	Latin America and the Caribbean	Middle East and N Africa	East Asia and the Pacific	Sub-Saharan Africa
Urbanization Rate	41%	41%	37%	37%
Comparable Year	1950	1968	1994	2013
Per Capita GDP (2005)	$1,860	1,806	$3,617	$1,018

Source Lall et al., World Bank (2017: 17)

will continue to feature prominently in the economy, as traders distribute and sell consumer goods in an indigenous capitalist market system. After all, in 2018 (see Table 3.3), consumer goods, in the aggregate, constituted almost 40% of imports in urbanizing sub-Saharan African countries. Along those lines, commercial centers, such as Onitsha, will continue to play an important role in the economic history of these areas, and this trend may continue. You see, before he received the Nobel Memorial Prize in Economic Sciences in 2008, Krugman (1994) had argued that importing from low labor cost countries could (understandably) threaten the productivity and prosperity of the US and, we may add perhaps, other developed countries. Critics may demur and wonder if it is then acceptable and defensible for low labor cost countries to continue to import finished goods from developed countries, often at inflated prices, without significant and unjustifiable negative effects on their economies?

SPATIAL ORGANIZATION

This section will examine the land use system, including an evaluation of how the marketplace is organized and a discussion of the structure of the mobility system. The existing conditions will resonate with traders in Accra, Ghana; Lusaka, Zambia; Nairobi, Kenya; Harare, Zimbabwe, and elsewhere in Africa and for that matter, in several cities in the developing areas. The discussion will provide a better understanding of how urban market traders depend on and/or are controlled and constrained by the existing land use structure, as they navigate the space created by it.

The Uses of Land

A generalized land use in Onitsha is characterized by mixed use. However, the northeastern portion of the city is substantially residential. This is the area known as Inland Town where the original migrants from Bini live. The remaining parts of town mainly consist of mixtures of residential, commercial, processing, financial, light manufacturing establishments, and other services. The recognizable markets tend to have geographically-defined boundaries but some commercial activities are still carried on all over the place, albeit at different scales. The evolution and growth of the Express Road Corridor markets were influenced by the delayed and protracted reconstruction of the Niger Bridge after the Nigerian Civil War (1967–1970), and more important, by the extension project of the express road from the bridge to the Upper Iweka Road junction. In addition, the establishment of industrial and housing estates and the construction of military barracks on adjacent properties played significant roles in promoting the growth and prominence of the corridor. The two major markets located along the corridor are also served by motor parks or terminal transit stations for inter- and intra-urban transport services. The Fegge and areas to the east and to the southeast of Inland Town are residential with neighborhood shops and commercial strips serving pedestrians and adjacent residents. Government administrative offices are located closer to the Inland Town, perhaps, a result of the early monopoly and grip on urban administrative machinery by those often referred to as Onitsha indigenes. They are the major inhabitants of Inland Town around the palace of the Obi of Onitsha, the traditional ruler.

For a long time, land use laws have not been seriously enforced, or when they were, it has increasingly been by force or punitive, ad hoc, and generally for a limited time and sometimes transactional. For example, in 1985, the new military government informed traders that they were forbidden to expand the size of their sheds by building 'attachments' for personal use or for rent. Attachments provide temporary (but soon permanent) badly needed additional trading space. They construct them with any available materials such as discarded planks, corrugated zinc, plastic sheets, and bricks to anchor the pulsating plastic sheets. As a routine, all offenders were cited and their goods often confiscated by the Market Master. Increased enforcement of this and similar land use laws affect the environment of the trader and tend to contribute to the need for intra-urban trips, even when traders may not be aware that there is a Land Use Master Plan or city laws forbidding such non-harmful uses of land for personal benefits, they would argue. To substantiate their claim of ignorance of the law (which is no legal excuse to flout the law), Aribigbola (2008: 1–14) has conducted a study in Akure a town of about 556,000 inhabitants in western Nigeria and found that 79.5% of urban residents were unaware of the existence of a master plan for the town, while only a mere 19% were aware of such a plan. It is inconceivable, therefore, that a zoning ordinance, which implements a master plan, will be common knowledge among these citizens. So, what you get is an amalgamation of an erratic enforcement of zoning code violations that encourages the continuing expansion of commercial activities onto the public rights of way. As a result, it converts open spaces to selling stations that obstruct the roadway by various sellers. International agencies (UN Habitat, 2009) have condemned the weak land use system, and the state governor Peter Obi has also condemned its effects on urban space that he has described Onitsha as an "unorganized entity." This is part of the reason why the state government in October 2019 commenced the clearing of street sellers and illegal motor parks from areas in the northeast part of town, and set up mobile courts to prosecute offenders, another example of punitive ad hoc land use enforcement regimen. The effective enforcement of land use regulations requires it to be institutionalized, routine, and continuous. To address the bad land use control system for commercial activities, the UN Habitat-state government collaborative development plan proposes to enhance commercial activities by improving and upgrading existing markets and allocating land for new markets to address expanding market activities. We will argue that in allocating land and building new markets, any failures to plan with facts could lead to the repeat and/or intensification of prevailing conditions, especially near the market(s), and the coalition appears interested in addressing the situation.

One significant feature of the land use system is the characteristic absence of major manufacturing establishments within residential neighborhoods, Fig. 3.2. Such establishments tend to surround and/or are adjacent to the built-up areas. Perhaps, the original land tenure system in which land is held in trust for the family could have been a factor. In Onitsha, the indigenous population had laid claim to an extensive land area and perhaps were more inclined to parcel them out in small holdings for development of residential properties, rather than for industrial purposes. Moreover, the early lead and continuous interest in Onitsha for

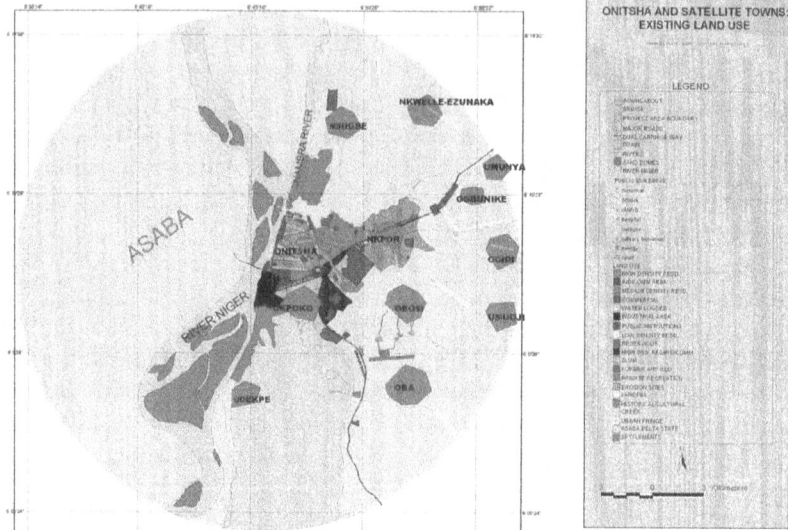

Fig. 3.2   Onitsha generalized land use

commerce may have reduced the interest in development of a tangible manufacturing sector—an activity the original land owners may have unfortunately considered incompatible with healthy living. For example, a review of the 1957 Map of Federal Nigeria Department of Commerce and Industry Supplement of manufacturing establishments shows that there were no manufacturing establishments in Onitsha, despite its regional importance. Mind you, this map was published about 36 months before the country's independence.

Onitsha still has relatively few manufacturing industries and they are based on processing agricultural and tree products (beverages, food-stuffs, rubber products, saw milling), and consumer goods (textiles and footwear), and printing. Apparently, industries must have been late arrivals due to the center's head start in commerce. Other studies (Okafor, 1986) have also found issues with land development planning and enforcement processes in Onitsha. In a more recent review of the land use structure, Emoh et al. (2013) find that government believes it is bringing order to an unorganized land use system by focusing on the issuance of building permits and certificate of occupancy, instead of monitoring incompatible uses and enforcing other violations as stipulated in the zoning ordinance. The resultant effect of this spurious argument is the sprouting of illegal structures and emergence of unauthorized uses, especially when traders own a significant proportion of the real state in town and may be reluctant to discourage kindred activities on their property. However, there are proposals for 15 residential layouts within and around the periphery of town, where residences will be truly segregated from other land uses. This will suggest that there are plans for urban renewal projects to update the look of the city, as the city grows and modernizes its land use structure that has drawn the governor's angst and the determination to regenerate and revitalize Onitsha. In any case, regardless of what has produced the present land use character and associated problems (Okafor, 1986: 221–229), in the absence of an overall enforceable development plan (Obi-Ani & Isiani, 2020), the spatial unorganized distribution of different land uses—schools, hospitals and health centers, warehousing, government administrative offices, financial establishments, religious institutions—and other community activity centers have created gravity zones that attract traders during business hours. We will evaluate the structure and characteristics of the resulting interactions in a later chapter.

The UN Habitat-sponsored urban development plan has developed a new land use structure that, if implemented as planned, is positioned to better serve and support the economic growth in the ONA corridor, the Onitsha-Nnewi-Awka industrial and manufacturing corridor. The proposal is that the corridor will spatially distribute urban development within the geographic area. Although traders constitute a major component of the local labor force, notice that the plan describes them merely as "petty traders" while justifiably emphasizing the need for manufacturing and industrialization, even though community members who are traders in Ijesha argue that trading leads to the development of industry, according to Trager (2001: 151), a point overlooked by these planners. One plausible interpretation of the commentary is that Trager found that Ijesha traders are willing to diversify into manufacturing which makes us believe that Ijesha community members also are aware that traders could enter manufacturing of goods they used to import, or other ventures, especially if the process is simple and not too capital intensive, such as manufacturing umbrellas, lady's handbag, or footwear. Despite the petty trader label, the plan also recognizes that planning for Onitsha is synonymous with planning for commercial activities—quite a contradiction—and the goal is to reinforce the vision of Onitsha as the foremost commercial nerve center of national and international repute, the plan stresses. As a leading indicator, it is certainly understandable why the UN Habitat would prefer to emphasize the manufacturing sector, while appearing to, undeservingly, under-value actors whose present activities constitute a major force in the local economy. Perhaps, this could be a coordinated strategy to encourage the city to "open its doors to the world." Besides, manufacturing will readily grow government coffers as it is widely known that tax collection cost is much cheaper for the government for manufacturers than for those engaged in 'petty trading.' That notwithstanding, they deserve equal attention, including a better appreciation of their current contribution to the local economy. After all, small-scale enterprises, including small-scale commerce, generally generate more employment per-unit of capital than do large-scale enterprises, according to studies in Latin America (Lanjouw, 1999: 92).

No matter how the document describes traders, the UN Habitat and other stakeholders should revisit the problem of "The Leap" associated with African businessmen (and certainly women). This is the reluctance to transition into a larger business organization because of the fear of losing existing intricate social web of relationships established in the current business. Sayre Schatz warns of the potential for reduced interest by traders to leap into relatively large, impersonally-managed formal (manufacturing) enterprises (Schatz, 1977: 97). This serves as a warning to planners and practitioners who are working with governments to build new markets and/or refurbish existing markets to diligently ensure that traders do not lose customers due to relocation and to be sensitive when discussing formalization issues with this "crowd," to borrow from Robert Dahl.

Market Organization

According to J. Beajeu-Garnier and Annie Dolobez, any commercial transaction is comprised of (a) making available the resalable goods; (b) the types of trading relationships and how they function; (c) the mechanics of the exchange process; and (d) the financial implications. Now, let us review how trading in Onitsha addresses each of these components in commercial transactions that are often fleeting and strictly cash and carry.

The marketplace is a special identity found in urban commerce in Africa. The infrastructure that defines the market plays an undeniable function in organizing African cities (Gantner, 2009) and that is the marketplace institution. Markets dominate distributive trade in (West) Africa as it is the functional foci for collection and distribution of goods produced by formal and informal economies. The marketplace serves as the major shopping center where individuals also meet to renew friendships and share information. It serves as a place for socializing, and for those in the apprentice program, a training institution for sharpening mental skills necessary for negotiating prices. Even with the emergence of mini shopping malls, marketplaces still serve individuals of different socio-economic status because of the heterogeneity of goods, including quality and price, and provide that opportunity to get a good deal by haggling over the price of good. The market has high order and lower goods that are sold, albeit in different zones.

In evaluating some of the factors responsible for the growth of the market town of Onitsha, J.O.C Onyemelukwe discovered that eight out of ten times Onitsha has lower prices for manufactured goods than the other centers in Ibadan, Enugu, Port-Harcourt, and Lagos. Even for agricultural food products, the prices in Onitsha are lower than what producers receive in their village markets where, in addition, they must attend various periodic markets and may sell on credit. Moreover, Onitsha has a wide areal trade influence in Nigeria. Fertile soils are an endowment that allow the hinterland to produce food staples. The settlements along the flood plains of the Niger also support rich agricultural farmlands. The producers in these areas have easy and quick river access to Onitsha. This has compelled the Oxford Business Group (2012) to observe that as an established commercial center, Onitsha serves as the main hub for goods coming upstream from the River Niger delta and those transported downstream from towns on the Niger and River Benue.

Commenting on the organization of trade in Onitsha, Margaret Katzin observes that each stall generally consists of the principal trader, usually the owner of the stall, and several "boys" (and girls) ranging in age from twelve years to the early twenties. The boys are usually in an apprenticeship program arranged with the owner of the stall. There is a collective effort to manage the stall efficiently and individuals are groomed to contribute their shares. Whether all members of the stall have the same or varying reporting times is a business decision that stall owners/managers are most qualified to make, and that determines how long in a day each stall member could intersect with the mobility system. The boys (and girls) conduct market surveys by ferreting out price information from competitors and by gathering information on the latest line of goods that have the potential for fast turnover. This practice is beneficial due to limited marketing information from government or any other established trade groups, given the low levels of advanced communication technology. In this market, everything hinges on a quick turnover, observes Guy Hunter. The author continues (Hunter, 1962: 134), "a knowledge of prices in markets 100 miles around, and extras to be earned by breaking bulk and selling small quantities down to a single cigarette," whenever it is considered profitable. However, at some level, the use of the modern cell phone, locally referred to as handsets, when available, has enhanced the level of communication but collecting human intelligence is still a stall activity mainly performed by the boys and girls. The improved communication technology also allows the stall owner to maintain communication with local, national, and international suppliers and business associates, and consumers.

Irrespective of the level of communication technology, traders prefer personal physical contact because it allows them to renew trust and relationships. If members of a Line, that is a zone that makes similar goods available for sale, have a meeting, the stall owner must attend in person—you cannot depend on technology, despite what Zoom may make you believe, to attend from a remote location and still feel that you are contributing to strengthen relationships, or are still a strong Line member. The eyeball is king for authoritative and meaningful contact. Apprentices also act as decoys and serve as early warning system for the owner when necessary, such as the unannounced appearance of an unwanted visitor such as a debt collector, a government agent, or a demanding relative. To advertise the goods sold in the stall, apprentices, with their profiling skills, streamline the exchange process, as the stall owner expects them to contribute to increase sales by approaching passersby, pleasantly engaging them in a conversation and promising a lower price for whatever goods they are interested in buying. They will determine what this potential customer wants to purchase and lead them to the stall to negotiate a price with the stall owner. Haggling is based on the concept of price discrimination where the seller quickly assesses the buyer and makes a quick determination about what this buyer would be willing to pay for the merchandise. College students and young adults are easy prey. It is a form of marketplace profiling. They factor in the buyer's appearance and dressing, gender, speech pattern, and mannerism into the quick assessment based on previous experience. In some SE Asian, Yoruba, and other cultures, sale price negotiation or transaction starts from the lowest price while in the other areas, including Onitsha, it starts with the seller offering the highest sale price, like what happens with a car salesperson in the West. The customer must be familiar with the prevailing tradition to avoid embarrassment and ridicule. Haggling occurs because of the ephemeral buyer–seller contact where the customer may not return as a repeat customer (tastes change quickly); it allows the seller to gauge the seriousness of the buyer; seller has a desire to make a quick sale and accumulate capital and buyer is not certain about the quality of the merchandise because of lax laws related to standards in the marketplace that may be flooded with local and foreign counterfeit goods. Reporting on this problem in Kenya, Andrew England writes "From whiskey to cooking fat to batteries to clothes, the East African nation – like other developing countries – is being swamped with counterfeit goods, some made locally, most imported illegally (The Columbian, December 2, 2001)." Haggling also provides an opportunity for the seller to cultivate the buyer to determine if a long-term relationship could be beneficial. The practice has an underlying social benefit—it is a process to make the buyer feel comfortable and relaxed, and buyer does not consider seller a threat because the dynamics of the interpersonal communication creates trust.

Apprentices and stall assistants may also serve as domestic help to the principal trader, locally referred to as the '*Oga*' or 'Master', as in an individual who has mastered some body of professional knowledge in some special field of practice and, in this case, the art of marketplace dealmaking and associated nuances of the marketplace institution. Often, they are related by blood, even if distant, or by marriage. The familial affiliation is an insurance against theft or other business-damaging behavior. Moreover, the arrangement tends to preclude the hiring of outsiders who have no affiliation with the master and who might want to consider themselves 'employees' which involves a different type of stall relationship. When the master accepts a non-family member as an apprentice, it usually requires a sponsor who also serves as a surety to guarantee that if the apprentice causes any financial damage, the master holds the surety financially liable. The master has limited control over a non-family member and that implies less obligation with the financial welfare of the apprentice upon graduation from the apprenticeship program.

Apprentices are usually diligent in rendering their services in return for learning the nuances of the business, including sourcing of goods, shipment methods, suppliers, pricing and sales, and accounting, or as much as the master is willing to share. Observes Onyemelukwe (1974: 126), quite often a master may decide to remunerate the outgoing apprentice in a more concrete way—by finding him or her a stall and stocking the stall with goods worth as much as, if not more than, the apprentice would have hoped to receive. Generally, the duration of an apprenticeship program is determined by several factors such as the age at entry, prevailing economic conditions, availability of a vacant shed at a prime location, number of apprentices serving the master, and the level of mastery of the line of business (as determined by the master) and availability of seed money to stock the new stall. The last point may sometimes create unintended consequences. When the master does not have the capital or seed money, he could concede that the apprentice lacks mastery of the line of business and claim that he does not want any blame of business failure, should the apprentice terminate the apprenticeship too early and strike out on their own. That is a ploy to allow the master to continue to get unpaid labor while frustrating the apprentice, who, in some instances, would terminate the arrangement and leave the program in anger. If the apprentice is patient and the master runs out of delay tactics, the master could resort to violence, as was the case of a telecommunications equipment dealer at Alaba International Market, Lagos. The master was accused of killing his apprentice after 7 (seven) years of apprenticeship to avoid "settling him" and reported that the boy fell from the second floor of their building (*Daily Sun*, July 14, 2007). When a new stall is set up for the apprentice, it serves as a form of business expansion and the master often continues to provide free (un)solicited business counselling until such a time that the parties mutually feel it is redundant. Sociologically, the bond or linkage is rarely severed.

So, the organization of trade revolves around the stall with the Master as the CEO, with apprentices as frontline staff who support the operation of the business that includes exchange process that explains the relationships with customers. There are also assistants who have completed the apprenticeship program but because of limited funds may be retained to assist the master in running the daily operation of the stall which exposes the financial implication of the apprenticeship program for the stall manager. These frontline staff fulfill different roles in managing the stall, including verbal advertisement to passersby, and running errands, but the master serves as the key decision maker. When they finally separate from the master, they are handsomely rewarded with a stall stocked with merchandise—and a new market-stall trader is born, the traditional reproduction of entrepreneurs in the marketplace institution—and the cycle continues.

The Urban Transport System

The earliest pre-colonial riverfront market developed in Onitsha in response to the excellent river transport connecting Onitsha with potential trading partners nested along the Niger and Benue rivers, and those located overseas. With the advent of the lorry and other improvements in overland transport system, the intercity transport network boosted the ascendancy of Onitsha to a center of commercial activity. Here, we find that the successful retailing of goods and services is also tied to marine and overland traffic flows, as James V. Simmons of the University of Chicago has observed. So apart from the earliest (Main) market locating near the river, the construction of the express road linking Onitsha with important Nigerian urban centers opened up an efficient intercity transport system and turned the segment of the express road into a 'Route 128'[4] of urban markets with the establishment of the Head Bridge Market to the west and the expansion of the Ochanja Relief Market to the east (and other smaller markets in between), and the locational advantage has allowed them to compete with the Main Market in the CBD.

Onitsha, like many Nigerian urban centers, developed from historical nuclei that are still evident in the twisting narrow streets and old-fashioned business premises (Floyd, 1969: 63), especially in the downtown district. Writing in the *American Journal of Engineering Research*, Ayo-Odifiri et al. (2017: 41–48) observe that the existence of narrow roads near (African) urban markets in many cities have continued to cause congestion because there have not been commensurate road improvements to ease congestion around and near markets. This suggests a failure to recognize and address the significance of these marketplaces in urban economic and development space of cities and how improved access is a catalyst for economic activity. African population centers had existed prior to colonialism and had elaborate roadway system that connected different

---

[4] This is highway in Massachusetts known for its high concentration of high technology and research institutions within a relatively small land area.

neighborhoods in the community. Large (traditional) cities such as Benin, Kano, Zaria, Ile Ife, and Ibadan eventually developed with a high density of urban footpaths supplementing motorable or macadamized roads. In Onitsha, especially in the unplanned residential districts in inland town, there are similar footpaths in residential neighborhoods, often unpaved, that supplement city streets in providing needed access. Generally, road construction and road improvements have not kept pace with traffic increases and this has coincided with the growth of slums and increases in traffic congestion. In any case, only in the Fegge district were urban roads originally laid out and constructed before building homes which is not the case in other parts of town where thought was not given to first laying out the road system, providing necessary urban facilities, before new structures were built and issued with certificates of occupancy by government. The result is a hurried pace at which elegant homes are springing up around the city without provisions for adequate access and other urban amenities such as roads, sewerage, water, and electricity supply. In their absence, home owners who can afford to install some or all those amenities have individualized the provision of urban amenities. Constructing new roads as developments are occurring reduces congestion. The wholesale absence of such modern infrastructures has contributed to the development of slum condition, especially to the south of the city.

Onitsha has a dense road network closest to the river that radiates to the east in a pyramid, even as growth continues along the ONA (Onitsha-Nnewi-Awka) manufacturing and industrial corridor. The road system was developed in an era of expanding trade and in the absence of vehicle weight restrictions on local roads. The roads are narrow, often two-lane carriageways from early town development. They are not served by traffic signals or controlled at intersections, and there are no sidewalks or separated paths for bicycles or pedestrians. This configuration pushes all road users onto the pavement as they juggle for ownership of right-of-way. There are also sellers illegally hogging prime portions of real estate along urban roads. There are no pavement markings and no turn refuge, meaning that in order to make left turns those drivers will block traffic and drivers use intimidation or commonsense to obtain and/or share the right of way, and in all these, there appears some sense of organization and understanding for sharing the road that may be confusing to the uninitiated. It is similar to a driver from Small Town America experiencing traffic in Los Angeles for the first time.

Roadways are typically classified by type of use—residential/local, collector, arterial, and expressway or highway—but drivers, irrespective of vehicle weight, do not pay attention to such road classification, especially in the absence of advisory signs restricting use based on vehicle weight or size; therefore, drivers feel free to use any road of their choice. All these have contributed to unmanageable damage to the road surface.[5] This is compounded by government's low/no appetite or interest in the upkeep of urban roads in a culture where the perception that (large) capital projects that are visible have exaggerated social benefit spread for constituents, and so those benefits (government is doing something) tend to outweigh mundane maintenance activities that keep societies safe, enhance economic activities, and reduce friction or the cost of travel. Of course, such an outdated development philosophy contributes to observed increases in congestion on almost all urban roads (Ikeagbunam, 2014: 250–256). This is occurring even though since the 1985 Development Plan government has attempted to reduce the level of congestion through various policies embedded in different national development plans, up to and including Vision 20:2020—the goal that the country would be in the top 20 of world's leading economies while consolidating its economic leadership in the continent by year 2020. The jury is still out on that goal as 2020 has come and gone. Government has developed other goals to focus attention on maintenance of urban roads while de-emphasizing the construction of new roads, except where it is in the interest of local and/or national economic development. Little wonder why the progressive UN Habitat plan for Onitsha talks about "redevelopment and maintenance" of key projects, including transportation, to promote a managed land use system (UN Habitat, 2009: 59) in line with what government would like to see happen in this and other urban areas.

To improve urban traffic movement, various administrations have supported, in one form or the other, soft policies such as the use of task force of able-bodied citizens to organize cleaning campaigns of travel ways and neighborhoods. In addition, the national requirement is that all residents participate in the monthly (last Saturday) neighborhood cleanup campaign, for short, known as 'environmental.' The goal is to rid neighborhoods of yard debris that could be dumped on road sides and impede travel. Government has also attempted other methods of

---

[5] For details of the conditions of existing major roadways in Onitsha, see UN Habitat. (2012). *Nigeria: Onitsha Urban Profile* (section on Transportation), UN, Nairobi, Kenya.

compliance by enforcing the no-litter laws, especially on (major) road-ways, and (erratically) enforcing laws prohibiting individuals from locating business premises that may encroach onto the public right-of-way. Such businesses reduce available road space for the safe movement of goods and individuals. Meanwhile, some property owners have gone the other way by converting their front yards to public parking lots which add to clutter on urban roadways. To enhance the enforcement of land use laws, government needs capacity building. As an example, training and deploying professional code violation inspectors would be useful, and if land use inspection is institutionalized, continuous, and visible, over time, the public may likely become aware of these regulations and the bene-fits of ultimately uncluttered travel ways. Perhaps, citizens would become more predisposed to collaborate with government officials to clear the streets for safe and convenient movement of goods and people.

Finally, the travel modes in Onitsha include walking, taxi, (mini)bus, private car, *keke* or tri-cycle (3-legged conveyors), and *okada* (motorcycle taxi). Almost 50% of residents depend on foot to get to their destina-tions. Taxi (21.6%), private automobile, and motorcycle (11.6% apiece) constitute the other major modes, Table 3.5. For those who choose to walk, this is probably due to their inability to afford the base bus fare of about N50-N100 (US.020-0.038, 08/2020 exchange rate), or a desire

Table 3.5 Onitsha: Working population by place of work and means of transportation

Place of Work	Foot	Bike	M/Cycle	Taxi	Pr. Car	Bus	Other	Total
Otu	743	14	270	381	243	128	3	1782
Odapku	313	0	33	70	31	17	1	465
Woliwo	8	1	1	10	6	7	0	33
Fegge	295	0	56	99	32	43	23	534
Inland Town	89	0	13	43	23	7	7	275
GRA	60	3	11	65	47	2	0	188
Onitsha	41	1	18	44	17	16	5	142
Other	56	3	26	84	30	30	36	265
Total	1704	22	428	796	429	250	55	3684
% Total Sample	46.3	0.6	11.6	21.6	11.6	6.8	1.5	100

Source Published Onitsha Master Plan Document

to avoid the extra charge for their personal effects, or perhaps they are concerned about how long the trip might take due to traffic congestion or they are plain just worried about their safety, or the absence of bus service to their destination. Elsewhere in Pune, India, 41% cite overcrowding as their major concern for not taking the bus, which could also contribute to explain the low percentage use of that mode in Onitsha. Incidentally, walking is typically the major mode of choice in African and Asian cities, and in Latin American cities, where it constitutes 10–35% of all trips (Venter et al., 2019). In Nairobi, Kenya, 70% of city residents walk or take the matatu (private minibus) to work. Perhaps, as in Nigeria, the congested city streets slow down the speed of traffic that makes walking an attractive mode of choice. Astrop et al. (1996) reports that road congestion, shortage of road space, and a lack of road discipline in Pune, India, hinder bus operation and the same will be said of Onitsha today. Taking a taxi may not be a better option because poor pavement integrity limits their service to few neighborhoods with relatively better road surface but cab fares are also much higher in the age of TNCs, Transportation Network Companies, but because of the convenience it is a favored mode of choice by almost 22% of the population. Bus routes are also limited to a few thoroughfares so that the UN Habitat plan for Onitsha proposes ten (10) routes to serve the entire city when implemented. The routes will connect the markets and key urban activity centers. The motorcycle (*okada*) taxi system was established in 1985 and was banned in 2018. Operators had a license and were required to wear helmets, and they were adept in dodging potholes. They were also good at weaving through congested traffic and were not actually competing for patrons with other modes because they accept passengers often refused by the other modes. But their demise was in part due to the same aggressiveness and willingness to accept all customers, as some of them engaged in snatching purses/handbags, and sometimes colluding with their 'customers' to commit the crime. The underground informal economic activity of these miscreants is an outgrowth of the poor condition of the road system that created its original need as a travel mode.

For comparison, Table 3.6 shows the modal share in selected African cities. Notice that minibus, walking (even though the mode is absent in some cities and rated high in another city), and the private automobile appear to be the most popular modes. Because these are capital cities, it is not surprising that the personal automobile is a preferred mode of

Table 3.6   Shares (%) of various modes in transport in use in selected African cities

City	Large bus	Mini bus	Taxi	M/Cycle	Pr. Car	Walk	Other
Abidjan	11	19	29	0	18	22	1
Accra	10	52	9	0	13	12	4
Addis Ababa	35	20	5	0	7	30	3
Bamako	1	10	5	56	19	-	9
Conakry	1	14	6	0	1	78	0
Dakar	3	73	6	6	11	-	1
Dar-es—Salaam	0	61	1	1	10	26	1
Kigali	1	75	10	0	10	5	0
Lagos	10	75	5	5	5	High	0
Nairobi	7	29	15	2	-	47	0

Source Kumar et al., World Bank Group (2008: 13)

choice for many individuals. Capital cities boast a high concentration of high and mid-level administrators, independent contractors, formal sector workers, and consultants whose income or job situations allow them to own and operate a personal automobile. Besides, the ownership of an automobile is a proxy for measuring and advertising the individual's success. As another social norm, society tends to describe individuals in relation to the type of automobile they drive or denigrate others by reminding listeners about the person's failure to purchase an automobile, despite the number of years working as a professional. There is, therefore, a race to the top to own and operate an automobile to elevate one's status in social circles. The taxi and motorcycle are not good mode choices because they are slightly worse than the use of large buses. The winding, narrow, and congested city streets are not conducive to operating big buses. Observe that more than half of the population in Bamako, Mali (56%), a desert region, depend on the motorcycle mode when 78% of residents in Conakry, Guinea, a coastal region, prefer the walk mode. In any case, the minibus features prominently in all the cities, as city streets grow narrower and more congested (Kumar et al., 2008), making it easier for drivers to maneuver on city streets.

In summary, in Onitsha, the walk mode is the most prominent mode of choice. Overall, the private automobile has a low score with taxi mode scoring almost twice as much. It is conceivable that traders making out-of-stall contacts might also find the walk mode attractive, especially for traders located in the CBD with several zones of attraction.

REFERENCES

Aribigbola, A. (2008). Improving urban land use planning and management in Nigeria: The case of Akure. *Theoretical and Empirical Researches in Urban Management, 3*(9), 1–14.

Astrop, P. C., Maunder, D., & Babu, D. M. (1996). *The urban travel behaviour of low-income households and females in Pune, India.* Center for Transportation Research, Crowthorne, Berkshire, UK.

Ayo-Odifiri, O. S., Fasakin, J. O., & Henshaw, F. O. (2017). Road connectivity to ease traffic congestion on market roads in Benin. *American Journal of Engineering Research, 6*(6), 41–48.

Crowther, M. (1966). *A short history of Nigeria.* Frederick and Praeger.

Emoh, F. I., Ayotunde, O. O., & Egolum, C. C. (2013). Prioritizing residential land value determinants in Onitsha, Nigeria. *International Journal of Academic Research in Business and Social Sciences, 3*(3), 201–214.

England, A. (2001, December 2). *Kenya in battle to fight fake-goods trade.* The Columbian, Portland, Oregon.

Floyd, B. (1969). *Eastern Nigeria.* Praeger.

Gantner, G. (2009). The urban market: Social and spatial configuration in the African city. Conference Paper, *African Perspectives*, Pretoria.

Hodder, B. W., & Ukwu, I. U. (1969). *Markets in West Africa.* Ibadan University Press.

Hunter, G. (1962). *New societies in tropical Africa.* Oxford University Press.

Ikeagbunam, F. I. (2014). Onitsha urban road transport system: Implications for urban transport planning. *International Journal of Applied Science and Technology, 4*(4), 250–256.

IMF. (2019). *Regional economic outlook: Sub-Saharan Africa.* Washington, DC.

Izueke, E., & Eme, O. (2013). Urban planning problems in Nigeria: A case of Onitsha Metropplis in Anambra State. *Singaporean Journal of Business Economics and Management Studies, 1*(1), 41–59.

Kennedy, P. (1988). *African capitalism: The struggle for ascendancy.* Cambridge University Press.

Krugman, P. (1994, July–August). Does third world growth hurt first world prosperity? *Harvard Business Review.*

Kumar, A., Foster, V., & Barrett, F. (2008). *Stuck in traffic: Urban transport in Africa. World Bank Group, Washington, D.C.* http://documents.worldbank.org/curated/en/671081468008449140/Stuck-in-traffic-urban-transport-in-Africa

Lall, S. V., Henderson Jr., M., & Venebles, A. (2017). *African cities: Opening doors to the world*. The World Bank, African Regional Studies Program, Washington, DC. http://documents.worldbank.org/curated/en/854221490781543956/Africas-cities-opening-doors-to-the-world

Lanjouw, P. (1999). Rural nonagricultural employment and poverty in Ecuador. *Economic Development and Cultural Change, 48*(1), 91–122.

Lewellen, T. C. (1995). *Dependency and development: An introduction to the Third World*. Bergen and Garvey.

Obi-Ani, N. A., & Isiani, M. C. (2020). Urbanization in Nigeria: The Onitsha experience. *Cities, 104*(September) https://doi.org/10.1016/j.cities.2020.102744

Okafor, F. (1986). Land use dynamics and planning problems in an urban fringe environment: The case of Onitsha Nigeria. *Land Use Policy, 3*(3), 221–229.

Okezie-Okeh, C. (2007, July 14). Puzzle: Man murdered, thrown down from second floor, death certificate hurriedly procured by accused who says it was an accident. *Daily Sun*.

Onyemelukwe, J. O. C. (1974). Factors in the growth of West African urban market towns: The example of pre-civil war Onitsha. *Urban Studies, 11*, 47–59.

Oxford Business Group. (2012). *The report: Nigeria*.

Pedersen, P. O., & McCormick, D. (1999). African business systems in a globalizing world. *The Journal of Modern African Studies, 37*(1), 109–135.

Rapley, J. (2002). *Understanding development: Theory and practice in the Third World*. Lynne-Rienner.

Schatz, S. P. (1977). *Nigerian capitalism*. University of California Press.

Teltscher, T. (1994). Small trade and the world economy: Informal vendors in Quito Ecuador. *Economic Geography, 70*(2), 167–187.

Trager, L. (2001). *Yoruba hometowns: Community, identity, and development in Nigeria*. Boulder, CO.

Udo, R. K. (1970). *Geographical regions of Nigeria*. University of California Press.

UN Habitat. (2009). *Structure plans for Awka, Onitsha and Nnewi and Environs 2009–2027*. Nairobi, Kenya.

Venter, C., Mahendra, A., & Hidalgo. (2019). *Towards a more mobile city. From mobility to access for all. Expanding urban transport choices in the Global South*. World Resources Institute, Washington, DC.

CHAPTER 4

Challenges Facing Urban Marketplace Traders

Now that we have explored the characteristics of a large representative (West) African urban market, and the likelihood that, as the region continues to urbanize, trading and traders would most likely continue to dominate the urban economy, the purpose of this chapter is to assess the ecology of market trading to shed light on challenges facing micro-entrepreneur traders. The discussion will include an exploration of how traders negotiate the operational space defined by the marketplace institution in order to maintain a financially-healthy business operation. This is especially true when Hodder and Lee (1974: 144) have since concluded that it cannot too often be emphasized that markets in the towns of the developing countries will continue to play the vital role as media in the social and economic life of the people. Along those lines, Chamlee-Wright (2002) has shown how urban market women in Zimbabwe have developed adaptive mechanisms to assist them to enhance capital accumulation in order to remain economically relevant in society; therefore, the discussion will explore the prevailing constraints, associated coping mechanisms, and how traders are manipulating institutional norms to their benefit.

There appears to be a debate in the literature (Africa Development Bank Group, 2018; Chamlee, 1993; Kossler, 2007; Muller, 1982; Teltscher, 1994) regarding the classificatory position of market-stall traders vis-à-vis the informal economy. Does the operation of permanent market stalls on public land where traders pay rent and taxes place them in the formal or the informal economy? As a result, Yinka Adegoke (Quartz Africa, December 6, 2019) is wondering why economists are still struggling to figure out where Africa's informal economy starts and where it ends. Consider that most urban market traders have permanent structures and operate legally-sanctioned business that are often registered (a prerequisite for stall allocation) in a highly competitive market without any real or quantifiable invisible hand (of government) reaching out to assist them. The size of the operation may be relatively small and the stall is often staffed by members of the household or individuals who may be (un)related but are not technically considered employees. This description fits the structure of many minority-owned businesses in the US where 88.60% of businesses that are owned by minorities (Black/African American, American Indian, and Alaska Native, Asian, Hispanic, and Native Hawaiian and Pacific Islander) have no employees (SBA, January 2016). They are often sole proprietors and have unpaid assistant(s) who are often relatives. The market-stall owner may not directly pay his/her 'staff/employee' a monthly salary, per se, but the business owner is responsible for their welfare and the value of those expenditures reduces the monthly gross income of the business. Those are indirect payments. Even though they may not show up in the calculation of the total output of the local economy, the exclusion of the monetary value illustrates the incomplete accounting system in these areas, as those expenditures generate known multiplier effects in the economy nonetheless. As the debate rages on, India has recognized the significance of traders in the economy that on May 31, 2019, the cabinet approved a pension scheme for shopkeepers and traders to safeguard their financial health, upon retirement.

Continuing the theme of income and the economic well-being of traders, Table 4.1 shows the gross margin or income of business services in Onitsha that may help to illustrate the impacts of traders on the (local) economy. Furthermore, the information in the table contributes to illustrate why these formal–informal market-stall businesses, with the complexity of their business structure and operation, are typically found toward the most privileged end on the social welfare spectrum. From the profits' column, it is understandable why some well-off traders would engage in both wholesale and retail trade. After all buyers from the Cameroon and other parts of Nigeria travel to Onitsha to buy in bulk, other customers buy retail; therefore, concurrently selling wholesale and retail generates the maximum profit, as the group has the

Table 4.1 Comparative annual gross margin/income from services

Type of activity	Sales receipt (Naira)	Cost of goods (Naira)	Gross margin (Naira)
Wholesale trade	N127,489,799	N103,992,711	N23,297,088
Retail trade	N126,551,510	N94,994,016	N31,557,494
Wholesale/Retail trade	N237,747,044	N180,845,508	N56,901,536
Restaurants	N10,132,167	N6,769,517	N3,362,650
Hotels	N49,925,403	N26,628,034	N23,297,370

Source Data is projected to 2016 from published *Report on the Survey of Distributive Trade*, Anambra State
Note Nigeria Average Monthly Middle-Class Income 2016 = N1.3 mill.—3.0 mill

highest gross margin. Separately selling wholesale or retail is not as lucrative as combining the sale of the two categories of merchandise, according to the table; otherwise, the next best option is to solely focus on retailing, as an alternative avenue for an enhanced rate of capital accumulation. The income information confirms that stall marketplace trade provides a pathway to upward economic mobility. By taking advantage of the marketplace, many traders, irrespective of gender, have prospered in business[1] and one method of advertising their success is by taking up traditional salutation titles, after performing some customary rites, often chaired by a traditional chief, and surrounded by family, friends, and well-wishers. Traders participating in these traditional ceremonies are bestowed upon with titles such as *Oji Moto Eme Ogo* (the one that gives personal automobile as gift), *Chief Ome Ego* (the traditional ruler who lavishes money), or Young Money. At such gatherings, to further demonstrate their business success, they will be 'spraying' one-dollar notes on dancers—'spraying' is the art of tossing paper money in the air and letting them descend on or around the intended recipient. Trager (**2001**) has documented how being a trader in Ijesa (western Nigeria) has also overemphasized individual's success to the neglect of communal advancement, a finding that allows us to peer into the social construct of the

[1] For additional strategies deployed by traders to maximize profit, see Uchendu, E., & Agbo, C (2015). Profit and profit making among Onitsha Market Traders. *Journal of Third World Studies, 32*(2), 219–240.
Robertson, C. (1974). Economic woman in Africa: Profit-making techniques of Accra market women. *The Journal of Modern African Studies, 12*(4), 657–664.

relationship between the established trader genre, individualism, and the community. It appears that there is a distance between 'made traders' and the community when they believe they have worked so hard to independently achieve financial success. This aligns with the knowledge that it appears that formal–informal trade is succeeding for some and is competing for economic power with the formal sector, as the income of stall traders is very competitive with those in formal employment. It also suggests that the sector is no more perceived as an 'unproductive' sector. Elsewhere, Kiteme (1992: 148) discusses the socio-economic impact of market (stall) traders in Kenya. The author found, for example, that Kenya market women and their 'employees' account for 80% of all bus ridership and at least 50% of all truck rentals for commercial purposes in north-eastern Kitui district of Kenya. That must have a significant impact on the district's mobility system and the local economy and specifically in the transportation services sector.

Now, let us briefly return to the informal–formal economy debate because it will assist us in understanding the problems faced by traders. Faced with the dilemma of how to avoid applying the all-encompassing "formal" or "informal" label without misrepresenting the true charac-teristics of the informal economy group, and not necessarily quelling the controversy surrounding the debate, Maria Muller suggests the term "small scale," while Potts uses "second economy" in her study of the Limpopo area of southern Africa (Potts, 2008: 151–167). In a more recent work on the subject, ILO (2018) notes that others have used terms such as "shadow economy," "black economy," and "unreported economy" to describe the informal economy, but McDade and Spring (2005) prefer the terms "micro" and "small scale," while the OECD (1991) believes that "popular economy" and "domestic economy" are more enlightened terms. As indicated earlier, we prefer to address them as *non-formal* small business men and women because traders reminded this author several times that they "are small entrepreneur businesses" who need support from the government—labels are not important in their circle. In their defense, the International Labor Organizations (2018) does not care anymore what you call the sector—"unorganized sector, or informal sector, or something else"—their interest is in working with actors in the sector because their activities are still central to the orga-nization's mandate of social justice. Others (Chukwuemeka et al., 2017: 55) would argue that perhaps the formal–informal economy is succeeding as a viable economic activity and there is basis to reconsider the stigmatization because after all "there is informality in the upper echelons of the society from financial capital to political relationships," they insist. The current position taken by ILO on this debate validates the rising economic importance of actors in the sector. They want to reduce the importance of fixation on labels previously attached to the sector in order to perhaps present it as an underclass, below par, non-productive segment in a pro formal sector-dominated culture and debate. To Breman (1985), however, it never appeared that appending a label would add to resolving the problem anyway. In fact, current arguments in the literature (Banks et al., 2020: 223–238) is that there is an informal–formal continuum instead of a dichotomy that allowed for pigeon-holing disaggregates of urban economic activities. This resurrects the argument by Breman who notes that "it is rather a continuum in which borderlines between the composite parts are drawn almost arbitrarily and are almost difficult to locate in actual situation." In other words, the difference, Breman concludes, between the two sectors would be that of "structural inequality," and we concur. That indeed is the milieu in which the Onitsha market-stall trader and their counterparts in other African cities operate. Taken together, we prefer the term non-formal because it will distinguish it from formal and separate it from underground activities that are often referred to as informal activity. In Onitsha, as in other (West) African cities, non-formal economy actors are often required to abide by certain regulations such as paying rent and maintaining hours of operation.

Viewed as structural inequality, the concept helps us in understanding and scaling the differences between subsystems in the two business typologies—one is a small-scale (formal–non-formal) trader business and the other is a large-scale (principally formal) manufacturing, financial or transportation business. In fact, the small-scale operator has no subsystems while the typical large business has different components which function collaboratively, and in tandem with each other, to enhance the efficiency of the system. This difference suggests that while the small-scale operator is responsible for all phases of the operation, the large-scale operator has different sections or departments (subsystems) that are responsible for different functions necessary for the successful management and operation of a 'modern' business. Furthermore, while the typical small-scale trader, for example, must compete with big trading houses and other formal businesses to obtain bank loans, government support, and grants, at another level the small-scale trader will queue

with other customers to seek access to government or other bureaucratic services, such as buying stamps at the post office, or paying rent
at the secretariat. In addition, while the trader must make financial decisions with family and business in perspectives, financial decisions by a
large-scale formal business is likely guided by a board of directors whose
members are probably all experienced (ex) business persons who have only
the interest of the business and its shareholders to consider. Moreover,
while the typical trader often solicits operational and/or working capital
from acquaintances and accepts and trains apprentices and is responsible
for the success or failure of the business, it is not so for the chief operating officer of a large-scale formal business who does not suffer a direct
loss, if the business flounders and/or fails. Unlike small-scale trader operators, large-scale businesses are often organized into separate divisions
to deal with recruitment, training, accounting, shipping, and receiving,
advertising, sales, and public relations, and often depend on and utilize
non-face-to-face communication, legal agreements, and commitments to
manage business responsibilities. Due to structural inequality, the small-
scale trader or small businessperson, who is also engaged in similar array
of business activities, manages all those responsibilities in a more informal
setting, and often face-to-face with the other parties. Therefore, in order
to financially survive, the trader must develop and deploy survival mechanisms to respond to the myriad of demands and challenges associated
with operating a non-formal business within the marketplace institution
and, in the shadow of large enterprises.

Typical challenges facing the stall microenterprise trader include
finding and recruiting adequate labor in a changing world where technology and information flow are going high tech, but where the trader
still relies on relatives or family members to staff the stall and those staffers
may be technologically-challenged; planning and managing the stall with
individuals who, collectively, have limited accounting and management
skills and should learn everything on the 'job'; and accessing finance to
maintain and expand the business. Other intervening issues include how
to juxtapose familial and business expenditures and still stay financially
afloat; storage space and warehousing; the absence of infrastructures such
as water and power supply, and affordable modern telecommunication
technology; properly managing the supply of goods from local, national,
and international sources to ensure that customer needs are continuously met; responding to the whims of government authorities; paying
for security services and information; and accessing information from

(non)government sources (Mwaanga and Chewe (2016); Nnabuife et al. (2018); Thiam (2007)). Though not exhaustive, we will organize these problems around three key themes for orientation: (a) marketplace environment and trader relationships; (b) intersection with government; and (c) challenges related to staffing. This will help us to better understand the backdrop of the business operation, and hence, trader adaptation methods in a highly competitive and capitalistic marketplace arena.

Marketplace Environment and Trader Relationships

The items sold in the markets include foodstuffs, provisions (packaged general household goods) and health supplies, textiles, readymade clothing, and hardware, some of which are acquired from foreign manufacturers in America, Europe, South Africa, or China. This arrangement requires initial capital outlay followed by maintenance of an excellent relationship and credit history with the seller for an enduring supply chain, a relationship that Trager (1981: 133–146) has described as "dyadic." These suppliers will ship goods commensurate with paid-up capital or a commitment (based on trust) to pay. But before evaluating the constraints associated with acquiring supplies, we will first examine household income distribution for context because it is intertwined with the business income that determines the durability of the supply chain.

In reviewing indigenous enterprises in distributive trades in Nigeria, Olakanpo (n.d.: 55) reminds us that despite their apparent success "The assessment of profitability of the business (of trading) is further rendered difficult by the tendency to mix up family and household expenses of the proprietor with businesses expenses." This will, for example, impact the decision to order supplies and, on the other hand, regulate the ability of the trader to develop a strong relationship with established financial institutions. Put differently, what transpires at the household level often has direct impact on the financial status of and the financial stability and ability of the business that prompted Lowder (1986: 184) to make an observation regarding the propensity of traders to accept bank loans, viz. "The acceptance of credit requiring interest payments and collateral is seen by many (traders) as unjustifiable risks for the family resources," suggesting the persistent inseparability of the family from the business. What emerges is that a typical trader must balance business with household financial interests in managing the stall. The trader must juggle revenues and expenditures to ensure that the financial health of each branch (family and business) of the enterprise is always in good standing. To stay solvent, the trader often resorts to non-traditional sources such as money lenders for capital support, a choice, for example, that will inform how the trader will deploy capital and manage issues surrounding stock acquisition.

As Olakanpo (n.d.) sees it, combining these demands with traders' managerial deficiencies compounds their capacity to adequately determine what, where, and when to buy, and the quantities to purchase, as the ability to keep the size of the business within limits is dictated by available capital, existing knowledge and experience of the sources of supply, the wherewithal to competently assess risks and develop strategies to reduce or preferably eliminate them, and the conviction that accurate record-keeping is as important as buying the right merchandise at the right price and quantity. The smallness of the operation and the neglect to track all transactions increases the trader's inability to deal with economic uncertainties related to irregular supplies, the failure to meet payments on schedule, sagging customer demand, and declining sales revenues (Muller, 1982). Taken together, the trader is faced with this incessant demand to toggle between the financial health of the business and the family, and walking that tight rope creates stress that affects stall operation.

Table 4.2 shows the distribution of income groups for wage earners and self-employed households in Onitsha. Traders appear to have the largest proportion of households in the middle-income category, while

Table 4.2   Household income by occupation (*number in sample*)

Occupation	Lower	Middle	Upper	Total
Public service	38	25	23	86
Contracting	14	-	1	15
TRADING	120	63	28	211
Teaching	7	2	3	12
Farming	6	-	-	6
Driving/Touting	24	1	-	25
Laborer	9	-	-	25
Salesperson	2	-	-	2
Tailoring	10	-	-	10
Mission Worker	1	-	-	1
Hotel Industry	2	1	-	3
No information	2	-	-	2
Total	235	92	56	383

Source Onitsha Master Plan

they are second to public servants in the upper-income category. In Nigeria, the average annual middle-income earner (2020) makes between N16 million to N48 million (US $42,105–$126,315).

From the table, we can infer that 43.1% of traders included in the table are in the middle- to upper-income bracket while 56.9% are in the lower-income category. It is certainly plausible that formal–informal traders are experiencing success in this marketplace. Traders in the lower-income category have quite a presence in the economy, but the income data in Table 4.1 make us believe that these lower-income traders will majorly include traders who may not have permanent stalls in the marketplace and/or are merely street vendors, hawkers, and other itinerant pavement capitalist sellers. We are, therefore, compelled to suggest that the fairly large proportion of middle—to upper-income trader categories shown in Table 4.2 is a confirmation of and co-terminus with the same middle—to upper-income trader earners previously identified in Table 4.1, lending additional credence to why stall traders deserve attention. In a Western economic and social system, this is the income group that is most likely to place demand on the system and the arc of public policies tends to bend toward their interests. The social structure and economic system in these areas create dissonance between the governors and the governed that make government to often discount and subvert the ability of such groups to organize and wield political power. Although numerically fewer than itinerant traders in the sample, it is certainly acceptable to infer that the combined income of the 43.1% of traders found in the middle- to upper-income cohort will be larger than the combined income of the 56.9% of itinerant vendors and other street sellers, given the value of stock typically owned by these travelling salesmen, petty traders. So, stall traders appear to be reaping the financial benefits of the consumption culture inherent in most (West) African cities that allow them to create formal manufacturing jobs overseas to satisfy their appetite for consumption. Confirming the trend, in Benin, Nigeria, stall traders have been shown (Ogeah & Omofonmwan, 2013) to belong to the top-earning bracket of businesses in the informal economy who use their income to pay household rent, feed the family, pay tuition for their children, purchase personal automobiles, and build their own homes—typical middle-/upper-income lifestyle—especially relevant when you consider the cash outlay required for purchasing an automobile or building a family home in a country where almost every financial transaction is cash and carry.

Researchers (Lowder, 1986; Schwimmer, 1979; Ikelegbe, 2005; Udegbe, 2007) have established that there are various market distributive systems—simple to complex, fairly organized to highly organized, and rationalized systems—related to foodstuffs supply—and perhaps by extension the supply of other products for sale. Different modes of social organization also exist in the distribution of other marketplace goods—pure competition, ethnic monopolization, and associational monopolization. Traders take advantage of these relationships in seeking out suppliers to competitively obtain stock to maximize profit. Even when they source supplies from international sellers, they depend on these types of relationships, in one form or the other, even when it involves working with middlemen who may or may not have ethnic ties to the foreign seller, to obtain supplies. Onitsha traders are mostly migrants from other parts of Nigeria and they maintain their ethnic linkages in the marketplace as a form of coping mechanism. The organizational affiliation and associated monopolization (over certain types of saleable goods) provide necessary social and financial structures for obtaining support. For example, most sellers, according to Onyemelukwe (1970) in the *mangala* (dried) fish lines, come from Ichida-Igbo Ukwu district near Awka in today's Anambra State, whereas food grains sellers are mainly from areas around Orlu, in Imo State. This ethnic solidarity facilitates the sourcing of goods. At another level, the trader could belong to a market traders' association for raising capital. The associational relationship is even more common among traders selling the same types of good even though one would wonder about the wisdom of a trader developing associational relationships in such a competitive marketplace. But one of the benefits is that it minimizes the acquisition cost of market intelligence and facilitates communication in an environment where the cost of reliable information is quite high. Moreover, it increases the value of the information because of the trust quotient associated with the source of the information due to the commonality of business interest. For example, one of the reasons that some small traders remain small is that big distributors and manufacturers often impose differing standards or terms of purchase which some traders may independently find difficult to meet because of the pure competition. One of the results is that these "bare foot managers," to borrow from Michael van den Bogert, would often source saleable merchandise from third parties, often at a higher price, which affects the rate of capital accumulation, or band together through associational ties to place orders in order to meet capital requirements of suppliers. In the end, various associations are formed between traders in the same line of trade or dyadic relationships between traders and sellers at different economic levels. A dyadic tie is formed between a trader(s) and supplier(s), even when the supplier is another trader, and between traders and customers (Trager, 1976/1977). Each mode of relationship enhances the ability to meet acquisition, processing, pricing, demand evaluation, and other market needs. In other words, the marketplace serves more than just a place of business; it contributes to community development.

At a higher level, the general trader association offers another form of social cohesion. The association performs a regulatory role by controlling the behavior of traders, either within the market or in sourcing saleable stock. The largest umbrella statewide organization is AMATAS, Amalgamated Market Traders Association of Anambra State, which replaced OMATA, Onitsha Market Traders Association, a local traders' association. The association has a chairperson at each of the major marketplaces. And, to serve as the chair of that market, the individual must own and operate a stall at that market. Following leadership meetings, these are the individuals who are responsible for disseminating information about new rules, regulations, and other decisions to members through established intermediate leadership. The association maintains a code of ethics and operational guidelines and enforces etiquette among traders through zonal leadership committees, working with the elected leadership. Often, it adjudicates between members and ensures that adopted market rules are adhered to, such as pricing, handling the intersection of daily religious prayers before the start of business to minimize business interruption, and handling issues related to returned merchandise. The organization is continuously interested in promoting the welfare of traders. It often hires security guards to safeguard personal property in the marketplace and provides guidance during local, state, and national elections since the outcome of these elections affect the welfare of traders. These time points serve as mileposts to monitor trader behavior, choices, and relationships within the marketplace institution, and AMATAS is a looming time point in the environment of the trader that it has to navigate and adhere to in the marketplace.

So, what we have in the social field of "an accomplished entrepreneur" trader, to borrow from Ahmed B. Yusuf, is a complex web of relationships between occupants of the marketplace institution and other institutions, groups, and entities. From this discussion, the different relationships affect the choices made by the trader which in turn affects the finances of the trader, and any mis-steps can and will have a bad financial impact on the business and the family. Suppose the trader runs afoul of AMATAS' rules and regulations, dealing with the stress could affect the trader's ability to manage the stall and that could affect sales, in addition to the loss of reputation that could drastically affect overall income. The constraints imposed by these relationships and opportunities created by them contribute to explain why the price of goods sold by traders tend to remain consistently lower than elsewhere even though Onitsha is by no means the geographical center for the production or manufacture of those products. The ultimate reward is ascendency to a relatively higher income level that will help to reduce financial stress on the trader. This will explain why in Ghana (Lyon, 2003: 11–23) urban food traders will sustain cooperation over many years with each other and their supply sources in contrast to limited interest in general community associations. Traders are aware of the financial rewards of those prolonged and expansive individualized relationships they maintain in a very competitive marketplace in comparison with general community associations with no obvious immediate remuneration. Within this context, the following is an exploration of the problems facing marketplace traders.

INTERSECTION WITH GOVERNMENT

The intersection of traders with government involves a different type of associational relationship that creates restraints and constraints on the trader. On July 31, 2020, Anambra State, Nigeria, inaugurated *Operation Clean and Healthy* and associated Special Task Force on Revenue Enforcement for the collection of (non-stall) revenues in markets. Elsewhere, in Abubakar Gumi Central Market and Kantin Kwari Market in Kaduna, the government of Kaduna State (Nigeria) had previously initiated the collection of N50 to N100 daily tax per spot from pavement capitalist traders within the marketplace district. These types of ad hoc revenue collection regimes are inimical to market operation because such direct and indirect non-institutionalized government tactics create fear and uncertainty and cause disruption in marketplace operation. When you add the practice of allocating permanent *deminimus* business spaces in the markets to these unstructured taxes, government is incrementally criminalizing market activity, to paraphrase Emily Chamlee (1993: 79–99), through unnecessary control and intimidation that cannibalizes this economic activity. One of the results of insufficient, therefore high rent, and inadequate stall space—a typical stall measures about 4.6 sq. meters (or 6 × 8 feet)—is growth in the number of non-permanent stall traders. A combination of these conditions is inimical to overall growth of the small-scale trader, unless government decides to allocate a proper amount of attention to planning and urban development issues and concerns of traders. Meanwhile, numerous apprentices are annually graduating from the program and may not separate and start managing their own stalls which creates further drag on the reproduction of entrepreneurs in the local economy.

Until the advent of non-State-owned community banks, in the 1990s, banking institutions were owned and managed as government subsidiaries, but they did not pay attention to supporting small businesses, including traders. The inclination to de-emphasize support for traders has not changed with the introduction of private banks because most of the private banks are owned by wealthy individuals who may not have real interest in the local community, and that means that traders have continued to struggle to grow their business. The introduction of microfinance institutions a few years later to increase access for small and medium-scale enterprises did not eliminate the traditional methods of funding microenterprises as 65% of microenterprises still depend on informal sources, such as credit and savings association, other traders and money lenders, to initiate and grow their business, according to an evaluation of how microenterprises have benefited from microfinance banks since their inception (Moruf, 2013: 505–517). In Dar es Salaam Kariakoo Market, traders have expressed skepticism for bank and microfinance loans because of high interest rates and short repayment periods and, therefore, tend to prefer traditional informal credit system over such formal loan programs (Bruhwiler, 2014: 29). Consequently, traders have learned to accumulate start-up capital other than through commercial lending houses, Table 4.3. In fact, according to McKinsey Global Institute (2014: 10), some 85% of microenterprises in Nigeria are funded with personal savings, and less than one-tenth receive bank loans. Notice that even though the table refers to all small businesses, the results are a good proxy of how traders finance their business, given that often there is a preponderance of traders in a 'small business' classification. For context, Table 4.4 shows how microenterprises, small enterprises, and medium and large enterprises are financed in sub-Saharan African countries.

Traders in Onitsha appear to fall into the same financial conundrum faced by other small enterprises in sub-Saharan Africa as (personal) savings

Table 4.3 Sources of small business finance

Source	% Of all establishments
Personal savings	82.2
Money lenders	1.9
Cooperatives & Institutions	1.0
Banks	5.7
Shares issued	0.2
Government	1.0
More than one source	8.0
Total	100.0

Source Onitsha Master Plan

Table 4.4 Sources of start-up finance (percent of firms using this source)

Source of start-up finance	Came roon	Cote d'Ivoire	Ghana	Kenya	Tanzania	Zambia	Mozambique	Nigeria
Savings	66.0	83.3	75.9	71.1	78.4	83.8	78.5	79.8
Friends or relatives	5.1	7.3	16.1	5.74	9.3	4.0	5.9	1.8
Foreign bank or donor	3.4	3.2	0.5	2.15	3.0	4.2	0.9	2.0
Local bank	8.8	2.9	2.6	16.1	3.6	5.0	8.2	8.5
Money lender	1.1	0.4	0.3	0.67	0.0	0.1	0.0	0.0
Supplier	4.1	1.2	1.4	0.90	1.5	1.5	1.02	0.0

Source T. Biggs & M. Shah: In Pathways Out of Poverty, World Bank (2003: 161)

appear to constitute the major source of financing an enterprise and governments appear oblivious to the economic advantages of supporting small non-formal businesses such as traders, especially given their role in the local urban economy. Of course, there will be no surprise at the low levels of support by foreign banks and donors. In any case, factors contributing to low levels of bank support include high processing cost, high interest rates, and the need for collateral which will explain why these businesses may continue to depend on informal sources such as credit and savings association, and other traders, relatives, and friends for financial support. After all, about 8% of small businesses depend on "more than one source" for financial support. Notice the very low rate of financial support from money lenders—globally, entrepreneurs tend to understand that these are not very nice folks for establishment of business relationships, especially in Tanzania, Mozambique, Nigeria, and Zambia. For Onitsha traders, the largest form of financial support comes from personal savings which includes savings from family and friends, because it is most unlikely that the trader would exclude 'the family' (relations, spouses, friends) in decisions related to starting a new venture, given the prominence of the family institution in the life of the individual in the culture. In Table 4.4, if you add friends and relatives to the Savings category, the contribution of Savings will increase by an average of about seven percentage points in each country, and that will make the savings source very comparable to those of Onitsha traders. As the business begins to prosper, the effect of a built-in social reciprocity emerges as the same relatives or 'shareholders' would be expected to benefit from the business profits and that creates additional stress on the financial situation of the business. What this suggests is that the imminent financial position of the trader is indeterminate, when the trader applies for a loan. Banks have often lost money in the past on unsecured trader loans and have reason to be cautious. This continues the forward linkage between small businesses and financial institutions when small businesses deposit funds but mainly large business tend to qualify for bank loans. That was why government originally approved the establishment of community banks that were later supplanted by microfinance banks (see Armendariz & Morduch, 2007, Chapters 4 and 5) to emphasize lending to small enterprises without collateral. However, without adequate controls and monitoring these institutions have ended up behaving as the big commercial entities they replaced as a capital source for small businesses (see Moruf and Ashamu, 2014: 179–193). But, realizing the lack of support from financial institutions, the Nigerian government (2019–2020) initiated "TraderMoni" (meaning money for traders) lending program that provides no-collateral loans of about N10,000 to N100,000 ($27.50–$275). The program will not benefit many of the traders we are focusing on because of the very small size of the loan, but our pavement capitalists might derive some benefits from it.

There is a school of thought that believes that these microenterprises would enhance their chance of obtaining institutional loans, if they followed the advice of Hernando de Soto as outlined in an IMF (2001) book review by placing 'value' (via documentation) on everything associated with their business. The aggregate value is known as capital—every piece of equipment, inventory, land, and building. Documents connect everything to the rest of the economy, De Soto opines, as these assets live a parallel invisible life and therefore can be used as collateral for loan. This is a method to end dead capital or undocumented capital and undercapitalization. As a reminder, property laws emerged in the US in 1820 for this same reason and capital accumulation has grown by maximizing the benefits accorded by the concept. In 2009, Lagos State, Nigeria, assisted by the Institute of Liberty and Democracy that is headed by the same Peruvian entrepreneur and economist, De Soto, initiated land titling registration scheme to assist small businesses and home owners by speeding development and placing value on hitherto dormant landed property (*Daily Independent*, June 6, 2009). Whether this method has worked for small business operators depends on the willingness of commercial institutions to accept the documents when presented where there is no disincentive (punishment) for unscrupulous borrowers to procure and present bogus documents to commercial institutions. This is where trader intersection with government needs to strategically evolve to strengthen the capacity of traders (and other microenterprises) to expand their business, if documentation and acceptance regimes are institutionalized for all assets owned by traders, such as business inventory, and a language developed on how to penalize offenders to the full extent allowed by law. Meanwhile, an evaluation of the land titling policy in Ogun State (Oyedeji et al., 2016) shows that homeowners are dis-satisfied with the process. They observe that government agency staff are high-handed with the process and homeowners could not get the certificate of occupancy through the normal process that, in addition to being costly, is also not transparent. In the absence of transparency, it is often difficult to justify what is going on inside that 'black box' of the titling processes. That is how an institution loses its capacity and ability to enforce legitimate rules and regulations.

It is not that those traders do not currently have collateral, but suppose the trader provided their landed property for a bank loan and the economy sours (think COVID-19) and the business falters, stories abound about wealthy traders who lost everything, including their homes, their visible trophy from a successful business life. The failure is not just the individual's failure, but society tends to tag the family because it demonstrates a sign of bad judgment to turn over one's property to the bank for 'an ordinary loan,' some critics in the trader community might muse. Taken together, traders may appear risk averse at a fundamental level which militates against their growth potential and (eventual?)

transition to formalization. Remember that trading is considered a profession and the idea of 'transitioning' is suspect because it might appear as if traders are being asked to abandon their profession and journey into the unknown. Chamlee-Wright (2002: 980) observes that women urban market "Traders in Southeastern Ghana have developed elaborate systems of accumulating capital, and they have used their matrilineal kinship ties to secure long-lasting economic relationships that enable them to develop their businesses, withstand economic hardship more effectively, and plan for exit and *retirement* (emphasis added) from the market." This observation reflects a long view plan for an extended professional career as a trader. The stress that will be placed on traders through engineered formalization is antithetical to urging governments to reduce regulatory burdens on entrepreneurs that interfere with business growth in the developing economies. The Decent Work (ILO) Agenda could be a ruse to cause chaos for small businesses in these areas who can least afford to incorporate the costs of the new layer of requirements into business operation, as the race to replicate Western formalized workplace traditions escalate. But the ILO (2018) fully understands the benefits of a useful enabling condition for formalization because it notes that "Informality seems to fall with the level of income likely reflecting higher government capacity and better incentives toward formality in higher income countries" which are scarce in the Global South. This is refreshing because combining general increases in overall poverty levels in many (West) African countries with associated decline in capacity building; it remains questionable when this transformation would be expected to commence in these areas. Traders prefer diversification over formalization because morphing into a single, relatively larger business means that if that single business fails the entire family also suffers. Traders are often not keen on proper financial record keeping, as we have noted elsewhere, for tax reasons, and many lack capacity necessary for managing the paper flow required for satisfactory documentation of income and expenditure balance sheets for government internal revenue officers, and monitoring business plans. All these may be related to their educational achievement, Table 4.5.

Although the highest literacy achievement is in the 10–19 (41.3%) and 20–28 (25.9%) age brackets (accounting for 67.2% of total literate population), it is not likely that a majority of stall ownership and decision-making responsibilities are co-terminus with the members of those groups who are likely to be completing the apprenticeship program. Because they

Table 4.5 Overall population by age and literacy, Onitsha

Age	Literate	Illiterate	Total	Percent, %
0–9	613 (9.5%)	2,158 (48.7%)	2,771	25.4
10–19	2,673 (41.3%)	792 (17.9%)	3,465	31.8
20–29	1,679 (25.9%)	689 (15.5%)	2,368	21.7
30–39	815 (12.6%)	424 (9.6%)	1,239	11.4
40+	694 (10.6%)	371 (8.4%)	1,063	9.7
Total	6,474 (100%)	4,434 (100%)	10,906	100.0%

Source Onitsha Master Plan

could be excluded in other decisions related to disbursement of funds, this could exacerbate the illiquidity of traders. Their exclusion provides an additional dimension as to why records may often be poorly kept to help track, guide, and direct stall expenditures. We have also pointed out the comingling of business and personal (family) accounts, facts banks need in order to intelligently asses the credit worthiness of an applicant. So, it appears that the two groups, traders and bankers, may not have developed a common ground rule, a working formula, to mutually promote the business of each other and minimize the incidence of forward linkages. Traders, therefore, have tended to distrust banks that even though many traders have incomes that are deposited in the bank to yield interest, some others may elect to save with a rich or older relative or simply keep the money at home to assure liquidity. This is because traders prefer to 'touch' the money instead of electronic (bank) transactions that some believe could go awry (someday) and make them lose their money. In addition, going to the bank to conduct financial transaction could take a good part of the business day because of low levels of technology and the general lack of supportive customer service for small-deposit customers at local banks. One of the results of these constraints is that traders have developed coping mechanisms by investing in real estate and collecting annual rents, ahead of time for reinvestment in real estate, or engaging the services of full-time farmer share croppers to allow them to sell excess produce for capital, or operating transportation services with paid drivers who make daily returns to vehicle owners, or owning rental trucks. They may also own chicken farms or fish ponds. Accordingly, some traders have developed the habit of terminating trading early in the day or taking off on Saturday afternoon to attend to those other businesses. And from there they will return directly to the market on Monday. Even during the day there are occasions when the trader's attention may be needed at any of those businesses which creates the need for out-of-stall contact. Diversifying, instead of expanding at one location, creates the impression of a 'small' businessperson for traders and serves as a tax management tool. Traders may also engage in light manufacturing such as bakery, soap making, label printing, and production of plastic bags. Income from these formal activities is easier to tax so traders would transfer and hide the income in the informal trading activity and disguise themselves as regular stall traders. These sources of income serve as a cushion in the topsy-turvy world of a dualistic economic system prevalent in the developing areas.

Located close to the markets is the Market Master's Office. A market master is part of the local government administrative structure. The major responsibilities of the office are to ensure that markets are constantly kept substantially in good and sanitary condition, allocate stall/sheds and collect rents, maintain law and order through the state police, treasury, finance, and administrative departments (Ogeah & Omofonmwan, 2013), and enforce right-of-way regulations. They ensure that street vendors not display their goods in such a manner as to impede pedestrian and vehicular circulation. Based on conversations with these officials, they are weary that the traders' organization is "militant" and would take the laws into their own hands and work directly with elected officials at the state level, instead of collaborating with the market master to properly channel complaints and concerns to resolve issues. This affects the potential working relationship, including collaborating on such things as the need to provide additional stall space for traders that will contribute to addressing urban transportation problems. The Market Master represents the State and oversees and coordinates the activities of the state with the union. He (usually) serves as the chairman of the market union. When there are complaints from customers about bad actors, the market master's office gets involved to arrange for refund or replacement of faulty merchandise. The office of the market master becomes a destination for traders whose (bad) choices in managing the stall compel them to visit the office.

With all these, what government actions could enhance the capacity of traders to cope in the marketplace to address these issues arising from intersection with the same government? Traders complain that the conditionalities for importation of finished goods are too onerous without realizing that the government is using those as an incentive to encourage local manufacturing. But, if traders were interested in manufacturing, which they indicated they are, production cost is too high for acquiring equipment and raw material in a country where the availability of water and electricity is questionable. For another point of view, we go to market traders in Techiman Market in Ghana. Nezic and Kerr (1996: 1–12) interviewed traders to determine their marketplace priorities. The authors observe that long hours spent at the market has led to the formation of community among market traders. They were interested in understanding and evaluating which parameters limit the ability of Techiman Market traders to improve their welfare in the marketplace. We do not have any reason to believe that the welfare needs of these traders will be any different from traders in Onitsha, or for that matter in other West African markets, given their understanding of government functions and the urban development process. As in Onitsha, the traders have steady supply of and demand for goods by customers from neighboring towns, regions, and countries. Asked if they were willing to contribute to market development, Techiman Market traders volunteered an average amount of 14,860 cedis (1991 value)—a coping mechanism. Traders placed the highest priority on facilities and amenities such as toilets, shelters (aka market stalls), water, and electricity that will improve their quality of life and income, with loan facility and paving the market in the second tier, over improvements that would indirectly benefit them such as improving public lorry park and providing refuse disposal facilities or those improvements that will generally benefit the 'public' that traders will become part of after leaving the marketplace. Traders would like to separate the warehouse from the marketplace as far as it is possible but close enough to the market for strategic reasons such as avoiding loss during market fire or theft in the stall; or, to conceal their true worth, critics might be quick to add. So, like their counterparts in Onitsha, traders can articulate their needs and want to exercise their voice to attract development to the markets and smoothen the jagged edge of the intersection with government, but the need for more and better market stalls is prominent on their list. It is widely known that AMATAS has developed an excellent relationship with Anambra State government (Nigeria) by contributing to elect a major party candidate as the state governor in past election cycles beginning in 2003. Irrespective of this relationship, we will argue that for an enduring development practice, there must be institutionalized collaboration and cooperation between government and traders in order to produce continuous desirable results like processes followed in the upgrade of Durban Warwick Junction Market, South Africa (Maassen & Galvin, April 5, 2019). Traders worked with planners and government to identify trader needs and participated in the design and implementation of the project that yielded mutual terminal satisfaction—an example of a well-aligned intersection between traders and government.

CHALLENGES RELATED TO STAFFING

In every business organization, both public and private, the success of the enterprise is a function of successful recruitment, training, and retention of a skilled workforce. In the marketplace, very often labor is foisted upon the trader from relatives and friends. There is limited opportunity to 'screen applicants' because they are often recruited through the apprenticeship program. As you review Table 4.6, you will notice that there is a correlation between age distribution and the number of years individuals have been in trading which will reflect the level of professional experience. The additional significance and relevance of this observation will become more revealing when we discuss out-of-stall contacts (in Chapter 6) because it impinges upon the propensity of the individual to impact the transport system. Meanwhile, what the table shows is that:

1. Over one-half of traders have been in business for less than 10 years;
2. Only 10.5% of the traders are 15 years or younger;
3. Over 78% of traders are 40 years or younger, when almost 86% of the urban population is in the same age category;
4. Generally, traders are represented at a greater proportion in each cohort than they occur in the general population, except for children 15 years or younger who are probably enrolled in school.

Table 4.6 Age and number of years in trading

Age	Under 5	5–9	10–14	15–19	20+	%	% Urban population
15 & under	10.5	0.0	0.0	0.0	0.0	10.5	43.7
16–30	24.9	15.3	5.3	4.0	0.0	49.2	30.4
31–40	0.5	4.5	6.5	5.5	2.0	19.0	11.6
41 & over	0.5	0.5	1.5	2.5	16.3	21.3	14.3
Total	36.4	20.3	13.0	12.0	18.3	100	100

Source Field work and published State Government documents

5. The greatest proportion, 49.2%, of traders are between 16 and 30 years of age, even though they constitute the second largest component of the urban population. This suggests that this is the most active group in the urban labor market.

6. Of those 41 years and older, a larger proportion (16.3%) has been in business for over 20 years while the distribution is much more diffused for those between 31 and 40 years of age. Only about 9.3% of traders between 16 and 30 years of age have been in business for over ten years, suggesting a delayed entry into trading, perhaps due to extended apprentice programs. This age distribution chart is also a pointer, based on cultural norms, about who could be responsible for what activity in the stall that involves business contacts, in order to maintain a smooth operation of the unit.

The general ease of entry into the business is illustrated by the declining percentage of those in business for over 20 years. It suggests that as more individuals enter the business, the proportion of those in the business for longer and longest time declines. Notice, for example, that while 56.7% of traders have been in the business for less than ten years, only 25.0% have been trading for ten years but no more than 19 years. It does not appear that older adults participate in the apprenticeship program at the same rate as younger individuals, given the proportion of older adults who have been trading for less than five years, which is just about 1.0%. This is the period reserved for teaching new entrants about the complexities of the business, including sourcing supplies, how to price-discriminate and maximize profit, customer service skills, and how to spot new trends. Perhaps, several adults would feel uncomfortable learning these basic skills and information about the institution from other adults and may choose to remain in their non-trading occupation, irrespective of how quickly they could make money being a trader, all things being equal. We can surmise that the lack of skills, based on number of years in trading, would accentuate challenges related to managing the stall business. But, within the 16- to 30-year age group are typically individuals who may have finished high school or completed tertiary education, but because they have been in business for less than five years, it may suggest that in the future, stall management could benefit from their academic but non-business training. Given this general staffing profile within the institution, the stall owner must exercise prudence in managing the stall to avoid making choices whose consequences will bleed into and also interfere with familial financial situation. It is certainly reasonable to suggest that the staffing 'problem' does more than influence overall stall operation; it controls and affects how the stall intersects with the transport system that leads us to make the following observations about the marketplace institution:

1. The size, measured by number of employees, of the business will influence the number of occupants who engage in necessary out-of-stall business trips;
2. The age range of occupants will influence not only the propensity of individuals to make out-of-stall contacts, but it will also affect the trip purpose of the individual;
3. The complex interpersonal relationships in the institution when juxtaposed against the three problem area themes discussed above would affect the number and frequency of out-of-stall contacts during business hours, as each stall member copes with relevant problems;
4. The variety and characteristics of different supply regimes and cultural norms will suggest that younger stall occupants, who may also be in the apprentice program, would be delegated the responsibility of collecting/delivering merchandise that most likely predispose the group to participate in a greater number of contacts. It could also influence mode choice;
5. The difficulty with which funds are secured for start-up and operation of the stall in conjunction with the desire to maintain financial balance between the business and the family exacerbates the need for older adults, perhaps the stall owner, to engage in finance-related contacts;
6. Traders would be expected to limit the volume of contact with state officials and trips associated with visiting government offices and financial institutions;
7. The tendency to diversify and disguise income, instead of expanding the business at one location, is another element that will influence the totality of trips from a stall; and
8. Separating the storage of bulk from retail goods for strategic reasons is a business choice for which the trader is willing to trade profit (push) for pain (pull) of retrieving the good, irrespective of constraints caused by the quality of the urban mobility system.

REFERENCES

Adegoke, Yinka. (2019, December 6). Economists struggle to figure out where Africa's informal economy starts and where it ends. *Quartz Africa.*

Africa Development Bank Group. (2018). *West Africa economic outlook: Labor markets and jobs.* Abidjan, Cote d'Ivoire.

Armendariz, B., & Morduch, J. (2007). *The economics of microfinance.* MIT Press.

Ashamu, S. (2014). The impact of microfinance on small-scale business in Nigeria. *Journal of Policy Development Studies, 9*(1), 179–193.

Banks, N., Lombard, M., & Mitlin, D. (2020). Urban informality as a site of critical analysis. *The Journal of Development Studies, 56*(2), 223–238.

Breman, J. (1985). A dualistic labour system? A critique of the 'informal sector' concept. In R. Bromley (Ed.), *Planning for small enterprises in Third World cities.* Exeter.

Bruhwiler, B. (2014). Trustworthy trader or creditworthy debtor? Competing moralities and trader subjectivities at the Kariakoo Market in Dar es Salaam. *Stichproben-Wiener Zeitschrift fur kristsche Afrikastudien, 27*(14), 27–53.

Chamlee, E. (1993). Indigenous African institutions and economic development. *Cato Journal, 13*(1), 79–99.

Chamlee-Wright, E. (2002). Savings and accumulation strategies of urban market women in Harare, Zimbabwe. *Economic Development and Cultural Change, 50*(4), 979–1006.

Chukwuemeka, C. V., Scheerlinck, K., & Y Schoonjans, Y. (2017). Collective spaces of informal and formal markets as drivers of self-organization processes of urban growth in emerging cities: Learning from Onitsha, Nigeria. *EU Human Cities,* 51–72.

Fields, G. S., & Pfeffermann, G. (Eds.). (2003). *Pathways out of poverty: Private firms and economic mobility in developing countries.* The World Bank/Kluwer Academic Publishers, World Bank, Washington, DC © World Bank. https://openknowledge.worldbank.org/handle/10986/25896 License: CC BY 3.0 IGO.

Finance and Development Book Review. (2001). *The mystery of capital: Why capitalism triumphs in the West and fails everywhere else,* by Hernando de Soto, *38*(1). IMF, Washington, DC.

Hodder, B. W., & Lee, R. (1974). *Economic geography.* St Martin's Press.

Ikelegbe, O. O. (2005). *The spatial structure of the supply and distribution of staple foodstuffs in the Benin region.* Unpublished Ph.D. Thesis, Department of Geography and Planning. University of Benin, Nigeria.

International , Labor, & Organization. (2018). *Women and men in the informal economy: A statistical picture.* International Labour Office.

Kiteme, K. (1992). The socioeconomic impact of the African market women trader in rural Kenya. *Journal of Black Studies, 23*(1), 135–151.

Kossler, R. (2007). Review article: Informal institutions in Africa: Economy, polity, and tradition. *African Spectrum, 2*(3), 557–568.

Lowder, S. (1986). *The geography of Third World cities.* Barnes and Noble Books.

Lyon, F. (2003). Trader associations and urban food systems in Ghana: Institutionalist approaches to understanding urban collective actions. *International Journal of Urban and Regional Research, 27*(1), 11–23.

Maassen, A., & Galvin, M. (2019, April 5). Urban transformations: Durban, informal workers design marketplaces instead of getting displaced by them. *World Resources Institute*, Washington, DC.

McDade, B. E., & Spring, A. (2005). The new generation of African entrepreneurs: Networking to change the climate for business and private sector-led development. *Entrepreneurship and Regional Development*, January, 17–42.

McKinsey Global Institute. (2014, July). *Nigeria's renewal: Delivering inclusive growth in Africa's largest economy.*

Moruf, O. (2013). Evaluation of the Nigerian microfinance banks credit administration on small and medium-scale enterprise operations. *International Review of Management and Business Research Results, 2*(2), 505–517.

Muller, M. S. (1982). The self-employed in Kitale: No easy way to success. *African Urban Studies, 12,* 1–15.

Mwaanga, C., & Chewe, L. S. (2016). Entrepreneurship development: Reflections on organizational challenges that hinder their growth. *Management, 6*(5), 137–145. https://doi.org/10.5923/j.mm.20160605.01

Nezic, T., & Kerr, W. A. (1996). A market community development in West Africa. *Community Development Journal, 31*(1), 1–12.

Nnabuife, E., Chigozie, P., & Ewah-Bassey, E. (2018). Family-owned businesses n Anambra State: Issues, problems, and prospect. *Asian Journal of Economics, Business and Accounting, 9*(1), 1–10.

OECD. (1991). *Preparing for the future: A vision of West Africa in the year 2020.* OECD.

Ogeah, F. N., & Omofonmwan, S. I. (2013). Urban Markets as a source of employment generation in Benin city Nigeria. *African Journal of Social Sciences, 3*(4), 62–78.

Olakanpo, O. (n.d.). A preliminary report on the indigenous enterprises in distributive trades in Nigeria. *Nigerian Institute of Social and Economic Research.* Ibadan.

Onyemelukwe, J. O. C. (1970). Aspects of staple food trade in Onitsha market. *The Nigerian Geographical Journal, 13,* 121–138.

Oyedeji, J. O., Abiodun K., & Sodiya, A. K. (2016). Citizen's satisfaction on land titling policy and regulation in Ogun State, Nigeria. *International Journal of Built Environment and Sustainability.* www.ijbes.utm.my

Potts, D. (2008). The urban informal sector in Sub-Saharan Africa: From bad to good (and back again?). *Journal of Development Southern Africa, 25*(2), 151–167.

SBA: Minority Business Development Agency. (2016, January). *Fact Sheet—US Minority-owned firms.*

Schwimmer, B. (1979). Market structure and social organization in a Ghanaian marketing system. *American Ethnologist, 6,* 682–701.

Simire, M. (2009, June 5). Lagos adopts land titling in reform package. *Daily Independent.*

Teltscher, T. (1994). Small trade and the world economy: Informal vendors in Quito Ecuador. *Economic Geography, 70*(2), 167–187.

Thiam, I. (2007). *Unlocking the potential of small and medium sized enterprises in West Africa: A path for reform and action.* Unpublished Master Thesis. MIT Sloan School of Management.

Trager, L. (1976/1977). Market women in the urban economy: The role of Yoruba intermediaries in a medium-sized city. *African Urban Notes, 2,* 1–11

Trager, L. (1981). Customers and creditors: Variations in economic personalism in a Nigerian marketing system. *Ethnology, 20*(2), 133–146.

Trager, L. (2001). *Yoruba hometowns: Community, identity, and development in Nigeria.* Boulder, CO.

Udegbe, S. E. (2007). *Spatial distribution of vegetable produce in Lagos Metropolis,* Nigeria. Unpublished Ph.D. Thesis, Department of Geography and Planning. Ambrose Alli University, Epkoma, Edo State, Nigeria.

CHAPTER 5

Attributes Impacting Out-Of-Stall Business Contacts

So far, we have focused on the milieu within which the trader operates in the marketplace to allow us to better understand the ecosystem in which the trader functions. To properly manage and maintain the financial integrity of the stall, the trader must leave the stall during business hours. Because the informal economy is expected to grow in (West) Africa, it is projected that the marketplace will continue to serve as a source of employment for a significant proportion of the urban labor pool. Moreover, the ability of the marketplace to provide income mobility is expected to broaden as more traders climb the ladder of economic prosperity. Faced with the spillover of urban commerce onto roadways and side-walks by sellers without permanent business locations, and pressured by stall traders who are clamoring for expanded stall space, cities in (West) Africa and elsewhere are attempting to decongest the street and respond to the needs of market-stall traders by building new shopping establishments or modernizing existing marketplaces. These new non-marketplace structures may not necessarily be responding to relevant needs of most marketplace stall traders despite providing protection from the elements and some urban infrastructures such as clean drinking water. A contrarian might suggest that sponsoring the construction of these Western-style multi-level shopping centers under the guise of providing modern marketplace facilities could be a structured strategy, a ruse, designed to stretch out the full-scale de-marketization of the unique African urban market-place experience and ultimately restructuring the non-formal economy, by starting with the largest and most dominant economic group. In years to come, it is plausible that the marketplace will be corporatized and most food items will be imported and, together with other household needs sold by large sellers (businesses), that is formalization. It also is plausible that with the shopping center/mall construction craze that developers repeatedly and unconsciously fail to meet real trader needs because of the lack of marketplace planning and design information and/or they are merely engaged in property development and may not have any interests in accounting for the preferences of beneficiaries. Consider this. The government of Lagos State (Nigeria) partnered with banks and developers to rebuild markets in Olu Wole, Alade, and Tejuosho in the last few years. As conceived microfinance banks would offer 30-year mortgage loans to traders to own stalls in the new structures. It is understandable why banks are willing to provide 30-year mortgage loans to traders to purchase stall space in a development project that will substantially benefit developers because the same developers probably borrowed the capital from banks for the project, but the same banks are reluctant to support traders to buy and own their own homes and use them as collateral to expand their business. This contradiction raises concerns about the mysterious circumstances surrounding the market fire in 2007, like the market fires in Onitsha in 1987. Anyway, the 5-story Tejuosho Market development (with a basement) is designed to house 4,048 shops and 1,700 traditional shops. It used imported design that Mary Kinyanjui, a senior Research Fellow at the Institute for Development Studies, University of Nairobi, has warned African urban planners to resist. The design replicates the architecturally-inviting but socio-culturally disengaging marketplace environment. According to the contractor, the new market was designed to meet the needs of the average shopper and seller in terms of functionality, accessibility, ease of navigation, and aesthetics with basic stall space renting for N1.2million/year ($3,175/year) for a 25-year lease (News of the People, May 21, 2012). Bigger shops rent for N525,000 per square meter in a facility that mainly accepts brand name retailers, and stalls range in size from 10.8 square meters to 129.6 square meters, meaning that stalls can rent for up to a whopping N68.0 million/year which is expensive even for traders who have edged into the middle class. Listening to posted video recordings of female traders, the refrain is that only the monied interests would acquire the stalls and most likely sublet them to others who, given their inability to pay the full rent, will end up sharing a single stall space with other sellers thereby making them smaller urban market-stall traders than they were before becoming shopping center retailers. With subdivided and therefore smaller stall space, the implication is that we will expect traders to continue to make out-of-stall contacts and their operation will continue to inadvertently present a challenge to the urban mobility system. Ordinarily, beneficiaries of such urban community development projects deserve to provide their input to planners which, in this case, will contribute to promote the sustainability of the marketplace. The story line *Beautiful Tejuosho market, yet to seduce traders, shoppers* (Gbenga Salau, *The Guardian*, July 23, 2017) supports our hypothesis that these developments obviously fail to meet the relevant needs of marketplace traders, or show any interest in promoting the structure of their business, as we know it. The story appeared three years after completion of two phases of the project and 10 years after fire destroyed the original market. The writer of the newspaper article observed that most of the stall spaces were still unrented and mall managers failed to provide substantive explanation about the lackluster occupancy rates and poor foot traffic. It appears that traders are not enamored by the mall design and high stall rental rates and, of course what most shoppers need are probably not offered by current retailers. Meanwhile, photos accompanying the newspaper article show pavement sellers doing business on the sidewalk across and adjacent to the shopping mall. These are potential traders who could rent affordable space in the mall, and their patrons are shoppers who are not providing foot traffic in the new shopping mall— and the cycle of forcing sellers onto the roadway and public rights of way continues. The marketplaces replaced by these modern structures were centers of human economic and social activity and always full of shoppers and sellers.

With this warning about the incipient trend in the desire to influence traditional (West) African marketplace shopping experience, let us return to indigenous marketplaces and evaluate selected stall attributes that frame the boundaries within which traders operate their business. In a study of traders in Ghana, Asante and Helbrecht (2019) observe that the marketplace possesses significant and complex spatial dimensions that are fundamental to the sustenance and capital accumulation of traders. Sustaining capital accumulation, we suspect, hinges on the trader making the right choices regarding out-of-stall business contacts. But, the quantity and timing of these contacts are constrained by the attributes of the stall that is the decision-making unit. Evaluating these attributes will equip us to better understand how they directly influence the choice made by the trader—a circular operational relationship. Just as the household serves as the decision-making unit for home-based school, work, leisure, and shopping trips that sustain the well-being of household members, so does the stall serve as the decision-making unit for contacts made from the business to sustain the financial well-being of its members. Based on our knowledge of marketplace operation and informed observations, the relevant attributes identified for evaluation are: market location, size of stall, availability of a means of transportation, gender, and the type of commodity sold by the trader. Following the evaluation of the attributes, the next chapter will model the attributes to demonstrate the existence of the linkage between the marketplace and urban transport. The veracity of the assertion will be based on whether these attributes are sufficiently strong (i.e., the r-square value) to induce stall members to make enough trips that are considered large enough to affect the transport system but so far are unexplored and therefore unknown but create unintended consequences on the urban transport system. It is the expectation that practitioners and policy makers will lean-in on the knowledge as they make plans for future traditional large urban marketplaces or remodel existing markets to minimize the propensity of traders to engage in these urban environmental-disruptive contacts. Achieving that goal will usher in a streamlined management process for the marketplace and the urban transport system.

Whether to make a trip involves decisions which are classified as games with associated risks, uncertainties, and payoffs. Individuals do not take a trip per se; rather, the benefits or utilities available at the destination provide incentives or payoffs for undertaking a trip. Take a traveler for example, from Apeguso, in Volta Region who engages on a trip from that hinterland to Accra, Ghana, three (3) hours away by road, in a full bus travelling on a country road punctuated by several police checkpoints and prone to bad road surface. The utility or the benefits of this arduous trip are the welcome, entertainment, and gifts from relatives upon arrival in Accra. The individual must deduct the cost—the bad road conditions, the 3-hour inconvenient ride and fare, stress associated with interacting with traffic police, sitting next to strangers, listening to everybody talking on top of their voices, congestion, nuisance during the line haul, and the opportunity cost (what else could this traveler be doing with her time) associated with the friction (distance)—from the benefits in order to justify the trip or the contact. This is like what Stuart F. Chapin describes as the "pull" versus the "push" factors in theorizing about movement behavior. The goal is to ensure that the trip maker maximizes her return on the travel because all the effort to get to an opportunity (visiting the relative at Accra) is part of the cost and that will help the trip maker determine the attractiveness of the opportunity; otherwise, the trip will be postponed or forgone if it is not worth the effort or cost. The trader will spend all the time in her place of business in the marketplace if the contact will not add value to the financial ledger of the business. Similarly, if the cost (push) of going to Accra is so low, then many residents in Apeguso will be making the trip very often and that will increase the fare, traffic, and road congestion. Transport service providers would quickly respond and charge higher fare to manage demand. In that case, the areal differentiation between Apeguso and Accra will diminish in value, in line with Stouffer (1940): "The number of persons going a given distance is directly proportional to the number of opportunities at that distance and inversely proportional to the number of intervening opportunities." In Onitsha, the existing intervening opportunities at different subareas or destinations—bad roads, traffic congestion, poor mobility system—would influence the level of potential reduction in the propensity of marketplace business operators to make out-of-stall contacts to meet the needs of customers, so the desire to make an out-of-stall contact is finally dependent upon what the trader determines as the net benefit or pull; that is, the total benefit must be greater than the cost in order for each contact to occur. In the aggregate marketplace, traders have collectively deduced that the benefits outweigh the costs of all those trips made from the stall during business hours as these daily trips have become essential and normalized like household members who make essential but routine trips to work or school.

Location of Marketplace

Typically, individuals at locations with attractive trip-inducing qualities would make more trips relative to other individuals whose locations have poor qualities. For example, attractive qualities for those taking a bus will include an excellent road surface and associated internally-connected wide sidewalks, low bus fare, short headways, a reliable service, and availability of a bus service. We know that bus ridership increases when bus frequency is increased because of the reduced wait time, irrespective of bus fare.

Therefore, transit services with headway scheduling attract higher rider-ship because riders know with some certainty how much time (cost) they will waste waiting for the next bus—a short wait time is a trip inducer. Outside of headways and bus frequency that are not germane to the current situation, in Onitsha, despite the bad roads privately-owned minibuses are plentiful along the limited bus routes and offer service at relatively low fares, if the traveler is willing to endure the numerous stop-and-go because there are no designated bus stops. The trader can use a motorcycle taxi (*okada,* if legally available) that provides door-to-door service or tricycle taxi *(keke)* but the trip maker is limited to what they can personally transport with them during the trip, but they will get to their destination quicker than if they took the bus or walked. For traders along the express road traffic speeds are relatively higher but for traders located in the CBD, there is more opportunity to use the bus and other modes because of safe vehicle refuge in adjacent streets, the availability of other modes, and slower traffic because of traffic congestion. Regarding road surface conditions, the poor road surface in the CBD has forced many taxi operators to refuse patrons to the CBD, or accept them if they are willing to pay for the inconvenience of the operator and the addi-tional wear and tear on the equipment. Combined together the location of a market appears to be an important factor for trip-making decisions and could have an impact on the number of contacts an individual could make in any given business day. There are other location-related issues to be considered.

The effect of location on business-related trip-making has been recog-nized and documented. In Lagos, Nigeria, Sada and McNulty (1981) found that there was an observed flow of traders to those sites with expanding opportunities for sale. The markets frequently favored by traders, the researchers found, "were large markets located in the main transport routes associated with high demands and they were also highly rated by the traders in terms of growth potentials." This would suggest that in relocating or building new (modern) markets, consideration might be given to locations that have potentials for traders to increase sales, but that is only a part of the story. For example, the finding suggests that increased access significantly contributes to the success of an enter-prise; yet, at another level, it implies that small-scale entrepreneurs who have selected, in several instances, legal/illegal locations that satisfice their needs to make contacts in order to service their customers should not be randomly relocated to another area with poor access because that could doubly affect the enterprise—poor sales in tandem with inability to make business contacts. Accordingly, Sada and McNulty will make us suspect that traders located near main transport routes may also engage in more out-of-stall contacts, for example, to restock the stall at a more frequent rate due to higher rate of sales. We, therefore, theorize that traders who are located along the express road and are spatially differentiated from CBD traders will be expected to make more stall-based contacts than CBD traders. The selection of spatially-differentiated markets will be useful in exploring whether market location is a significant factor influencing the choice to make out-of-stall contacts, and the number of contacts completed from a stall. The aggregate number of intra-urban contacts made by traders will directly affect the level to which traders contribute to off-peak-traffic in urban areas with large markets. This is critically significant as (West) Africa urbanizes and more individuals are absorbed into trading as a career, often intra-generational, especially for large urban marketplaces that appear to serve as agents of travel disruptors in the urban mobility space.

Several cities in Africa are growing outwards instead of upwards. The resurgence of low-quality residential districts mixed with better quality residences, estates, and new housing, together with other uncontrolled land uses, makes the periphery a vibrant part of the city. With the expansion of cities come increases in travel opportunities for city residents. But it does not mean the death of the CBD. Because the new areas tend to compete for economic activity, the CBD does not necessarily lose out to the periphery. In many African cities, the original center of town, the CBD, is still a fair competitor for new businesses because several institutions were originally located in or near the CBD to prop up colonial administration. Post-colonial governments and administrations have not mostly relocated the affected establishments because of the sunken cost, relocation cost, and potential of increasing the search cost for those accustomed to finding government services clustered in or close to the CBD. The existence of relatively newer roads and the emergence of new residences, firms, and businesses make us believe that urban marketplaces in the periphery would induce more trips as traders work harder to satisfy the needs of consumers who may find 'going inside town' onerous, in comparison with more accessible markets located along/near the expressway in the periphery and close to their residences. Peripheral growth will continue as large swaths of land are being gobbled up by real estate development away from the CBD because land is plentiful and affordable.

Ahmed, Mitra, and Rafiq (2020), in a study of trip generation rates of different land uses in Dhaka, Bangladesh, found that trips generated by a development are based on more than a single use factor associated with the designated land use. These include surrounding land uses, modes available, and prevailing economic conditions. Based on this finding, the researchers go further to question the appropriateness of trip rates published in the Handbook of the Institute of Traffic Engineers that is solely based on single attribute—type of use. For our purposes, this further suggests that the more variability of (uncontrolled) land uses surrounding markets in the periphery will translate into traders in periphery markets making more trips than traders in the CBD where land uses are relatively established. The two periphery markets are adjacent to evolving satellites or new developments with the expectation that the trip-making frequency of traders along the express road corridor would be greater than those other traders in the CBD, as the population of city continues to increase. Gihring (1984) conducted a study of out-of-outlet contacts by urban entrepreneurs in Zaria, northern Nigeria where the dominant market is the Sabon Gari Market near the railroad station. The study showed that entrepreneurs located in the major market center in the CBD participated in significantly fewer out-of-outlet contacts for all purposes than their counterparts in the growing periphery. The author took pains to remind readers that the level of spatial nucleation found in southern Nigeria urban centers may not measure up to those existing in the north; therefore, results may vary. This is instructive even though the researcher did not include and/or further explore the factors contributing to the trip-making behavior of entrepreneurs in Zaria, and neither did the researcher measure the impact of the trips on the transport system.

To be included in the model, the two spatial locations must be quantified: They could be measured with reference to the center of the city or population center, or by determining the distance from the administrative center, or from an intersection of a major arterial. Alternatively, location could be entered as a dummy variable. Determining the population center or defining a geographical center in Onitsha could be unrealistic in view of uncontrolled peripheral growth in the last decade, especially to the north and southeast. On the other hand, since the express road is the major traffic arterial, defining location linearly would yield only two scores, including a zero score. A similar dichotomous value will be obtained by scoring location as a dummy variable. We prefer to score location, LOC, as a dummy variable, 0 for CBD, and 1 (one) for periphery markets, given that a powerful model will be used in the analysis. The expectation is that the partial regression coefficient of location will be positive. But because of the nominal nature of the variable, we cannot statistically increase or decrease its value in tandem with total contacts made by traders. However, a positive value would be interpreted to mean that should CBD traders move to the periphery markets, they would increase their propensity to engage in non-home-based business trips.

THE INFLUENCE OF STALL SIZE

The number of individuals in the stall is an appropriate surrogate for measuring the size of the business unit, the stall. Daniels and Warnes (2006) argue that in the same way that household size and composition influence the number of trips generated in each period, the size of a factory or office, measured by the number of employees, affects the volume of traffic generated from the factory or office, particularly for non-work trips associated with the provision of services. In the oft-quoted work by Hurst (1970) on traffic generated by non-residential land uses, the analysis showed that total traffic generated seems to bear a strong relationship to land use measured by floor space and the number of people employed. However, according to Hurst, in the regression analysis, for all cases the correlation coefficients showed that occupants and workers are more closely related to trip production than floor area appeared to be. The findings are illustrative and useful because they point to the statistical significance of applying the number of employees in defining the size of the business and relating the variable to the frequency and number of trips generated. Incidentally, Olayiwola (2015), in a study of intra-urban trip generation in Abeokuta, Nigeria, found that a single attribute, the number of employed individuals in a household, out of six attributes, contributed 37% to explain the number of trips generated by the household. Though useful, we could alternatively use income to measure the size of the stall, but using income generated from the stall will be unproductive because it will be difficult to obtain reliable income data from traders who are fearful that the State will eventually appropriate the information for tax collection purposes.

Three stall sizes are selected for the analyses:

- Small – all stalls occupied and managed by one or two traders;
- Medium – all stalls having three occupants; and
- Large – all stall occupied by more than four individuals.

The selection of these sizes is based on observed number of occupants or traders in the stalls. Since most stalls are occupied by no more than four persons, it is reasonable to use those grouping to avoid a preponderance of empty cells. Size differentiation is one of the reasons why shop traders who are located outside the physical marketplace are not included in this evaluation. They tend to have more occupants and relatively larger business space for storage and display of merchandise as they trade business-based trips for large business premises.

In Africa, Katzin (1964) has observed that insufficient information exists on which classification based on the size of the business could be developed, such as the amount of invested capital or volume of business. We do not believe that there has been a significant change to traditional business operation to make us not to accept that statement. For example, (West) African businesses still engage in poor record keeping habits as they strive to stay clean from the prying eyes of others, including the State and those relatives who assisted with start-up capital for initiating the business. Moreover, there is still no separation between capital investment, profits and funds reserved for business and non-business purposes, information that could be applied in classifying businesses. This validates what McKinsey Global Institute (2014) means when it observes that in Nigeria, revenue from informal enterprises flows to the individual owners so that capital is not retained in the business and used for investment, data and information which could be used to better understand the size of the business. Not only that, attempts to obtain income-related data have often met with serious disappointment and have sometimes threatened the progress of a research project.

Another method of measuring the size of an establishment could be the amount of rent paid since it is tied to floor space. In the three markets, the one-time development fee and monthly/annual rent are individualized for each market, irrespective of stall size. Therefore, the rent-fee module does not provide any meaningful relief. As a result, at the interval data level, the size of stall was measured by recording the number of employees (or occupants), NEMP. The expectation is that there will be a positive relationship between trips generated from the stall and stall size. In other words, the regression coefficient for NEMP will be positive and not highly correlated with other factors that characterize the enterprise because the number of people in the stall is not a function of business characteristics such as revenue, salary, expenditure, amount of floor space, and the type of good sold that could create multi-collinearity. The size of the stall is solely based on the magnanimity and social field of the stall owner.

AVAILABILITY OF A MEANS OF PERSONAL TRANSPORTATION

In many societies, a means of transportation provides convenience, perceived or real time savings, freedom to choose preferred travel routes, and an opportunity to exhibit the social status of the individual. A personal means of transportation is particularly more than a mode choice in many African societies where many buyers typically pay cash for an automobile. The assumption is that stalls with a means of personal transportation will be associated with a greater number of trips. For example, traders prefer to use a means of personal transportation, despite the potential for (real) increased travel time. As a result, stalls which have a means of personal transportation will consist of a cohort of traders with a greater level of mobility potential and whose business operation would be characterized by a greater variety of contacts, even if it includes trips just to impress business associates. Second, as the number of personal means of mobility increases, the expectation is that there will be a corresponding increase in the number of trips generated from the stall, *ceteris paribus*.

This attribute was selected because we know that in such a status-conscious society, Onitsha traders attach high regard to the ownership of an automobile, being a proxy for measuring business success; therefore, the possession of an automobile could increase the number of trips generated from the stall because of the probability of making 'frivolous' trips such as visiting a friend during business hours for a non-business-related chat which the trader may consider non-frivolous. After all such trips strengthen relationships. We also know that competing public transit (bus) and paratransit (taxi service) modes are not close substitutes because of their poor quality of satisfaction, as automobile owners tend to place a premium on door-to-door service provided by a means of personal transportation. Accordingly, traders who own automobiles would make them the preferred mode for making business contacts.

It will be a misconception to assume that traders, especially stall traders, belong to the poorest income groups, and therefore, cannot afford a means of personal transportation. But studies (Peil & Sada, 1984; Nezic & Kerr, 1996; OECD, 2019, Ogeah & Omofonmwan, 2013) have shown that not only do traders receive a greater than a proportionate share of income as shown in Tables 4.1 and 4.2, but their income is relatively high, in comparison with workers in other sectors. Moreover, there are marked differences in income distribution between traders with stalls and those without stalls, with the former earning more than the latter, which explains why they cannot afford a stall in the first place. Because it symbolizes business success, the inference is that as a trophy for showing off success, many automobile owners may not ride the bus because minibuses are small, often associated with the very poor, and routinely transport both goods and passengers in the same vehicle. They are, therefore, congested and many buses are not well maintained or cleaned and are also filled with noisy passengers. Just as other many automobile owners in other developing economies, owners in Onitsha seldom walk because they consider walking demeaning and enervating.

To their credit, given the inconvenience of using public transit, it is understandable why a trader would prefer to move small freight using a personal means of transportation. Even though traders consider time as money, when it comes to driving their personal automobile, there is a dissonance as many West African residents tend to consider the opportunity cost of time as zero. Because of the convenience, traders would prefer to use their private automobile for out-of-stall contacts despite the slow traffic speed, increased travel time, and congested streets. For those who choose the motorcycle mode, their intra-urban trips could be completed in a relatively shorter time, depending on the dexterity of the operator. An then we are reminded by a Dutch study (Van derHoorn, 1979) that found that car ownership and availability have rather limited influence on the number of trips made in a total activity pattern for home-based and non-home-based activities. However, closer to home, Adedotun et al. (2017) determined from a study of six cities in western Nigeria that 69.9% of trips made by urbanites were made by households with personal automobile, but more importantly, most of the trips (67.8%) were made by households with only one vehicle, 22.6% with two vehicles and only 4.1% by households with three vehicles. In other words, the number of personal automobile available to the trip decision-making unit, the household, has an inverse relationship with its trip generation rates. As a reminder, these are home-based trips and we will find out through analyses whether this is also applicable to trips made from the place of business or non-home-based trips.

In evaluating the variable, we must distinguish between stalls with and without a means of personal means of transportation, on the one hand, and between stalls with different number of a means of personal transportation, on the other hand. The segregation will assist in analyzing whether a statistical difference exists between units without a personal means of transportation, scored as zero (0), and those who have it, scored as one (1); and if there is a difference in trip-making capacity, a subsequent model will assess the trip generating rates of stalls based on the number of a means of personal transportation to assist in contextualizing the findings relative to information in the preceding paragraph.

The first model scores the attribute presence/absence of a means of personal transportation, PETRPS, as a dummy variable with $0 =$ None, and $1 =$ Yes. The expectation is that the value of the regression coefficient will be positive for the presence of a means of personal transportation, in contrast to Van derHoorn. In a second model, the effect of the number of a means of personal transportation available, VEHAVA, is also expected to have a positive regression coefficient in that way, we can hypothesize that the number of contacts will increase as the number of vehicles available to the stall increases, contrary to Adedotun, Tanimowo, and Ibrahim. Multicollinearity is not expected to pose a problem, as income and stall revenue, for example, are not considered relevant attributes, as in the higher the income which is a function of stall revenue, the greater the chance of owning an automobile.

GENDER AS A STALL ATTRIBUTE

In a study of adult trip makers in New York, Bronso and Hartgen (1984) found that men make more trips than women in all categories of income and employment. Following this, we could hypothesize that the greater the number of males in a stall, the greater the number of contacts from the stall, but in many African marketplaces females generally tend to dominate. World Bank staffs, Barbinard and Scott (2011: 213–224), have warned us about the need for stand-alone transport surveys to enhance the availability of gender statistics in developing countries where there is limited household and individual level surveys. At the same presentation at the 4th International Conference on women's issues, they emphasize the dissimilarities that exist between males and females regarding trip purpose, mode of travel and mobility constraints to access services, and the complexity displayed by each gender in making such trips. Therefore, in managing their stall business, we would expect Onitsha female traders to engage in more complex trip behavior that will be exposed by the presence of trip chaining in fulfillment of traditional gendered expectations.

Typically, women start participating in trading at an early age to accumulate the experience of running their own business before marriage, realizing that they will manage the daily livelihoods of their matrimonial home (White, 1981). Chamle-Wright (2002: 986) observes that trading provides women in Harare, Zimbabwe, the opportunity for greater economic autonomy, if they can employ effective economic strategies for maintaining control of their resources, a trait acquired through experience. In Ghana, for example, among the Ga families, women are traditionally traders, and in several markets in Ghana and many other African countries, women are predominant in marketplace trade as men tend to focus on working the farms, except that the reverse is true in East Africa where women tend to be farmers or are engaged in craftworks. No matter which gender dominates in the marketplace, our interest is on stalls as a surrogate for traders and assessment of the number of stall-based contacts generated by occupants as part of daily business operation. In Onitsha, men have come to dominate the distribution of imported and locally-manufactured goods because of the early lead by male heads of household to venture to town to better the family, even as the town expands with new markets selling hardware and home improvement supplies where men also dominate; therefore, we are comfortable retaining the hypothesis proposed at the beginning of the discussion on gender as an attribute.

A consultant's survey of 3,934 participants in the labor force further confirms the preponderance of males over females in sales (trading), Table 5.1, with a ratio of almost three males to one female. Perhaps, because women are active participants in the agricultural economy in this part of the country, unlike Yoruba women in the western Nigeria, female traders in Onitsha are more often found selling foodstuffs. They may also be found selling other commodities such as cosmetics and fabric; therefore, it is plausible that women may not be completing as many out-of-stall contacts as men in similar market conditions. You must also realize that this is a culture where women are held at a different social standard by

Table 5.1   Overall Working Population by Sex/Type of Employment

Employment Type	Male	Female	Total	Percent (%)
Professional/Technical	37	10	47	1.2
Administrative/ Exec & Management	225	72	297	7.5
Clerical	91	29	120	3.5
Sales/Trading	1,656	605	2,261	57.5
Farming/Fishing	4	3	7	0.2
Transport & Communication	85	1	86	2.2
Produce processing/labor	132	22	154	3.9
Services	236	118	354	9.0
School/College	46	147	193	4.9
Others	262	153	415	10.5
Total	2,774	1,160	3,934	100.0

Source Onitsha Master Plan

society and other women, and that could affect their decision to make an out-stall-contact during business hours. In other words, women may still fail to make an active use of the urban mobility system to support their business, and therefore, have less impact on the system. Adedotun et al. (2017) have shown in a study of trip-making behavior of households in six (6) cities in western Nigeria with population between 65,970 and 355,000 that there is a significant difference in percentage of trips made by men and women to school, religion, and shopping destinations. On the aggregate, they found that males make ten times (91%) the number of trips made by women (9%). Realizing that women tend to be subjected to different treatments than men when using public transportation (OECD, 2019), we will believe that the finding could factor into their lowered impulse to leave the stall during business hours, in addition to societal constructs. For each stall, gender is measured by enumerating the number of males and females and scoring the result on an interval scale. The attributes, NMALES (number of males) and number of females, NFEMS, are each expected to have a positive regression coefficient. Furthermore, we expect NMALES to have a larger *bi*-value (value of the coefficient) as a demonstration of a higher trip-making quotient.

COMMODITY SOLD IN THE STALL

Since traders buy and sell different types of goods, it seems reasonable that the type of good sold will factor into the decision space for leaving the stall, as there is a different demand spectrum (quantity and rhythm) for different goods. The spectrum would compel sellers to make different choices, for example, in frequency of restocking saleable goods as a function of known seasonal demand for some type of commodity, or even making a trip to meet an immediate customer demand. As a result, even though all traders face similar generalized operational constraints, the type of goods sold creates another layer of constraint that will exert unique but global influence on trip-making choices for all affected members in that category that will make them behave differently from other traders in a separate commodity group. So, the expectation is that for traders selling similar commodities, aggregate out-of-stall contacts would be a function of the type of goods available for sale in those stalls. Ross (1982) has determined that villagers in Senegal have a propensity to borrow grains from their neighbors during periods of unforeseen shortages. We know that traders demonstrate similar behavior for merchandise sold in this marketplace to address immediate shortages. We have described how traders increase sales by disguising themselves as stall owners when they take a buyer to a stall that has a merchandise that is unavailable in their own stall, but another behavioral layer materializes when a single or easily borrowable merchandise (dress, shirt, a can of powdered beverage) is needed by a customer. In that case, the apprentice 'makes a market run' to a collaborating seller to get it for the customer. The borrower can replace the merchandise from the warehouse outside the confines of the market, or pay cash for it. Sellers of 'lumpier' merchandise such as bicycles and enamel wares and (breakable) plates (china wares) that cannot be easily borrowed, as seen from the list below, will impact the transport space at a relatively lower rate during business hours.

The following constitute the commodity groups sold in the markets:

1. General goods/Provisions and Articles – sugar, perfumery, patent medicine, toiletries including lotion and pomade, imported and locally-manufactured and packaged food items, watches, sewing accessories, school supplies, books, and canned goods;

2. Textiles – piece goods including cotton, bafts, printed cotton, wax block prints, woolen and synthetic materials, brocade, and lace materials;
3. Readymade clothing – men's and women's apparel and accessories, children's wear, beddings, and mosquito nets;
4. Hardware – bicycle and bicycle parts, small hand tools, kitchen utensils, small farm implements, small electric and electronic supplies, nails, enamel wares and plates; and
5. Foodstuffs – yams, garri, beans, dried fish and meat, onions and other condiments, vegetables, plantains, fruits, and other food ingredients.

The hypothesis is that commodity type will influence the number of contacts generated from the stall. For example, goods that are more likely to be borrowed will be associated with stalls with a greater number of trips and the provisions group may fall into that category. On the other hand, goods, such as textiles that come in bales and not easily borrowable, will be associated with fewer trips. Besides, food is a necessity and only after satisfying that need would income be spent on discretionary (luxury textiles, etc.) goods. This economic behavior may further diminish the propensity of affected stalls to generate trips, as those traders may make fewer sales. Hardware goods come in small pieces and may assume the same characteristics as provision goods, as some hardware goods are also sold in small quantities, for example, nails, hammer, or saw. Our expectation is that the trip rates of stalls in this category may resemble those of stalls selling provision goods. Finally, for foodstuffs sellers, the expectation is that relatively fewer trips will be made by the group. Over time consumers have come to realize that foodstuffs differ in quality, just like any other goods offered for sale. Sellers often take turns announcing the origin of their goods to attract buyers who demand a lot for their money in a society where many people survive on about $1.25/day. Consumed by this on-the-spot oral advertising activity or exhausted by it, foodstuff sellers may avoid making multiple trips in exchange for possible improvement in daily turnover and revenue, especially for perishables.

To include the different commodity groups in the analyses, each group could be (arbitrarily) ranked according to the propensity of its members to make a trip, or commodity groups could be scored as dummy variables. As a dummy variable, the provision group that is expected to

Table 5.2   Score for Each Dummy Variable

Number of Dummy Variables

Commodity Group	D_1	D_2	D_3	D_4	D_5
Foodstuffs	1	0	0	0	0
Hardware	0	1	0	0	0
Readymade	0	0	1	0	0
Textiles	0	0	0	1	0
Provisions	0	0	0	0	0

generate the highest rate of contacts is used as a reference or comparison group resulting in scores shown in Table 5.2. By referencing the number of contacts for each group to the comparison group, in causal terms, according to Blalock (1979), the score might be interpreted as the increments or decrements in the number of contacts that the other group members would generate, assuming the comparison group members were to change into that line of trade. Oberschall and Beveridge (1979) applied similar reasoning by scoring commodities, in this case, from 1 through 5, in a Multiple Linear Regression analyses of business success in Zambia, while Clark and Hosking (1986) applied nominal classification because the magnitude of the difference between the groups cannot be properly specified or ordered. Scoring the attributes as dummy variables with Provisions, PROVIS = 0; other variables = 1 will assist in model building and interpretation of statistical results associated with each commodity group. For skeptics, in comparing the statistical results obtained from scoring a variable nominally and as a dummy, Lewis-Beck (2015) found no difference in the regression coefficients, and Oberschall and Beveridge (1979) found that in no case were the results of the tests of significance affected.

OVERVIEW OF INFORMATION COLLECTED

We have presented the market-stall trader as an entrepreneur engaged in a duality of financial management. Considered separately, that is what all entrepreneurs and businesspersons do—improve the welfare of the family while running a successful business. But the lack of separation of the business from the family has contributed to the push to formalize these non-formal businesses. The International Labour Organization has been advocating "to curb the spread of informality" and address the negative aspects of informal economy employment "through protection and incorporation into mainstream economy (ILO, 2014: 12)." You see, traders in large urban markets, especially market-stall traders, already constitute a major proportion of "mainstream economy," at least in (West) Africa. The organization, in collaboration with other international development agencies, is couching the argument on protecting the rights of workers and providing them with social security, as outlined in Decent Work Agenda. Moreover, the cultural devolution embedded in the Agenda would allow for the deconstruction of existing cultural social security system found in several African countries that require family members to be their 'brother's keepers' and replace it with a 'modern' system that involves government intervention and control in these highly competitive capitalistic (West) African nations. The devolution could lead to family disintegration and contribute to the decline of the traditional extended African family system. Therefore, supporting a gradual evolutionary process will yield mutually-productive results devoid of resentment and suspicion from small business managers. For example, Benjamin and Mbaye (July 2020) report that in Senegal household employment in the informal sector was 92.6% in 2011 but fell to 90.9% in 2019 and for the formal sector, it was 7.4% in 2011 but rose to 9.1% in 2019, a mirror image of the decline in informal employment—formalization can actually be a gradual, painless evolutionary process, we will surmise but, it should be grounded on adequate structural foundation of support for these underserved entrepreneurs.

What type of data set can we use to clarify the station of market-stall traders in the urban economic space vis-à-vis the urban transport system? The clarification would also assist other researchers interested in similar work to contribute to wise urban development decisions. To evaluate the nexus between large marketplaces and urban transport, we offer the following hypotheses:

1. Stalls located along the express road will generate more business contacts than stalls located in the central business district;
2. Stalls with a greater number of occupants will generate a greater number of contacts;
3. Stalls which have a means of personal transportation will generate more contacts than stalls where none are available;

4. Stalls with a greater number of a means of personal transportation will generate a greater number of business contacts;
5. Stalls with male occupants will generate more contacts than stalls with female occupants;
6. Stalls with a greater number of male occupants will generate a greater number of contacts; and
7. Stalls specializing in the sale of provisions, which can be easily borrowed, will generate a greater number of contacts than stall specializing in other types of goods.

Specification of Attributes

The relationship between stall attributes and total stall-based business contacts is examined by applying the Multiple Linear Regression model. This model is selected because it has a powerful capacity to depict linear relationships where they exist. The assumption is that a linear relationship exists between total trips, TOTRPS generated from a stall and its location, the type of commodity sold, stall size, means of personal transportation, and gender.

In other words,

$$\text{TOTRPS} = f(\text{location, gender, personal transportation,}$$
$$\text{size of stall, commoditysold}) + \text{disturbance term}$$

Or, in a multiple linear regression expression, the equation will be of the type:

$$Y = a + b_1X_1 + b_2X_2 + b_3X_3 + b_4X_4 + b_5X_5 \ldots b_nX_n + e$$

Accordingly, markets are in the periphery and the central business district and will be recorded as such, and gender will be evaluated based on how males and females perceive the need to make out-of-stall contacts during business hours. Any difference in the number of contacts will only suggest which gender makes more contacts but not necessarily which gender places a higher value on the need to make out-of-stall business contacts. In part, this is because of cultural constraints that view a woman's behavior differently, if they make 'numerous' out-of-stall business contacts, as tongues may begin to wag. Recall that the type of commodity sold is measured on a binary scale, and therefore, the Provision category will not appear in the modeling because it is the comparison group in a series of binary variables.

The following is the list of specified variables that are applied in subsequent equations and interpretation of results:

LOC = location of stall

NMALES = number of stalls exclusively occupied by males

NFEMS = number of stalls exclusively occupied by females

MAFEMS = number of stalls exclusively occupied by combined gender

PETRPS = measures the presence/absence of a means of personal transportation

VEHAVA = measures the number of vehicles available to the stall, 1^+

NEMP = measures the number of occupants (size of stall)

FOODS = foodstuffs commodity group

HARD = hardware commodity group

READY = readymade commodity group

TEXTI = textile commodity group; and,

PROVIS = provisions commodity group (the comparison group)

Method Used to Determine Which Stalls Provide Information

A systematic (non-random) sampling methodology was used to select stalls, the units of observation and analyses, as reflected in the hypotheses, and they also serve as surrogates for traders. Stalls in the markets are arranged in rows and back-to-back. They are identified by block and stalls are individually numbered. A spatial sampling frame consisting of all registered stalls was used. A spatial sampling frame is one in which location is an essential part of the variability of individual observations, as in the different types of traders based on type of goods sold, and where, it is therefore, important that samples are representative of the full range of locational variability (Hammond & McCullagh, 1978: 110). All business premises in Onitsha are required to be registered and the database is used for revenue (rent) collection. Generally, due to low vacancy rates in the markets, traders often rent and pay for stalls several months in advance, to ensure undisrupted occupancy. The selection of the three spatially-differentiated markets is more a question of incidental design than a sampling technique. The selection is intended to facilitate the testing of hypothesis based on business location.[1]

All the required number of stalls were selected systematically following the identification of a random starting point. This methodology has not produced any bias which would render the results of the analyses suspect. This is because there is no inherent periodicity in the arrangement of renters. Traders are randomly assigned stalls within their respective commodity zones, usually based on first come, first served. The assignment is conducted by street-level bureaucrats, using stall identification numbers. That notwithstanding, the sampling methodology does not equate to a pure random sampling method because once the first stall is chosen, all others are fixed, but Hammond and McCullagh (1978) have argued that this type of bias in systematic samples is a small price worth paying for the time saved. Moreover, the application of this sampling methodology has not created any computational problems above and beyond those generally associated with mobility studies. Indeed, we are usually safe in considering a systematic sample as equivalent to a simple random sample.

Being familiar with the physical layout of the markets, the realization was that the numbers identifying each stall would not be visible to a casual observer, including an interviewer, but any attempts to verify those stall numbers would create an undue amount of suspicion from traders, irrespective of any assurances that the survey was unconnected with any government entity. As traders may be unaware of academic survey methods, they would perceive surveying as merely interviewing any number of eager, and perhaps, curious volunteers without necessarily attempting to identify their stall numbers, if the researcher has no ulterior motives. Therefore, the use of stratified sampling was reinforced to avoid inciting traders to non-participation. For each stall selected, all individuals or a minimum of one individual was interviewed who had full knowledge and accounting of trips made by stall members the previous business day. This was considered appropriate, given the size of more than a majority of stalls. The argument is that the statistical information obtained from the interviews are adequate for analyzing and explaining

---

[1] For those interested in sampling mobile market traders, see, for example, Leidich, A., Achiro, L & et al. (2018). Methods for sampling geographically-mobile female traders in an East African Market setting. *PLoS One*, NIH. DOI: 10.1371/journal.pone.0190395. January 11.

the overall movement of the trader population during business hours, at least for those conducting business in selected markets. In the end, data were elicited from 513 individuals, a statistically large sample size that will allow generalization.

Interviews focused only on trips completed the previous business day during daylight hours and while the trader was still in the workplace (marketplace). There have been attempts (Marble, 1967; Hoorn, 1979; Burnett & Hanson, 1982; Srinivasan & Rogers, 2005; Barbinard & Scott, 2011) to explain the travel behavior of individuals. The argument is that travel patterns may be a result of constraints, environmental and economic, or the avoidance of other choices for similar reasons. In order to evaluate the relevance of this argument, a non-structured interview of 5% of the sample was conducted. The interview probed participants to explore to what degree constraints such as traffic congestion, location, and available modes affect their trip-making behavior, and considering trip purpose and destination, how do the same factors affect the propensity to make contacts. It also provided an opportunity to examine whether there were other reasons for trip making that the questionnaire failed to capture. An additional purpose was to evaluate the extent to which multiple stops (trip chaining) characterized market operation, and whether trip-substitution was a possibility, where a mobile telephone was available to the stall.

Method Used to Collect Information

The primary source of data was travel survey material that assisted respondents in answering questions regarding the travel history of stall occupants during the previous business day. The survey material was also formatted to allow for pre-coding of responses. The questions were designed to reflect traders' understanding and knowledge of marketplace and trading conditions, stall choice making constraints, and market operational opportunities. Researchers should be aware and sensitive to inherent characteristics of market traders and marketplace environment. Culturally, most traders will be found in the conservative spectrum in terms of providing business (secret or guarded) information. The harsh and very competitive trading environment may have exacerbated the tendency to legitimately withhold private (business) information. Moreover, since haggling is the medium of sales, a trader may be consumed by the attempt to consummate a deal a lot the time and may appear stressed to engage in 'non-productive question-answering' exercise. So, collecting relevant marketplace research information becomes more problematic, especially for stalls occupied by single persons that they may consider the entire exercise intrusive. With those nuances, marketplace surveys might be best conducted away from the shed or during non-peak (trading) hours. This is where local knowledge of the slow period and rapport with the union leadership become useful.

Conducting research in a large marketplace is challenging, especially when you are interested in getting numbers from traders—it is not for the fainthearted. To reduce the challenge, the trader population should be informed in advance about the impending research through responsible communication channels. Even though every trader may not read the newspaper, those who read about it might share the information. It minimizes 'survey shock' when the researcher and her team arrive at the marketplace.[2] The pre-survey communication should include the purpose of survey, starting date and duration, and potential questions. The purpose is to allay any fears and reassure traders that government representatives are not disguising themselves as researchers, and that the survey material does not involve sensitive issues such as income and expenditures. This does not guarantee that the researcher would garner 100% cooperation from traders, but it will minimize the number of rejections, realizing that the percentage of return of travel-related questionnaires is dependent on (a) the degree of simplicity of the questionnaire, (b) the kind of questions asked, and (c) the mode of contact with respondents (Kansky, 1967: 283). In our case, the response rate was 95% which was far greater than if survey materials were mailed to respondents which is typically about 10–15%. According to those who failed to cooperate, the most often-cited reason was that the survey would not diminish the level of suffering associated with trading; interestingly, they stated that government was always sponsoring these surveys in one way or the other, or that they had no reason to cooperate with government agents. In anticipation of survey rejections, the sample size was expanded to accommodate a 5% rejection rate.

---

[2] For example, in their study of markets and vendors in Lusaka, Zambia, Todd, Mulenga, and Mupimpila (1979) write "The arrival of several people armed with questionnaires... was greeted with reactions varying from suspicion to instant flight. One market, Matero," they continue, "was abandoned after half a day as a large proportion of vendors deserted their stalls, while other refused to be interviewed or gave patently false answers.".

Sheskin (1985) has provided a useful guide for selecting sample sizes (n), based on different confidence levels and confidence intervals. The following formula is generally applied[3]:

$$n = \left(\frac{z\sqrt{PQ}}{c} \right)^2$$

where
Z = 1.96, for 95% confidence that a result lies within a given confidence interval, CI;
P = the percentage about which a confidence interval is computed, expressed as a proportion;
Q = 1−P;
C = the desired size of the confidence interval, expressed as a decimal number.

Applying a P = 0.8 for traders who have the attribute, that is stalls, therefore Q = 0.2, a CI of 5% yielded 245 stalls, while a CI of 8% yielded only 96 stalls. However, a CI of 6% produced 170 stalls. Applying a rule of thumb, 234 stalls were considered adequate, and by accepting a 5% rejection level, 246 stalls were finally sampled (implicitly the CI was set at 5%). A low rate of rejection was anticipated because of the face-to-face administration of the survey material. The number of stalls selected represented 2.8% of all stalls in the markets (8868 stalls) which yielded 513 responses, at a 95% confidence level, and that exceeds the number suggested by Sheskin (1985: 35). As a result, statements applicable to the sample will also apply to the entire trader population (Norusis, 2010).

The sample excluded traders scattered in the urban areas such as shops, neighborhood (sauce) markets, roadside kiosks in residential areas, or along business strips. They were excluded because they were not considered part of the "marketplace institution" which is geo-fenced and has its own subculture. Moreover, it was conceived that their business size and practice are incompatible with those of stall traders.

---

[3] Compare this to the work that differently calculated sample size, thus: Sample size (n) = N calculated using 1 + N (e)^2 where N = total population, e = margin of error. Total population of stratified population of 398. With N = 396, confidence level = 95%, margin of error (e) = 0.05 n = 398 398(0.05)^2; n = 398. 1.995, n = 200 Peprah, C., Abdulai, I., & Agyemang-Duah., W | David McMillan (Reviewing editor) (2020). Compliance with income tax administration among micro, small and medium enterprises in Ghana, *Cogent Economics & Finance, 8:1,* DOI: 10.1080/23322039.2020.1782074

In order to understand how traders make choices related to out-of-stall contacts while juggling other stall needs, the information collection was limited to the following data points—sex of respondent, stall location, type of goods sold, number of employees/males/females, category of trader (Master versus other occupants), number of vehicles available, travel history (previous market day), age, and years in trading. For future marketplace improvements and adequate amenity, there was also an inquiry about the number of adequate stalls necessary to support the growth and prosperity of urban marketplace trade by type of goods sold. Answers to the last question revealed the preferences of respondents, since the trader had no cognitive capability of discerning or channeling the thoughts of another trader.

Apart from the Master, other traders are labeled trader-in-training, assistant, owner/co-owner, or temporary help. Apprentices are traders-in-training. Assistants are apprentices who have completed their normal training but have not separated from the stall, and a temporary help is a trader who is intermittently providing labor in the stall. This category was included because of the assumption that teenagers or other adult family members often pitch in to assist in the stall, a corroboration of the non-separation of family from the business—a team sport where everyone contributes their quota and talent to achieve group success. What was found was that an adult trader who occupies the stall with the spouse tended to classify the spouse as a 'temporary trader,' perhaps, to avoid any potential future head tax on all adult full-time stall occupants, or it was an attempt to clarify the pecking order.

The travel report included information on the number of contacts completed the previous day, the origin, the destination, the time started, time ended, purpose of contact, and the mobility mode selected for the contact. The Origin–Destination question style assisted respondents in tracking and reporting relevant contacts—and focusing on trips that had their destination outside the physical boundary of the marketplace. It also helped to satisfy the researcher that reported contacts were non-home-based, occurred while the trader was conducting his/her daily business activity, and that the contact truly had a destination outside geographically-defined market boundaries. The purpose of contacts was segregated into defined categories and subcategories, that is, financial (buy stock, accept, and pay for shipped goods, go to the bank); personal business (pay/collect debt, run errand, pick up/deliver goods); leisure (eat a meal, socialize); and others (travel out of town, go to government offices including the post office). Mobility mode choice has four categories: walking; transit (bus, taxi); cycle and motorcycle; and automobile included van and truck (drive alone, passenger, and driver with passenger). The next chapter is focused on contacts made by traders, including a discussion of statistically significant attributes that affect the travel behavior of traders.

REFERENCES

Adedotun, S. B., Tanimowo, N. B., & Ibrahim, R. B. (2017). A study of socio-economic characteristics of urbanites and their travel pattern in Nigeria. *Economic and Environmental Studies, 17*(4), 831–848.

Ahmed, T., Mitra, S. K., & Rafiq, R. (2020). Trip generation rates of land uses in a developing country city, Transportation Research Record: *Journal of the Transportation Board, 2674*(9), 412–525.

Asante, L.A., Helbrecht. I. (2019, May). Urban governance and its implications for the micro-geographies of market trading in Ghana: A case of the Kotokuraba Market Project in Cape Coast. *GeoJournal*, 1–23.

Barbinard, J., & Scott, K. (2011). What do existing household surveys tell us about gender and transport in developing countries? In *Women's issues in transportation: Summary of the 4th International Conference, vol.2. Technical Papers*. The World Bank.

Benjamin, N., & Mbaye, A. (2020). The informal sector in francophone Africa. Africa Growth Initiative, *Policy Brief*, The Bookings.

Blalock, H. M., Jr. (1979). *Social statistics*. McGraw Hill.

Bronso, J. M., & Hartgen, D. T. (1984). An update on household-reported trip generation rates. *Transportation Research Record 987*. TRB.

Burnett, P., & Hanson, S. (1982). The analysis of travel as an example of complex human behavior in spatially-constrained situation: Definition and measurement issues. *Transportation Research, 16*(A), 87–102.

Chamle-Wright, E. (2002). Savings and accumulation strategies of urban market women in Harare, Zimbabwe. *Economic Development and Cultural Change, 50*(4), 979–1006.

Clark, W. A. V., & Hosking, P. L. (1986). *Statistical methods for geographers*. John Wiley and Sons.

Daniels, P. W., & Warnes, A. M. (2006). Movement in cities. *Routledge, London*. https://doi.org/10.4324/9780203716410

Gihring, T. (1984). Intraurban activity patterns among entrepreneurs in a West African setting. *Geografiska, 66*(B), 17–27.

Hammond, R., & McCullagh, S. (1978). *Qualitative techniques in Geography*. Clarendon Press.

Hurst, M. E. (1970). An approach to the study of non-residential land use traffic generation. *Annals, Association of American Geographers, 2*, 40–45.

International Labor Organization, (2014). *Transitioning from the informal to formal Economy*.

Kansky, K. J. (1967). Travel patterns of urban residents. *Transportation Science, 1*, 261–285.

Katzin, M. (1964). The role of the small entrepreneur. In M. J. Herskovits & M. Harwitz (Eds.), *Economic transition in Africa* (pp. 179–198). Routledge and Kegan Paul.

Lewis-Beck, M. (2015). *Applied regression*. Sage Publications.

Marble, D. F. (1967). Transport inputs at urban residential sites. Papers and Proceedings. *Regional Science Association, 5*, 253-266.

McKinsey Global Institute. (2014, July). *Nigeria's renewal: Delivering Inclusive Growth in Africa's Largest Economy*.

News of the People. (2012, May 21). Tejuosho, Alade Markets project consultant Olaide Omotola in fraud scandal. *News of the People*.

Nezic, T., & Kerr, W. A. (1996). A market community development in West Africa. *Community Development Journal, 31*(1), 1–12.

Norusis, M. J. (2010). *PASW statistics 18 guide to data analysis*. Prentice Hall Press.

Oberschall, A. A., & Beveridge, A. (1979). *African businessmen and development in Zambia*. Princeton University Press.

OECD. (2019). *Women and trade networks in West Africa*.

Ogeah, F. N., & Omofonmwan, S. I. (2013). Urban Markets as a source of employment generation in Benin City, Nigeria. *African Journal of Social Sciences, 3*(4), 62–78.

Peil, M., & Sada, P. O. (1984). *African Urban society*. John Wiley and sons.

Ross, C. G. (1982). A village level study of producer grain transactions in rural Senegal. *African Studies Review, 4*, 65–94.

Sada, P. O., & McNulty, M. L (1981). The market traders in the city of Lagos. In P. O. Sada, & J. S. Oguntoyinbo (Eds.), *Urbanization processes and problems in Nigeria*. Ibadan University.

Salau, G. S. (2017, July 23). Beautiful Tejuosho market, yet to seduce traders. The Guardian *Sunday Magazine*.

Sheskin, I. M. (1985). *Survey research for Geographers*. Research Publications in Geography.

Solanke, M., & Olayiwola, S. M. (2015). Socio-economic characteristics of urban residents and intra-urban trip generation: An illustration from Abeokuta, Ogun State, Nigeria. *Ethiopian Journal of Environmental Studies and Management, 18*(5), 593–606.

Srinivasan, S., & Rogers, P. (2005). Travel behavior of low-income residents: Studying two contrasting locations in Chenai, India. *Journal of Transport Geography, 13*(3), 265–274.

Stouffer, S. A. (1940). Intervening opportunities: A theory of relating mobility and distance. *American Sociological Review, 5,* 845–867.

Todd, D., Mulenga, A., & Mupimpila, C. (1979). Market vendors in Lusaka, Zambia. *African Urban Studies, 5,* 45–70.

Van DerHorn, T. (1979). Travel behaviour and the total activity pattern. *Transportation, 8,* 309–328.

White, E. F. (1981). Creole women traders in the Nineteenth Century. *The International Journal of African Historical Studies, 14,* 626–642.

CHAPTER 6

A Geography of Contacts in a Large Urban Marketplace

As a surrogate for traders, the market stall is the decision-making unit of the business. The decision to make a contact is only but one of the clusters in the decision space of the stall manager. The result of those operational choices shows that mean daily contacts generated by a stall is 2.7 trips with some stalls generating up to a mean of 8 trips on the typical business day prior to the interview. The excellent South African Government 2018 *National Household Travel Survey* has data on travel and travel constraints of rural and urban households to allow for transportation service improvements and subsidies, but it lacks information, for example, on travel rates from non-household origins for similar subsidies. Perhaps, the survey was not designed to address the urban economic impacts of non-home-based travels of the same household members from their businesses that would have enhanced our understanding of the interface between marketplace traders and the mobility system, for example, in South Africa. Government agencies that are interested in improving the local urban economy would like to know that almost forty percent of market stalls in this large urban marketplace make more than three contacts every business day, meaning that almost 70% of trips have their origin and destination in the stall. Realize that when respondents are subjected to an interview situation and are forced to recall travel history, there is a tendency for either an under- or over-reporting of trips. The estimate is that at least 10 percent of actual trips often go unreported. This implies that the mean daily trips of Onitsha market-stall entrepreneur traders should be assumed to be higher, especially given their sociological lean to the conservative side. This will make the research results more relevant for both development planning and policy making. Excluding the ten percent error factor, we found that characteristically 61.8% of stalls generate less than three (3) trips/day while 22.0% of stalls generate 3 (three) to 4 (four), and 16.2% of stalls generate five (5) or more trips in a typical business day. So, traders in this large urban marketplace do not appear to spend all the time in the market-stall consummating deals—they make numerous out-of-stall, non-discretionary contacts that suggest a linkage between marketplaces and urban transport. Given their similarities, we believe that the results will not be any different for stall traders in other large urban marketplaces in (West) Africa. The findings also reveal that there is limited stall 'co-habitation' in this marketplace—a super majority (89.4%) of stalls are exclusively occupied by male or female traders, and 70 percent of stalls are occupied by one or two traders, only.

The geography of out-of-stall travel behavior of urban market traders will be examined at the aggregate (stall) level, using identifying stall strata of size, location, type of good sold, gender, trader category, and a means of personal transportation. Taken together, the attributes will contribute to clarify the balancing act between the pull and the push faced by marketplace traders in their quest to maintain financial buoyancy, given the operational lift facing the trader. The attributes are modeled using a Multiple Linear Regression model, a powerful descriptive and predictive model.

Quantifying Out-Of-Stall Contacts

A. Effect of Location

The hypothesis is that stalls located along the express road will generate a greater number of contacts than stalls in the CBD. The resulting model for this attribute is

$$\text{TOTRPS} = 1.618959 - \underset{(12.8)*}{1.0077257} \text{ LOC} + \underset{(20.9)*}{0.535140} \text{ NEMP}$$
$$+ \underset{(27.3)*}{1.342905} \text{ VEHAVA} + 0.365711$$

$$FOODS - 0.065537 \ TEXTI + 0.1888003 \ READY + 0.568586 \ HARD \tag{6.1}$$

$$R^2 = 0.6044 \ F = 10.77 \ Sig \ F = 0.0012 \ N = 246$$

*Significant at the 0.001 level (1-tailed);
(All F-values of regression coefficient will be shown in parenthesis for all equations).

As predicted, the variables are not multi-collinear (see Appendix). The coefficient of multiple determination, R^2 value is 0.6044 and the model is statistically significant at 0.001, an indication of the positive effect and direction (1-tailed) of location on the incidence of trip making. About 60% of variation in total contacts by location is explained by these attributes. Our goal is not to get a higher value close to $R^2 = 1$, but rather to demonstrate that these attributes contribute to business contact-making behavior of traders in an urban marketplace, and that for financial viability stall occupants, irrespective of their location, most likely take these attributes into consideration (consciously or unconsciously) when making a choice whether to make an out-of-stall business contact.

The sign of the regression coefficient for LOC is opposite our predicted direction, meaning that contrary to our expectation, traders in CBD stalls engage in a greater number of contacts than stall traders located along the express road. In addition, the regression coefficient of VEHAVA indicates that total contacts from the stall will increase by 1.3 units if you add one more vehicle unit to the stall. But total contacts will increase by 0.54 units or times if you increased stall size (measured by the number of occupants) by one unit which is understandable from operational and management perspective—the additional body will help to complete other money-making trips that were forgone due to labor shortage. In the commodity group, only in the hardware group do we observe a positive increase and a relatively larger (0.57) value even though it is not a statistically significant attribute when paired with location. For total daily contacts produced, CBD stalls generate a mean of 4.4 contacts while stalls along the express road generate a mean of 2.1 contacts (std. dev = 0.47) in a typical business day.

Realizing that the spatial difference creates a difference in the propensity of stalls to induce contacts, two additional models (equations 6.2 and

6.3 below) were run to further evaluate the direction of that difference. The results will shed lights on the value of means and coefficients:
For CBD location:

$$\text{TOTRPS} = 1.320975 + 1.669072 \underset{(19.3)*}{\text{VEHAVA}} + 0.808183 \underset{(22.0)*}{\text{NEMP}}$$

$$- 0.104151 \text{ TEXTI} - 0.084232$$

$$\underset{(3.3)**}{\text{FOODS} - 1.208509 \text{ READY}} - 0.671877 \text{ HARD} \qquad (6.2)$$

$$R^2 = 0.6724 \ F = 4.04 \text{Sig } F = 0.05 \ N = 83$$

*Significant at the 0.0000 level (1-tailed)
**Significant at the 0.06 level (1-tailed)

For Express Road location:

$$\text{TOTRPS} = 0.942537 + 0.960118 \underset{(8.67)*}{\text{VEHAVA}} + 0.420864 \underset{(6.52)*}{\text{NEMP}}$$

$$- 0.715578 \underset{(1.83)**}{\text{TEXTI}} + 0.146635$$

$$\text{FOODS} + 0.352009 \underset{(4.59)***}{\text{READY}} + 0.917665 \text{ HARD} \qquad (6.3)$$

$$R^2 = 0.4780 \ F = 3.69 \ \text{Sig } F = 0.05 \ N = 163$$

*Significant at the 0.01 level (1-tailed)
**Significant at the 0.1 level (1-tailed)
***Significant at the 0.03 level (1-tailed)

Both models are statistically significant at the 0.05 level, but a prediction based on the CBD model would be about 67% accurate and better than an equation solely based on express road location with 48% accuracy. In other words, these factors will explain 67% of trips generated by CBD stalls but only 48% for express road traders. Moreover, not only are the regression coefficient values for VEHAVA and NEMP larger for the CBD model, we also have a much smaller critical region for the variables. For a unit increase in TOTRPS, there would be an induced change in VEHAVA of 1.70 units, and 0.96 in NEMP for the CBD model compared to a much smaller change in the express road model. Along the express markets (Equation 6.3), a unit change in the number of vehicles available to the stall will only increase the number of contacts by 0.96 units compared to 1.7 times in the CBD. Similarly, if one more individual were added to the stall in the CBD, the stall will generate twice as many contacts than a similar stall along the express road (0.8 vs.0.4).

Information from the two models show that if stalls selling provisions changed into selling hardware goods, HARD, along the express road their rate of making contacts will increase by 0.9% but if they changed their minds and started selling textiles, TEXTI, they will reduce their level of contacts by 0.7% which will be even much lower if they sold ready-made, READY, in the central business district. In any case, we cannot predict with confidence the contact-making behavior of traders along the express road markets as we would for the CBD market by relying on these variables because of the relatively lower R^2 value. The superiority of a CBD-type environment for market location is instructive for planners.

Finally, additional results show that while stalls in the CBD generate 3.96 mean trips daily, the mean value for express road markets is 2.12. With a standard deviation of 2.41, we can suggest that there is minimum variability between the data set and, in general stalls in the CBD, despite the high concentration of activities and associated congestion, tend to have a greater propensity to generate contacts than stalls in the periphery. This is contrary to intuitive expectations and our hypothesis because location has a negative value for the coefficient of regression in Equation (6.1). This finding also contradicts Gihring (1984) who studied traders in Zaria, Nigeria. Perhaps the difference in the results may be attributed to spatial nucleation in southern Nigeria, as suggested by that researcher (Table 6.1).

B. Effect of Stall Size

NEMP, number of employees, was used as a surrogate to model stall size, and the regression result is shown in equation (6.4).

$$TOTRPS = 1.618959 - \underset{(12.8)*}{1.007257} \ LOC + \underset{(20.9)*}{0.535140} \ NEMP$$
$$+ \ \underset{(27.3)*}{1.342905} \ VEHAVA + 0.365711$$

Table 6.1 Impact of Location on Propensity of Traders to make Out-of-Stall Contacts

Units measured	CBD	Express Road	Location as a Variable (Eq. 6.1)
No of stalls	83	163	246
R^2	.6724	.4780	.6044
Mean trips	3.96	2.12	2.1 to 4.4
Coefficient of Regression*			
a.NEMP	+ .808183	+ .420864	+ .535140
b.VEHAVA	+ 1.669072	+ .960118	+ 1.342905
c.HARD	NA	+ .919665	NA
d.TEXTI	NA	−.715578	NA
e.READY	−.208509	NA	NA
f.LOC	-	-	−1.0077257

*Only applies to statistically significant variables, and direction

$$FOODS - 0.065537 \ TEXTI + 0.188003 \ READY + 0.568586 \ HARD$$
$$(2.2)**$$
$$(6.4)$$

$$R^2 = 0.6044 \ F = 10.77 \ Sig \ F = 0.0012 \ N = 246$$

Pearson's R = 0.4277 (ordinal); Pearson's R = 0.4699 (Interval scale)
*Significant at the 0.000 level (1-tailed); **Significant at the 0.1 level (1-tailed)

The R^2 for the model is 0.6044, and the F-value of 10.77 (sum of the predictive power of all independent variables) is much greater than the significant F-value of 0.0012 for the model, meaning that we are confident that the attributes are best fitted in predicting total trips or contacts than if we added more attributes to the model. The model is significant at the 0.001 level which means that the null hypothesis must be rejected; that is that the size of a stall has no effect on the number of business contacts generated from the stall in any given business day. And, as expected, NEMP has a positive or direct relationship with total trips generated from the stall, significant at 0.000 level, one-tailed.

The frequency results show that about one-half (56.1%) of stalls sampled generate either two or four trips while only 4% generate either one or three trips daily. These suggest that more than a majority of traders, at least those in the sample, who leave their business locations during business hours tend to also return to the stall. The results also show that about 83% of stalls generate four or less trips per day. Irrespective of this, trip frequency decreases appreciably beyond four trips per day since only about 16% of stalls generate five to ten trips per business day but when you consider the absolute numbers, there are still significantly many trips from this unofficial city that impact the transport system.

For practical purposes, some critics may suggest that there may be only two-stall sizes in Onitsha markets, namely small and large. This is because there is a preponderance (70.3%) of stalls occupied by either one or two traders. Stalls occupied by three, or four, and over category is roughly similar, 15.5% vs. 14.2%, respectively, so with that proportionality, a third category was created—medium size—to avoid empty cells in the model.

Two slightly different results of trip characteristics were obtained when stall size was measured at an ordinal versus interval level scale. Tables 6.2 and 6.3 show the results for the two types of measurements: There is a dramatic increase in trips produced between small and medium/large

Table 6.2 Mean Trip (Contacts) and Stall Size

Stall size	Mean trips	Standard Error	95% CI*
Small (1–2 traders)	2.0	0.1422	1.8 to 2.3
Medium (3 traders)	4.3	0.3867	3.5 to 5.1
Large (4+ traders)	4.5	0.4627	3.6 to 5.4

*CI = Confidence interval; N = 246

Table 6.3 Mean Trip (Contacts) and Number of Employees

Number of Employees	Mean Trips	Standard Error	95% CI
1	1.5	0.1393	1.2 to 1.8
2	2.9	0.2605	2.4 to 3.4
3	4.3	0.3883	3.5 to 5.0
4	4.2	0.5506	3.0 to 5.3
5	5.6	1.1096	2.9 to 8.3

N = 246

stall categories. The data suggest that as stall size increases, the number of contacts tends to increase. In fact, the number of out-of-stall contacts doubles as stalls increase their size beyond a minimum of two occupants (small size). Notice that when the measurement is limited to interval scale, the results, Table 6.3, are more representative of intuitive expectations and much easier to visualize.

It appears that the third occupant has a relatively large disproportionate marginal effect on number of contacts generated from the stall. The business manager appears to effectively deploy the newest employee/apprentice to complete out-of-stall contacts that may have been forgone due to the relatively high opportunity cost for existing stall occupants. It is certainly permissible to assume that generally, should the average size of stalls increase from the current average size of 1 to 2 employees to a new level of 3 and above, the transportation system in the commercial center of Onitsha would be expected to experience a significant stress due to increased use—that is what linkage will do to an urban transport system when marketplace activity is not considered in conjunction with what is going on the street. This presents a reason to justify refocusing attention on urban markets and traders' operation and, pairing it with the transport system, as it illustrates the need to manage stall operational characteristics in order to minimize trader impacts on urban transport, even as new trading (business) units are formed.

There is a positive correlation between the number of trips generated and the number of occupants in the shed, irrespective of the scale of measurement (correlation coefficient, Pearson's $r = 0.42774$ for ordinal level data and Pearson's $r = 0.4699$ for interval level data). Meanwhile, there is a significant marginal increase in the number of trips produced as stall size increases which lends credence to the altruism that a third individual is a 'crowd'—the utility of forgone contacts increases so quickly that the stall manager decongests the stall more frequently (to perhaps improve access for shoppers). To keep impacts on transport at a minimum, it then confirms that for most effective stall operation, the ideal size of the stall should be kept at a minimum of two individuals. In any case, it is reassuring that the findings are consistent with expectations (hypothesis) regarding the linear relationship between non-homebased (business) trips and size of an establishment that is stalls in the marketplace which serves as a workplace.

C. Availability of a Means of Personal Transportation

The first model (Equation 6.5) evaluates whether there is any statistical difference in trip production rates between stalls with and without a means of personal transportation. Note that PETRS is coded as a dummy variable to differentiate it from VEHAVA, number of vehicles, 1^+, available to the stall to measure the influence of the attribute on trip production.

For PETRPS, the resulting model:

$$TOTRPS = 1.850317 + 1.813394 \underset{(27.0)*}{PETRPS} + 0.787967 \underset{(18.6)*}{NMALES}$$

$$+ 413245 \underset{(9.8)**}{NFEMS} + 388881$$

$$MAFEMS - 1.027891 \underset{(5.9)***}{LOC} - 308740 \underset{(12.9)*}{TEXTI} + 0.383943 \ HARD$$

$$- 0.048502 \ FOODS + 0.117010 \ READY \qquad (6.5)$$

$$R^2 = 0.6020 \ F = 13.42 \ Sig \ F = 0.0003 \ N = 246$$

*Significant at the 0.000 level (1-tailed); **Significant at the 0.002 level (1-tailed)
***Significant at the 0.01 level (1-tailed)

confirms that there is a statistical difference ($p = 0.0003$) in trip generation rates between stalls when a means of personal transportation is present and when it is unavailable. The F-value (13.42) confirms that the null hypothesis is false, and we will conclude that the population coefficient of variation is indeed greater than zero. The expected positive value for PETRPS is also obtained and in fact, a unit change in its value will trigger a 1.8 increase in total contacts. Stalls with a means of personal transportation generated a mean of 4.5 trips in a typical business day, while stalls without a means of personal transportation eked out a mean of 2.0 trips (standard deviation PETRPS = 0.45). The value, therefore, has less than a 50% chance of deviating from the mean which is worse than the performance of a fair-minded coin. And notice that the positive value of PETRPS shows the potential for an increase in trips making if stalls without a means of personal transportation suddenly own an automobile, that is, switching from a 'No' to a 'Yes' coding.

Having established a statistical difference due to the availability of an automobile to the stall, a model to determine the direction of the difference, VEHAVA, number of vehicles at 1^+ was then modeled:

$$\text{TOTRPS} = 1.618959 - \underset{(12.8)*}{1.007257} \text{ LOC} + \underset{(20.9)*}{0.535140} \text{ NEMP}$$

$$+ \underset{(27.3)*}{1.342905} \text{ VEHAVA} + 0.365711$$

$$\text{FOODS} - 0.065537 \text{ TEXTI} + 0.188003 \text{ READY} + \underset{(2.2)**}{0.568586} \text{ HARD}$$

$$(6.6)$$

$$R^2 = 0.6044 \ F = 10.77 \ \text{Sig } F = 0.0012 \ N = 246$$

Pearson's R = 0.48575
*Significant at the 0.000 level (1-tailed); **Significant at the 0.1 level (1-tailed)

Total trips generated and number of vehicles available to the stall are strongly correlated because the measure of relationship Pearson's r has a value of 0.48575, and VEHAVA has a positive value and significant at 0.000 level (one-tailed, showing direction) that confirms the hypothesis. However, almost 70% of all stalls have no vehicles available to them, and the maximum available is two, Table 6.4. We find that there is a significant increase in mean trips from 2.0 trips to 4.3 trips as a stall acquires the first unit of a means of transportation. This is the reverse of data obtained from a homebased trip generation study in six cities in western Nigeria (Adedotun et al., 2017) where researchers found an inverse relationship between number of automobiles available to the household and the number of trips generated by the household, meaning that household movement needs may be quite different from those of stall businesses in the marketplace in these areas. In Onitsha, limiting

Table 6.4 Mean Trips of Stalls by Number of Vehicles

Number Vehicles	Mean Trips	Standard Error	95% CI
0	2.0	0.1396	1.7 to 2.3
1	4.3	0.2965	3.7 to 4.9
2	5.6	1.0456	3.2 to 8.0

access to the number of vehicles available to the stall will reduce the impact of traders and marketplaces during business hours on the urban transportation system. Even more dramatic is the increase in the number of contacts as the number of personal means of transportation increases from zero to two. Mean trips increase almost three times from 2.0 to 5.6 trips. This is instructive because no other stall attribute has exerted such a strong influence on total trips produced in the marketplace which is why the knowledge of the percentage of stalls with a personal means of transportation is important, and more so in absolute terms regarding total trips dumped on the system. The result also suggests that not only do stalls with a means of personal means of transportation maximize the use of those vehicles, perhaps in response to the 'socio-auto fact,' but vehicle owners also disproportionately impact the existing transportation infrastructure, given the frequency of their contacts with the system in a typical business day. Evren and Muran (2001) have commented on how cars use 70% of road space while carrying 20% of travels, while buses use only 4% and serve 35% of road users. Stakeholders should be pondering this finding in view of the level of use of the automobile by marketplace traders.

A Westerner in Onitsha may not resist observing the magnitude and domineering influence of personal automobile owners who (un)consciously exert power over other road users. There is incessant use of vehicle horn to warn other road users to relinquish their right of way. Often owners of personal automobiles verbally abuse recalcitrant pedestrians and motorcyclists, *keke* (tri-cycle) drivers or force them off the road, especially if the personal automobile is of the modern (big) sports utility vehicle type. Over time, these classes of automobile owners have come to expect that their 'rights' should be respected by other road users. By usurping the rights of other road users, those who own and operate a personal means of transportation are implicitly predisposed to use the system at a greater rate relative to, in this case, other marketplace traders. Adding this privilege to the traits of middle income-earner traders with the ability to afford other businesses outside of the marketplace, we can appreciate why they would have the desire for additional business contacts, albeit disproportional. Most often sharing valuable business tips and/or providing operational information to employees at those other establishments is better accomplished face-to-face. The visits also serve as disguised unannounced inspection and maintenance of a control regime. We subsume that the average urban market trader is probably unaware of the impacts of these contacts on the urban mobility system. In any case, these unscheduled visits by the owner of the business keep subordinates on their toes.

D. Effect of Gender

The hypothesis is that for stalls occupied by both males and females, the greater the number of males, the greater the number of contacts generated by the stall. However, a pre-test of the survey material confirmed that in Onitsha markets, stalls are not integrated, rather, both sexes appear to be naturally segregated, irrespective of goods sold, with males occupying 58.5% of all stalls and females occupying 30.9%, while only 10.6% of all stalls are integrated. As a result, a decision was made to re-evaluate and extend the hypothesis without changing its thrust. With the expectation that males will generate more trips, the selected method for recording the number of males and females was retained. Accordingly, the number of males and females was then recorded on an interval scale at the stall level; otherwise, it would be difficult to statistically score stalls with more than one male or female trader.

It would be reasonable to assess the effect on trip making when stalls are exclusively occupied by (1) males, NMALES; (2) females, NFEMS; and (3) both males and females, MAFEMS. But because of the small sample size (26) of stalls occupied by both males and females, no useful statistical information will be gleaned from modeling MAFEMS, but the result is shared.

In order to evaluate whether there is any statistical difference in trip rates between stall samples occupied by males and females, the coefficients of the two models were compared, Equations 6.7 and 6.8:

For NMALES:

$$TOTRPS = 2.681600 + \underset{(11.3)*}{0.571397} \ NMALES - \underset{(21.5)*}{1.358978} \ LOC$$

$$+ \underset{(49.0)*}{1.925919} \ VEHAVA - 0.282002$$

$$FOODS + 0.620066 \ HARD - 0.511478 \ TEXTI + 0.263348 \ READY \tag{6.7}$$

$$R^2 = 5754 \quad F = 41.22 \quad Sig \ F = 0.0000 \quad N = 144$$

*Significant at the 0.000 level (1-tailed)

For NFEMS:

$$TOTRPS = 2.383537 + 1.524533 \underset{(24.7)*}{VEHAVA} - 1.324510 \underset{(18.7)*}{LOC}$$
$$+ 0.199823 \underset{(2.5)**}{NFEMS} + 0.602420$$

$$FOODS + 0.776162\ HARD + 0.487450\ READY + 0.049845\ TEXTI$$
$$(6.8)$$

$$R^2 = 5509\quad F = 21.07\quad Sig\ F = 0.0000\quad N = 76$$

*Significant at the 0.0001 level (1-tailed)
**Significant at the 0.1 level (1-tailed)

The results of the two models are strikingly different: statistically significant NFEMS, ($p = 0.1$) contributes to a relative reduction in the regression coefficient of VEHAVA and overall R^2 value of the model (Equation 6.8). The regression coefficient value for NMALES is larger (0.6) than that for NFEMS (0.2) even though both models have statistically significant F-value 0.0000, pointing out a greater, albeit, propensity of males to make more trips from the stall. As a result, for a unit increase in the number of males, total contacts will increase by 0.6 while total contacts made during business hours by females will increase by only 0.2 units.

For confirmation, a third model, Equation 6.9, considers only stalls occupied by both males and females, MAFEMS, and the resulting regression model is shown below.

$$TOTRPS = 3.010393 + 0.113854\ MAFEMS + 1.681974 \underset{(43.2)*}{VEHAVA}$$
$$- 1.365345 \underset{(23.0)*}{LOC} - 291508TEXTI + 344856HARD$$
$$+ 0.010605\ READY + 0.028157\ FOODS\qquad (6.9)$$

$$R^2 = 0.5583\quad F = 56.76\quad Sig\ F = 0.0000\quad N = 26$$

*Significant at the 0.0001 level (1-tailed)

Notice that the regression coefficient for MAFEMS is not statistically significant even though the overall model is significant at the 0.0000 level. The model has an R-square value of 0.5583 and an F-value of 56.76. It is plausible that the small size of the sample may have contributed to the statistical insignificance of the value; otherwise, the result could be interpreted to mean that mixing both sexes in the stall does not produce any statistical difference in total contacts generated from stalls. Put differently, the amount of variation in TOTRPS accounted for by stalls occupied by both males and females is only 11.4% (Equation 6.9), compared to 57.1% for NMALES (Equation 6.7) or about 20% by NFEMS (Equation 6.8). Additional data from frequency tables show that mean trips produced by the attribute MAFEMS is 3.8 trips (STD DEV = 1.0) even though a single stall produced 8.0 trips while six (6) stalls produced 4.7 mean trips. In any case, based on the sample size, we cannot make any definitive statements about the sample or implications of mean trips produced. In all three models, though, multicollinearity posed no statistical problems.

The confirmed difference in trip generation rates of exclusive male- and female-occupied stalls is instructive because it appears that even though they may sell similar types of goods and are subjected to similar operating conditions, females tend to have better coping mechanism by resisting the impulse to make out-of-stall contacts, even when it could benefit the business. We are not sure if social constructs are contributory factors, as neighbors watch the going-ons' at each other's stall—too many absences would delight the gossip crowd, including other women traders, as their keen observation skills are deployed to record and comment on 'unreasonable' absences from the stall. Or, maybe there are just fewer employees in stalls exclusively occupied by female traders since we have established that stall size is a good predictor of trip production (see equation 6.4). But, the positive side of this is that female traders appear not to impact the transportation system at rates like those of male traders, Table 6.5. Notice the value of the standard deviation between the genders as there is more variability (1.44) in mean trips score for NFEMS—female traders appear to make trips for varied reasons than male traders whose trips purpose appear to be more similar. This may be because female traders may have developed alternate arrangements to service the needs of the stall such as hiring out labor. Some female traders revealed that those whose husbands are in the same market tend to receive assistance from the husband in the daily operation and management of the stall. The husband, for example, would provide lunch for the spouse and coordinate

Table 6.5 Summary of NMALES and NFEMS

Model results	NFEMS	NMALES
Mean trips	2.0	3.0
Pearson's r	0.03908	0.35956*
Std dev	1.44	0.89
R^2 value	0.5509	0.5754

* The values for Pearson's r, correlation coefficient, show that the attribute/independent variable NMALES has a stronger (positive) relationship with total trips than NFEMS

the delivery of stock to her stall. This is normal, as husbands are known to collaborate with their spouses to capture a larger market or customers by locating at different zones in the same market, therefore, when they leave the stall, the reasons are more varied. There is also the issue of the quality of the transportation/transit system. Females tend to perceive the difficulty associated with trip making different from their male counterparts. The narrow-congested roads are unkind to pedestrians, and minibuses are known to exceed recommended and acceptable crush load factors. According to other female traders, several taxi cabs are also decrepit. It is unlikely that nursing mothers or females with infants would engage in 'un-necessary contacts' under those conditions, given the potential enervating and psychological strain on the traveler. Therefore, a rational choice will be to make that contact when the utility clearly outweighs the cost; otherwise, many female traders appear to decide to stay back in the stall and improve revenues to assist then to support their families.

E. Type of Commodity Sold

As a result of the scoring system used for this attribute, the regression coefficient of each commodity can be interpreted as the difference in the intercepts between the commodity and the Provisions category, the comparison group. The intercept represents, in a causal term, the increments or decrements in the number of contacts that would be generated if traders selling provisions were to reestablish themselves in that commodity group. We will illustrate this statement with the foodstuffs group, FOODS, based on what the resulting model shows for the group.

But first let us examine a general model for types of good sold.

$$\text{TOTRPS} = 1.592166 + \underset{(19.15)*}{1.386491} \text{ NVEH} + \underset{(20.26)*}{0.525884} \text{ NEMP}$$
$$+ \underset{(2.5)**}{0.598784} \text{ HARD} + 0.227701$$

$$\text{READY} + 0.407032 \text{ FOODS} - 0.027671 \text{ TEXTI} - 1.012450 \text{ LOC}$$
$$(6.10)$$

$$R^2 = 6080 \text{ F} = 10.470 \text{ Sig F} = 0.0014 \text{ N} = 246$$

*Significant at the 0.000 level (1-tailed)
**Significant at the 0.1 level (1-tailed)

Then the model for the foodstuffs group,

$$\text{TOTRPS} = \{1.592116 + 0.407032\} \text{ FOODS} + 1.386491 \text{ NVEH}$$
$$+ 0.525884 \text{ NEMP} - 1.012450 \text{ LOC} \qquad (6.11)$$

as each attribute in the commodity group would score 0 while the foodstuffs category would score 1, and so on. The R^2 value is 0.6080, and the model was found to be significant at the 0.0001 level. Only in the hardware group does an appreciable change occur (0.6) for a unit change in the dependent variable, if traders selling provisions reestablished themselves as foodstuffs sellers, because it is the only variable that is statistically significant. A statistical run of models for the other categories made us realize that the other types of good sold in the marketplace would not affect total contacts produced, should provisions sellers transitioned into that category; therefore, the failure to show any level of statistical significance, equation (6.11) suggests that a single statistical model suffices for assessing the propensity of types of good sold in the marketplace to induce contacts during business hours.

Other empirical data indicate that a typical stall selling provision goods will generate 3.3 mean trips (standard deviation = 2.51) in a typical business day, while a stall specializing in foodstuffs generates 2.1 mean trips (standard deviation = 2.09). The values are close to the mean suggesting a good sign of less variability in the data set. Intermediate results exist for other categories. Apart from stalls selling provisions and those stocking hardware, other commodity groups generate less than

Table 6.6 Mean Stall Trips by Type of Goods Sold

Commodity Group	Mean Trips	Standard Error	95% CI
Foodstuffs	2.1	0.2969	1.5 to 2.7
Hardware	3.3	0.3324	2.6 to 3.9
Readymade	2.6	0.3324	1.9 to 3.3
Provisions	3.3	0.1496	2.6 to 3.9
Textiles	2.4	0.3427	1.7 to 3.1

overall mean contacts. One of the implications is that hardware and provision goods are relative over-producers of trips while stalls specializing in other commodity groups are under-producers of contacts that impact the transport environment, Table 6.6. In fact, additional empirical data, Table 6.7, for example, indicate that when the comparison is limited to evaluating differences in trip-making rates between commodity groups by percentage of stalls, we find that 48% of foodstuffs group and 47% of readymade group relatively generate more journeys daily. On the other hand, for those stalls generating 4 (four) trips, hardware sellers (27.5%) lead the pack followed by the provisions group (24.5%). Stalls selling textiles do not appear to present any clear pattern of travel behavior except that this is the only group that has about the same proportion of stalls with sellers that stay in the stall all day (32.6) as those other stalls where traders only make two trips per day (30.2%).

Notice that only 0–4% of stalls produce three trips meaning that journeys which begin in the stall tend to have the stall as the destination suggesting that traders take their business seriously because they tend not

Table 6.7 Percentage of Stall Trips by Type of Goods Sold

Total Trips	Foodstuffs %*	Hardware %*	Readymade %*	Textiles %*	Provisions %*
0	30	15.7	22.5	32.6	17.0
1	0.0	4.0	0.0	2.3	7.6
2	48.0	27.5	47.5	30.2	24.4
3	0.0	4.0	0.0	0.0	1.9
4	12.0	27.5	18.4	21.0	24.5
5–10	10.0	21.6	12.3	14.0	24.4

* Percentage of total stalls where N = 246

to leave the stall and engage in other activities that will force them not to return to the stall. While a relatively large percentage (32.6%) of textiles sellers lead the group of stalls that do not produce any trips, the foodstuffs group is within the range at 30%. Perhaps, the absence of refrigeration is a factor as small quantities of (fresh) produce must be bought and sold each business day and spending more time in the stall may translate to higher sales volume. The data further confirm that within this group, we have the lowest percentage (12%) of stalls generating four trips but the largest proportion (48.0%) producing two trips. Stalls selling textiles have the highest zero-trip generation rate which may also suggest that stacking bales of fabric allows for larger storage/display of inventory, or they have more predictable clientele that allows traders to anticipate sales and accordingly stock their stalls, or they may have (unrevealed) alternatives for meeting stall operational needs that minimize their interaction with the transport system. The readymade group tends to have similar characteristics, as they sell substitute and/or complimentary goods, implying that market factors that affect one group would be expected to affect the other group. And, indeed, there is no appreciable difference between the groups in the proportion of stalls generating four trips, viz 18.4% for readymade clothing against 21.0% for textiles goods. A common practice among traders, especially those who sell provisions, is the establishment of neighborhood shops, when they could afford it. Neighborhood shops allow traders to continue the business after closing from the major business in the marketplace. In fact, these neighborhood convenience shops are locally known as 'Provision Stores.' Elsewhere, they are known as convenience shops. A stall whose owner operates such neighborhood shop could generate daytime trips to restock the shop and use the opportunity to supervise shop attendants. This behavior may point to the leadership of the group in the 5–10 contacts/day category.

Now that we have established the existence of these largely unexplored and unknown trips that result from operation of marketplace-stall businesses, we can safely state that the data seem to confirm the unmistakable linkage between the marketplace institution and urban transport. This empirical information has so far eluded planners, researchers, and policy makers. The lack of information and knowledge about these trips and therefore the position of the marketplace institution in the urban development space is the source of the existing paradox that is, despite the impacts of the marketplace institution, over time it has been routinely disregarded and ignored in the urban development ecosystem. This is because very often, (West) African Urban Marketplaces are contextualized as urban spaces occupied by "petty traders" whose actions are inconsequential on the state of urban roads and urban traffic. Consider the work of John Howe and Deborah Bryceson for the World Bank. The work reviews transport in metropolitan areas (Nairobi and Dar es Salaam) and secondary cities (Morogoro and Eldorot) in Kenya and Tanzania, East Africa, where according to the authors, "(i)n relative terms, and in some cases absolutely, formal sector employment is declining relative to informal sector activities (2000: 21)," so, naturally the emphasis of the study is on the cities and their poor. Where would you think is the income source of urban residents engaged in those informal activities? The authors remind readers that the "(t)he poor's *petty trading* (emphasis added) and service activities... tended to be over oversubscribed and highly competitive, (thereby) affording very meager earnings (2000: 27)." As long as city residents are typically engaged in petty trading, the desire and typical (research) goal are often to provide transport investment that allows "the poor" to access basic needs, as the authors did quite well. They argue that the urban transport "users have little expectation that things will get better (p. 11)" and therefore, it is justifiably proper to provide additional or marginal (capital) transport investments that will reduce household travel costs. There is nothing inherently wrong with focusing on the urban poor and their transport needs, but as long as there is this vision of African cities with substantially petty traders hogging the urban informal sector, there appears to be no incentives to differentiate between traders and to further explore how they actually function in the informal economy relying on the existing transport system, and it would be farfetched to consider whether their economic activity produces meaningful impacts on the same transport system. As long as the universal assumption is that informal sector's undifferentiated 'petty traders' have no impacts on the urban transport system, there will be no concerted efforts to identify any methods for addressing the impacts of their travel behavior to assist in reducing urban transport investment. The authors have also identified the travel behavior of informal sector actors and simply labeled it "irregular" which is true, but that is the characteristic of non-peak temporal trips made by traders to support their economic activities, as the preceding empirical data show. Being irregular does not mean being insignificant, but that has been the strategy to dismiss, with prejudice, the magnitude of trips made by informal sector actors. Over time, the conventional wisdom has morphed into this universal and over-riding concept that these poor informal sector actors, including market-stall traders, have no significant additional travel behavior outside of accessing their places of business. Urban development experts should reconsider and question whether this neglect has contributed to their inability to address perennial urban traffic problems in these areas, especially in cities with large marketplaces. Elsewhere, in evaluating policy responses to informality in urban Africa, Rogerson (2017: 1179–1194) notes that "most Africans make their livelihoods in the informal economy." The author examines how Maputo, Mozambique responds "to informality through the lens of street traders," a research emphasis that tends to propagate the stereotype that informal sector actors who dominate the urban economy are majorly *street traders,* our pavement capitalists. Sustainable Mobility for All, a World Bank advocacy platform for international cooperation on transport and mobility issues, projects that by 2045 the additional two billion people that are expected to live in urban Africa will place stress on public transport and that might limit "access to economic and social opportunities (2017: 7)." What is missing is a suggestion for an exploration of the dynamics of activities within those economic and social opportunities because transport users, such as marketplace-stall traders, today do not just access those economic opportunities and spend all day in place. If researchers make such an assumption, it is a poor substitute for additional rigorous investigation of dynamics within differentiated informal sector activities. They must support their livelihoods and the exploration of the inner workings within those opportunity areas will be essential, if the development community is interested in updating the framework for managing urban development in Africa for the twenty-first century and beyond (see also Evren & Akad, 2001). What we are observing is the unstructured economic system that is manifesting itself in an unstructured (also known as "irregular") travel frame that most advocates have failed to grasp, but are too eager to dismiss, as they focus on familiar theoretical areas of discourse—preponderance of docile petty traders and the poor in Africa.

Next is the exploration of the purpose of marketplace trips to determine if some or all of the needs that induce trader trips could be accommodated within the marketplace. Doing that will minimize their intersection with the urban transportation system and serve as a useful and indirect method in improving the quality of urban travel of community members to economic and social opportunities, to borrow from the World Bank advocacy group.

REASONS FOR OUT-OF-STALL CONTACTS

So far, the assumption is that stall-based trips completed during normal business hours are business-related. To assess the veracity of the statement, we examine the distribution of trips by purpose, Table 6.8.

At the macro (trip purpose data collapsed) level, the data suggest that for all daily activities associated with operating the business, a large proportion of stalls, 41.1%, generate contacts associated with paying/collecting debt, running errand, picking up/delivering goods (categorized as personal business), and completing finance-related duties, 30.2%, which consist of buying additional goods, or going to the bank. On the other hand, in a fairly large number of stalls, 82.6%, the occupants could not identify any other reasons for making out-of-stall contacts other than traveling out of town, socializing, or visiting a government office. This suggests that traders take their business seriously, as trips are mainly

Table 6.8 Percent of Stalls Producing Contacts by Purpose of Contact

Percent of Stalls Generating Contacts

Purpose of Contact	Not Connected with %	Connected With %	% Of Times
Financial: Go to bank	69.8	30.2	10.2
Personal Business: Pay/collect debt Run errand Pickup/deliver goods	58.9	41.1	7.3 22.3 22.3
Leisure Socialize Eat Meal	88.7	11.3	27.2 14.2
Others Travel out town Visit govt. office	82.6	17.4	10.6 1.6
Total			115.7%*

* Total is more than 100% because responses combined (almost 16% of time) running errands with picking up/delivering goods which to traders are semantically the same. This is correct as they have similar frequency score of **22.3%**

related to operating and managing the stall. Accordingly, traders do not consider the existence of government offices essential to daily business operation (1.6%) compared to spending 22.3% of their time acquiring additional supplies for the shed. Additional data reveal that either stall traders do not extend credit to their customers or if they do, those who get credit tend to come in and make payments because traders appear not to deploy useful business time chasing down debtors or paying their own debt (7.3%). This points to the existence of a cash and carry transactional structure that characterizes the economic system. Generally, traders spend 10.2% of their time making contacts with the bank/post office in a typical business day, and a similar proportion has its occupants making out-of-town trips (10.6%). Meanwhile, contrary to what we thought would be frivolous trip making—socializing—traders use more than a quarter (27.2%) of business hours socializing. This partly confirms the importance of nurturing relationships through face-to-face human interaction in a competitive urban marketplace. Finally, while 22.3% of the time stall members engage in running errands, 14.2% of their time is spent to eat a meal. This should not be surprising since most traders purchase their meals from mobile food sellers, or they bring their lunch from home or have it delivered by another family member.

The profile of trader activities demonstrates a highly focused non-formal sector actors engaged in reproducing capital and mostly making trips to meet that goal. We now have facts to allow us to theorize that traders do take their business very seriously in the informal portion of the economy. Based on activity distribution by percentage of time, it appears that planners can accommodate trader needs within the institution and quickly absorb 50% of the damage traders place on the urban transport system, as that is about the percentage of time spent dealing with personal business. By reducing the incentive to leave the stall, it is expected that over time, the value of the pull would diminish and traders will further cut back on stall-based travel, as more incentives are provided within the institution. For example, safely warehousing supplies and providing banking needs in the marketplace will go a long way to minimize trader impacts on the transport system (Chapter 8 has additional discussion). Pairing those improvements with other transport infrastructure enhancements will contribute to show why refocusing attention on the economic significance of the marketplace institution in the urban space is a good urban development policy for cities.

Multi-Purpose vs Single-Purpose Trips

Another area for further exploration is whether traders who leave their businesses make only a single stop or several stops at different destinations, also known as trip chaining, before returning to the stall. Put differently, are traders averse to multi-purpose trip making, even when bad roads and wildly traffic conditions, for example, may serve as deterrents? Surprisingly, empirical results suggest that only 28% of stalls generate multi-purpose trips. The traffic character in the urban area is expected to place operational constraints on traders so, as a coping mechanism, a reasonable person would expect traders to engage in more multiple-purpose trips to reduce stress and conserve resources. Apparently, the inherently economic person, the trader, is wedded to satisficing her daily operational needs as whenever necessary. There is a similar dissonance in trip purpose when over a quarter of their time is devoted to socializing as a form of socio-psychological coping mechanism because it assists traders in fomenting marketplace relationships. However, it tends to question the hypothesis that the proportion of multi-stage journeys made by an individual increases as the individual's total number of journeys increases (Bentley et al., 1977). Could this be a function of that cultural difference with the Global South in social and economic structures that are being manifested in a different travel behavior by marketplace businesspersons? This observation points to another justification for the need to continuously assemble indigenous database for appropriate planning in these areas. In any case, this finding is surprising; therefore, the matter was further pursued with respondents, mostly owners and co-owners. The question posed to them simply was, why do traders prefer single purpose trips, in spite of travel difficulties presented by the transport system?

Traders believe that a lot of time would be wasted completing multiple-purpose trips. They argue that it would be more cost-effective to truncate trips to minimize aggregate trip times. In other words, the relatively smaller chunks of time spent during each trip create the illusion that the trader is saving time. The rationalization is quite hard to understand but they were puzzled about why this author could not understand or appreciate their reasoning because they believe that they can just "go and quickly come back to the store instead of wasting a lot of time going from one place to the other." It may be a pretext for spending more time in the stall to provide the constantly needed stall supervision, management, and operation; otherwise, it would be mathematically difficult to justify how returning to the stall prior to initiating an additional trip would reasonably lead to time savings when the two destinations might as well be closer to each other than returning to the trip origin to initiate a new trip. But there is a better explanation. Suppose the stall owner wants to resupply the store, it does not make any sense to ask an apprentice to visit other destination(s) before returning to the stall. It encourages truancy, and the stall owner will lose the ability to 'track' the movement of the apprentice as the stall owner can easily gauge how long it takes to complete that single journey. Adding more destinations dilutes the original trip purpose and encourages other stall members, in the future, to engage in other non-productive and unauthorized trips that may cause delays in servicing the needs of the stall. Other traders indicated that it will create a poor impression on colleagues in adjacent stalls and on customers if a trader is rarely available in the stall because the trader is trip-chaining (obviously discounting the saved time the trip maker would spend in the stall). Apart from losing invaluable customers, a trader could be perceived as an unreliable business person. The expectation that neighbors should assist in making business decisions in the absence of the stall-owning trader, and perhaps, coach any abandoned stall staff would not sit well with adjacent traders, especially if it becomes routine. Traders prefer that colleagues 'baby-sit' their stalls only when it is absolutely necessary, for example, in an emergency, and preferably for a short duration of time. Engaging in multi-purpose trips will, therefore, produce the opposite effect and generate undesirable results and bad impression, traders emphasized. To effectively impart required business skills and knowledge to apprentices and assistants, and to maintain an orderly stall operation, the presence of the stall owner is essential, traders opined. Taking a single purpose or multi-single purpose trips is better than engaging in multi-purpose trips that would disrupt stall operation, and besides the longer the trader is out in the public space and away from the stall, the greater the chances of getting into an 'accident' such as running into an angry (ex)-lover or get accosted by a creditor, they joked. It frees them to properly discharge stall responsibilities such as coordinating and supervising trainees and planning, and executing other logistics that will contribute to enhance profits and revenue. Finally, since some contacts involve acquiring additional stock or delivering merchandise, it would be unreasonable for a trip maker to haul the merchandise from one trip origin to another trip destination before returning to the shed. Even a bank visit would be better accomplished in a single trip, given the amount of time bank customers spend at the bank to deposit and/or withdraw cash. And for trips involving running errands, which apprentices and assistants may engage in, they are expected to promptly return to the shed to report the trip outcome to the master. All these combine to make Onitsha urban marketplace traders justifiably averse to multi-purpose contacts, irrespective of road and traffic conditions.

Purpose of Contacts and Category of Trader

Because of the culture, there is the possibility that the trip purpose of the master category could be different from the trip purpose of the non-master category because of the social structure within the institution. To evaluate any differences, stall-trader groups were cross-tabulated with trip purposes, the premise being that the visual display of the collapsed data will make the data more understandable, for comparative purposes, Table 6.9. The results affirm the expectation and are consistent with previously discussed empirical evidence. An appreciable proportion of contacts made by the master category appears to be associated with financial matters. Typically, bank customers are known to spend a disproportionate amount of time at the bank before completing a transaction. If you are a 'known' bank customer, such as the master, bank tellers are more lenient and reduce customer wait time with expedited service. Besides, we should expect the master to engage in contacts that deal with handling business finances, as it also affects the family. Most errands (within the sub-category of personal business) are run by non-masters, often at the request of the master, and that is part of the reason why we observed that a relatively greater proportion of trips in this purpose category is dominated by the non-master group. Notice that there is a greater sense of coordination between Leisure and Others trip purposes, as there is only a one to two percentage point difference in participation rates between

Table 6.9   Category of Traders by Trip Purpose

Percent of Trip Purpose by Stall

Trader Category	Financial	Personal Business	Leisure	Others	Total
Master	31.3	37.5	12.1	19.1	100%
Non-Master	26.0	42.5	13.8	17.7	100%

non-master and master category, perhaps an attempt by the master to keep 'peace' in the family.

MOBILITY METHODS OR MODE CHOICE

We will turn our attention to mode choice or, the mobility options available and used by traders. Commenting on factors that determine mode choice, researchers (Almarsi, 2013; Brog et al., 1977; Racca & Ratledge, 2004) have found them to include total travel time, total trip cost divided by personal income, accessibility, the level of service, which includes frequency (transit service), speed of the mode, socio-demographic/socio-economic characteristics, purpose of the journey, and factors characterized as habitual, trusting, or induced by publicity of the mode. Do market-stall traders put these into consideration? As a large albeit unofficial business city, marketplace 'residents' are likely to be affected by some of these factors as urban travelers, but as we have noted, traders have a different key motivational factor associated with stall-based trips made during business operation—they are mostly motivated by profit maximization. Kumar, Foster, and Barrett (2008) have lamented the menace of minibuses and how large buses have disappeared from Africa urban transport system, including Onitsha. Other common public transport characteristics include road congestion, safety problems, unpredictable routes, and of course high crush load and the absence of schedules for service stops. For Onitsha market-stall traders, mode choice could simply boil down to habit that has been incorporated into running the business, and maintaining that business-familial financial health requires that trips must be taken as necessary. Empirical evidence reveals that most traders rely on the walking mode to complete a significant proportion of business-related trips. Table 6.10 shows the breakdown of mode choice

Table 6.10 Type of Mode selected by Stalls in completing Trips

Percent of Stalls Producing Trips		
	Not completed by	Completed by
Type of Mode		
Walking	58.9	41.1
Transit	76.4	23.6
Motorcycle	96.1	3.9
Auto	99.9	0.1

by percentage of stalls producing those trips.

The collapsed data show that walking (41%) and transit (24%)—bus and taxi—are selected most often while bicycle and motorcycle modes (4%) and the auto mode (0.1%) constitute miniscule proportions. This finding magnifies and illuminates the results reported earlier regarding the impact of the presence of a personal means of transportation and the number of trips produced by the stall, plus the linear relationship associated with increasing the number of that attribute. To reiterate, this single attribute has demonstrated quite a disproportionate amount of power on inducing stall trips. The preponderance of the walking mode is partly due to traffic congestion as negotiating city streets are best accomplished by the individual as a pedestrian, but the other reason is probably because the other modes are not affordable or available. It is certainly understandable that a high dependence on the walking mode will translate to reduced cost of doing business, as there is no direct out-of-pocket cost attached to the mode (until the pedestrian faces off with another mode and loses in the encounter, such as in broken limb). The un-collapsed data reveal additional information. While the taxi mode is the next best preferred mode, surprisingly the van is the second least preferred mode, although the reason has more to do with its unavailability than preference—after all it has comparable carrying capacity and comfort level of a personal automobile. Traders indicated that they ride the taxi more often than bus because it provides door-to-door service, not subjected to frequent stops to let off or pickup other passengers; is more convenient, and as a shared ride, it does relatively reduce exposure to strangers; it could even be chartered for a single stop non-shared ride. The preference for the taxi mode could also demonstrate interest in time saving which would be inconsistent with their logic for preferring single purpose over multi-purpose trips; therefore, it has more to do with convenience as it approximates a personal auto mode. In only 11.0% of the time (frequency), do stall occupants choose the auto mode or have the driver travel alone, but only in about 1 out of 33 times would a personal auto driver travel with a passenger.

The bicycle mode was never mentioned as a mode for understandable reasons of roadway congestion and the inability of the mode to allow the transportation of merchandise. Dodging pedestrians or running into them and negotiating right of way space with aggressive bus, taxi and auto drivers present quite a big challenge to a bicycle rider. The mode is touted as non-polluting, easy to maintain and operate and suitable for short distance (2–5 miles) trips, but it appears to be out of favor among stall traders. The road congestion would force traders to walk anyway than ride a bicycle because at least they can safely head-transport their supply or delivery.

Means of Movement and Category of Trader

Table 6.11 is a display of the relationship between trader category and mode choice. The table shows the proportion of times a given mode was selected by traders to complete business contacts. It shows that when the contact requires a master or business owner to complete it, 39.4% choose to walk. This is consistent with the other findings, for example, that masters more often deal with financial matters than non-masters. Many financial institutions are located close to the markets and it is understandable why the master category would choose the mode more often than non-masters. On other hand, they rarely (7.2%) choose the motorcycle mode which reflects the age distribution spread, as older adults, including females, tend to be stall owners/managers or co-owners. Older adults may perceive that riding a motorcycle can be unsafe—after all the data show that when stall members make out-of-stall contacts, non-masters tend to choose the auto, transit, and motorcycle mode more often than the master group. It should not be surprising that the non-master group chooses the auto mode more than the master group. One of the reasons is that often the group doubles as house helps and/or chauffeurs. When they are not shuttling the master between destinations, they may be sent on an errand that requires the use of the personal auto, such as delivering and/or picking up merchandise, or assisting family members. This is also in tandem with non-masters using the transit mode at a higher rate.

Table 6.11 Category of Trader by Mode Choice

Per-cent Choice by Trader category

Category of Trader	Walking	Auto	Transit	Motorcycle
Master	39.4	15.3	38.2	7.2
Non-Master	24.8	22.7	41.1	11.4

In conclusion, while 41.1% of stalls generate contacts completed by walking, only 28% complete out-of-stalls trips in which the taxi mode was specifically selected, and at the same time, 19.1% of stall trips were completed on the bus mode. However, as a combined transit group, bus and taxi accounted for 23.6% of all trips which is the average for the two modes. As expected, the three modes represent the principal means of travel in the intra-urban movement geography of Onitsha marketplace-stall traders, and together account for 76.7% of all trips in a typical business day. Until there is comparative data and information from other regions or large urban marketplaces, we can infer that this is a representation of how informal or non-formal marketplace-stall traders (in Onitsha) interact with the transport system, after arriving in the market at the beginning of the business day, in their quest to maximize profit and accumulate capital.

CONSTRAINTS ON CONTACTS

There is an on-going debate concerning the extent to which the built environment is a significant attribute in choice behavior of urban trip makers. Psychologists would argue persuasively that travel behavior is prevented by a host of constraints, such as a sense of responsibility, perceived behavioral barriers, the lack of automobile, place of residence, and income that Tanner (1999) describe as subjective factors and objective conditions. Hong, et al. (2012) have documented mixed findings on similar constraint issues with some studies reporting statistically significant effects, while several other empirical studies have reported insignificant correlations. However, after examining the literature at the end of 2009, Ewing and Cervero (2010) concluded that travel variables are inelastic in response to measurable changes this time in the built environment, with none scoring greater than 0.39 on a weighted travel elasticity band, and most of the other variables scoring much less. Our interest is not to settle the debate on these environmental issues that Burnett and Hanson (1982) collectively describe as "avoidance behaviors and habit," rather, our interest is to evaluate the extent to which the daily contact-making behavior of traders is influenced by location-specific environmental constraints. This is accomplished through a non-structured interview of traders. The relevant environmental constraints (perceived/real) include congestion and bad road conditions (operational constraints/infrastructure conditions), limited mode choice

Table 6.12   Ratings of Environmental Constraints on travel behavior

Response Rating (%)		
Factors Considered	*Yes*	*NO*
A.System constraints		
(i) Single circular bus route	33.3	66.7
(ii) Not enough taxi cabs	6.6	93.4
(iii) No other means of transportation	40.0	60.0
B.Economic constraints	20.0	80.0
C.Operational constraints	33.3	66.7
(i) Infrastructure conditions (bad roads)	26.7	73.3
D.Low level of Technology	46.7	53.3

(system constraints), out-of-pocket cost (economic constraints), and the presence/absence of modern communication services (technological constraints), Table 6.12.

From the table, the findings are consistent with Ewing and Cervero (2010), and in this case, that the existing environmental factors are not deterring traders from making out-of-stall contacts, resulting from out of habit of managing the stall business. Overall, a clear majority of traders overwhelmingly do not believe that the identified environmental factors are sufficient disincentives that will force them to forgo trips that will add value to the economic welfare of the enterprise. Perhaps, traders have internalized the effects of these constraints because they are intractable, and traders have accepted their emasculation to reframe them. For example, consider the sellers' market for public transportation in which despite the operational characteristics of the service, patrons appear not to be concerned or complain or organize to seek redress from micro-entrepreneur transit operators, and the multiplicity of operators is a major deterrent. Therefore, as transit-captive users, they are apathetic because they need the system to move themselves and their goods to sustain their livelihood. Traders appear not to be paying attention to environmental factors that have no direct relationships to their business, as their immediate need is to move goods and information via the system, and any ancillary benefits such as comfort and convenience are just that, and therefore considered inconsequential. In essence, instead of fleeing from the system, traders fight back by internalizing the negative traits of the system, but surely do not condone it. Their business contacts are obligatory, as they contribute to create urban economic wealth, as policy makers struggle to accept and promote the marketplace as an engine of development. Given the intense competition and low-profit margins, the choice to make trips will separate economic survival and longevity from economic capitulation and annihilation. To a rational trader, the preference is to discount friction and increase the utility value of each trip to justify the movement. The high negative scores in Table 6.12 should not be construed as an indication of unwillingness to accept a better travel environment. It is expected that the UN Habitat-Government collaborative efforts would seek and deploy best practices to provide meaningful relief to traders through meaningful urban development.

Dodman, Leck, et al (2017), in their work on African urbanization, observe that a conservative estimate is that African urban dwellers in sub-Saharan Africa pay 11–18% more for goods and services than for comparable cities worldwide, and for communication, it is 46% and 42% for transportation. Irrespective of the relatively high-cost of goods and services in urban sub-Saharan Africa, it appears that technology could assist traders to substitute business trips through the use of electronic communication and reduce their impact on the transportation system, but the strong preference for traditional face-to-face communication, as we have emphasized elsewhere, may have informed their responses regarding the usefulness of technology in trip substitution. This is a rational choice that may appear puzzling to a non-native but this is consistent with research findings in Lagos, Nigeria that shows that for Ikeja GRA residents, telecommunication technology is not diminishing the appetite for intra-urban travel (Olayiwola & Akinpelu, 2013). For example, traders feel more comfortable touching wads of currency, their wealth, than the invisible money in an electronic banking system. They insist that it just does not feel the same, a concept they admit might be difficult for non-traders to comprehend.

In summary, what traders appear to reflect is that they need to support their families, irrespective of some 'white noise' of existing negative environmental impediments to mobility. This suggests a corollary hypothesis that business opportunities and potential profits, rather than environmental constraints, present stronger controlling effects on travel behavior of marketplace-stall traders (think African migrants risking their lives on the Mediterranean Sea to reach Europe). Moreover, traders crave improvements to the system so much so that some traders, wrongly perceiving that this writer has access to public policy makers and leaders in development circles, implored the researcher to share the high mobility misery index (MMI) of traders and emphasize that an improvement in the transport system would improve market operation and enhance the economic well-being of traders. So, even marketplace traders understand the linkage between urban transport and the marketplace.

Constraints and Category of Trader

The information used for discussing constraints on travel behavior was obtained from stall business owner/co-owners who are often older than stall assistants, apprentices, and traders-in-training. Anyone who is knowledgeable about prevailing social structure and strata may demur at the responses because the expectation is that older traders may not truly constitute the bulk of stall members who make out-of-stall contacts. In socializing apprentices into becoming career traders, the expectation is that while in the apprenticeship program or upon completion but before separation, the bulk of trip-making activities would be their responsibility, in recognition of reverence for older adults in the society—the authority and judgment of an older individual, especially if they are family members, are rarely challenged. Although times are changing but the controlling factor is the institutionalized power relationship between the master and other stall members in a workplace considered an extension of the household, as what happens in the marketplace does not stay in the marketplace—at the end of the business day the work group often becomes the family group. This power relationship is more critical when you factor in the financial rewards that await a successful apprentice at separation. In other words, stall owners may not be experiencing the identified environmental constraints as much as non-masters, a skeptic would argue. However, survey results show that stall masters, who also provided responses to the structured interviews, participate in trip making at a greater rate than the other group of traders, non-masters. Table 6.13 provides the empirical evidence that affirms the validity of the assertion.

Table 6.13 Mean Trip by Trader Category

Category of Trader	Mean Trip	Std. Error	95% CI
Master	4.2	0.4527	3.3 to 5.2
Non-Master	2.3	0.3292	1.7 to 3.0

So, it appears that such skeptics may only have opinion but not facts. The marketplace institution has its own subculture as a business city because in the general city, a master will be expected to make fewer trips in running the households (outside of work trips) in reverence to cultural norms, but the business city functions differently. The value of the standard errors tell us that in fact, this cannot be occurring by random chance. The empirical data confirm that participants in the unstructured survey belong to the category of traders who generate almost twice the rate of contacts produced by non-masters, and, therefore, their responses are valid for the marketplace. Furthermore, the associated hypothesis offers a new vista into the life of stall traders in a large urban (West) African business or unofficial city. Our concern therefore is why, contrary to intuition and expectations, would the non-master group make relatively fewer trips than the masters' group?

Most traders in the master category have business experience that the other stall members lack, suggesting that the owner is better equipped to deal, for instance, with banks and suppliers than the other stalls members. The group may also have a better understanding of the institution and complexities of business operation, and may also have a greater involvement with marketplace politics and other daily institutional shenanigans. Members of the group are also rightly positioned to sign business documents on behalf of the business because they can easily provide the required evidence. Finally, being more knowledgeable about the overall financial status of the business (balanced against the needs of the family), group members are in a better position to make on-the-spot and informed decision about the quantities of goods to purchase and from which suppliers. A trainee, for example, due to inexperience, will not be delegated to discharge those risky financial and sourcing responsibilities. The non-master crowd is better positioned to handle non-monetary (business) matters, such as running errands or picking up/delivering goods—responsibilities the master group are often willing to delegate to trainees without outsourcing control of the financial health of the business. Moreover, apprentices are typically expected and are required to spend more time in the stall to learn what is considered the fundamental skills of marketplace trade—understanding and managing customer behavior to persuade them to spend money in your stall. This constitutes part of the socialization process. For example, commenting on African urban markets, Peil and Sada (1984: 254) argue that the large number of assistants in the market are not exploited youngsters but learners who are being adapted to the nuances of the trading profession including understanding the lingua franca of the marketplace. A trainee, therefore, must earn their wings. Trainees need to understand the virtues of perseverance and hard work, especially in a marketplace characterized by frequent economic fluctuations. They are expected to understand, practice, and perfect the equivalent of a marketplace filibuster—the art of tactfully delaying a customer while the other is dispatched to another stall to fetch the merchandise. They must learn that there is no 'other stall' and be aware of the delicacy of the ruse unless it will backfire on them with associated financial loss. The fact is that the trader is sourcing the merchandise by asking neighbors to loan them the merchandise for sale. No matter how long the apprentice takes to return with the merchandise, the master, who fully understands the intricacies of sourcing a merchandise, must 'berate' him for taking too long, a ploy designed to mollify the waiting customer. This is a quick consignment strategy where the seller takes a quick profit on top of the price quoted by the consignor. So, in addition to generating that immediate financial reward, the practice also produces a tripartite effect—it meets the needs of the customer, it makes the stall owner look good and look big with owning a non-existent 'other store', and if the merchandise is in short supply, impresses the customer who in appreciation, often vows to return for future purchases from a hardworking and dependable supplier. It also reinforces the spirit of camaraderie among friendly competitors that is characteristic of the institution.

Usually, a trainee or an assistant is expected to demonstrate tenacity in consummating sales, maintaining relationships with adjacent stall occupants, and efficiently recording sales. The successful and satisfactory discharge of such responsibilities contributes to how quickly the trainee graduates from apprenticeship and, for obvious reasons, is a relevant factor in deciding the monetary settlement received at completion of training. Offering and pliantly spending the extra and necessary time in the shed is one of the methods an apprentice could use to demonstrate a willingness and preparedness to learn and acquire relevant business skills and experience and a readiness to leave the nest and run their own market stall. Finally, the longer the amount of business hours a trainee or an assistant spends in the stall, the greater the probability that the trainee will understand and master the nuances involved in manipulating the pricing process, including practicing price discrimination—applying attributes such as age, gender, dressing, dialect, and mannerism of a potential customer to make an opening offer for the price of a merchandise—developing an aptitude for taking initiatives, and showing a general understanding of stall management practices and operation, essential skills that a trainee will transfer and deploy when they become an independent operator. For all these reasons, they spend relatively more time in the shed than the master, as shown by the proportion of trips made by each category.

There is empirical evidence that demonstrates that traders engage in a substantial number of trips from the stall during business hours to suggest the existence of a linkage between the marketplace institution and urban transport. Lumping all traders into the 'petty trader' category is an outdated stereotype and a form of devolution that allows the perpetuation of the orthodoxy that non-formal economy sector actors, especially urban market-stall traders in large urban marketplaces, are simply entrepreneurs whose travel demand only is to access their place of business and return home. The dynamics of their business operation has not been of interest and the subject of vigorous academic and professional evaluation. The isolation allows researchers time to focus attention on the familiar urban poor, since all urban petty traders are members of the impoverished group, the argument goes. It is rather a reluctance to engage in exploring and understanding the differentiation of informal sector non-formal actors, especially those engaged in distributive trade as the consensus is to push the familiar economic system—formal production and manufacturing with easily measurable outputs. In addition, there is reluctance to accept that the different socio-economic and cultural characteristics in the Global South are producing trip behavior that reflects the economic framework of the vast informal sector actors that is often manifested in an urban traffic that may be described as chaotic by the uninitiated. To wit, the urban traffic is merely un-patterned and reflects the un-patterned informal economy that is producing it. There is also data that reveal stall attributes that are statistically significant in inducing these un-patterned essential business trips. Urban marketplace stall operation involves an implicit division of labor as you would find in a large formal organization, and this appears to frame the type of contacts completed by different trader categories. Finally, the trip frequency results of different trader groups appear contrary to intuitive expectations of our knowledge of what obtains in a typical (West) African traditional society, a social framework and behavior that were expected to be transferred to the daily temporary marketplace city. Not so. It appears that the marketplace institution has its own subculture. However, on the whole, the magnitude and character of business trips completed from the stall suggest that The Marketplace is functioning as a city within a city.

REFERENCES

Adedotun, S. B., Tanimowo, N. B., & Ibrahim, R. B. (2017). A study of socio-economic characteristics of urbanites and their travel pattern in Nigeria. *Economics and Environmental Studies, 17*(4), 831–848.

Almarsi, E. (2013). Factors affecting mode choice of work trips in developing cities—Gaza as a case study. *Journal of Transportation Technologies, 3*(4), 247–259.

Bentley, G. A., Bruce, A., & Jones, D. R. (1977). Intra-urban journeys and activity linkages. *Socio-Economic Planning Sciences, 11*, 213–220.

Brog, W. et al. (1977). Psychological determinants of user behavior. *Economc Reserach Center*, OECD, Paris.

Burnett, P., & Hanson, S. (1982). The analysis of travel as an example of complex human behavior in spatially-constrained situation: Definition and measurement issues. *Transportation Research, 16*(A), 87–102.

Dodman, D., Leck Rusca, M., & Colenbrander, S. (2017, December). African urbanisation: Implications for risk accumulation and reduction. *International Journal of Disaster and Risk Reduction, 26*, 7–15.

Evren, G., & Akad, M. (2001, January). Transportation planning problems in developing countries. *JOUR.*

Ewing, R., & Cervero, R. (2010). Travel and the built environment: A meta analyses. *Journal of the American Planning Association, 76*(3), 265–292.

Gihring, T. (1984). Intra-urban activity patterns among entrepreneurs in a West African setting. *Geografiska. 66*(B), 17–27.

Hong, J., Nasri, A., Zhang, L., & Shen, Q. (2012). How built environment affects travel behavior: A comparative analysis of the connection between land use and vehicles miles traveled in US Cities. *Journal of Transport and Land Use, 5*(3), 40–52.

Howe, J., & Bryceson, D. (2000). *Poverty and urban transport in East Africa: Review of research and Dutch donor experience.* A Report Prepared for the World Bank. International Institute for Infrastructural, Hydraulic and Environmental Engineering. Balkema.

Kumar, A., Foster, V., & Barrett, F. (2008). *Stuck in traffic: Urban transport in Africa.* World Bank Group. http://documents.worldbank.org/curated/en/671081468008449140/Stuck-in-traffic-urban-transport-in-Africa

Olayiwola, K. O., & Akinpelu, A. A. (2013). *The role of telecommunication in urban travel in Lagos metropolitan area: A study of Ikeja GRA, A* paper presented at the Lagos Polytechnic SM & BS Conference on Poverty Alleviation, Income Redistribution and Rural Development in Developing Countries held between Monday 24th–Thursday 27th June, 2013, Lagos State Polytechnic, Isolo Campus.

Peil, M., & Sada, P. O. (1984). *African urban society.* John Wiley and sons.

Racca, D. P., & Ratledge, E. C. (2004*). Factors that affect and/or can alter mode choice,* Delaware Transportation Institute and the State of Delaware DOT.

Rogerson, C. M. (2017). Policy responses to informality in urban Africa: the example of Maputo, Mozambique. *GeoJournal, 82,* 1179–1194.https://doi.org/10.1007/S10708-016-9735-x

Sustainable Mobility for All. (2017). *Global mobility report 2017: Tracking sector performance.* http://creativecommons.org/licenses/by/3.0/igo

Tanner, C. (1999). Constraints on environmental behavior. *Journal of Environmental Psychology, 19*(2), 145–157. https://doi.org/10.1006/jevp.1999.0121

CHAPTER 7

Sustainability of the Marketplace Institution

In order to establish justification to sustain the marketplace institution in the (West) African urban economy, given the undeniable impacts of the institution on urban transport, we frame the argument around whether planners and other stakeholders.

a. recognize the importance of marketplaces in the mostly unfamiliar urban travel space and share a willingness to refocus attention on marketplaces on improved urban planning processes;
b. are committed to addressing marketplace-transport linkages for the mutual improvement of urban transport and the marketplace and
c. are inclined to minimize the effects of attributes that are inducing trips that create the un-patterned travel structure that characterizes many cities with large marketplaces mostly in the Global South.

Many readers would agree that it will be a monumental policy decision to discontinue the marketplace institution and disallow the resident entrepreneurs from engaging in their very important distributive services, after centuries of servicing consumers merely because they exert what many planners would consider manageable externalities on urban transport. As a rejection of that notion, studies (Nchito, 2006) show that the number of marketplaces continues to grow in African cities whether through formal government intervention or through community efforts,

K. Ochia, *Marketplace Trade and West African Urban Development*, https://doi.org/10.1007/978-3-030-87556-5_7

and in fact that these African marketplaces are projected to continue the undeniable function of organizing African urban areas (Gantner, 2009). But a formal intervention is required to allow these marketplaces to achieve a purposeful organization of African cities. To support this premise, in analyzing where cities can take Africa, the OECD (2016) suggests that African major cities and towns, where we find large urban marketplaces, are engines of growth that, if properly harnessed, that is with proper urban development planning, will be able to fuel the entire continent's sustainable (economic) development. The authors observe that cities, for example, account for 60% of the food market that is worth US180 billion (2010 dollars) that suggests continued expansion in the universe of entrepreneurs engaged in distributive trade. In fact, the Urban Institute (2008: 4) had earlier estimated that by 2030, urban areas will account for 75% of all purchased food that will be distributed in sub-Saharan Africa. Despite these projections, the African Union's refined position on urban development, as outlined in *Agenda 2063—The Africa We Want* (African Union, 2015), a 50-year strategic document, specifically appears not to identify this key African economic institution as an important, harnessable resource in its projected and preferred sustainable development framework for the continent. Outlining the Key Transformational Outcomes expected by Africans in 2023, the document identifies improvements in living standards, transformed, inclusive and sustainable economies, integrated Africa, empowering women, youth and children, and a well-governed, peaceful, and cultural-centric Africa in a global context. Agenda 2063 also emphasizes a preference for the creation of regional industrialization hubs linked to global value chains and commodity exchanges that should be in place by 2023. While highlighting an interest in establishing global linkages in areas such as manufacturing, space, education, financial institutions, and dual citizenship for Africans in diaspora is progressive, laudable, and forward-looking, but by its absence, the document forfeited the opportunity to embrace and promote the significance of the marketplace institution and, as a result, contribute to propagate the ongoing disregard of the marketplace as a resource, unlike the leaders of pre-colonial Trading Empires such as Ghana, Mali and Songhai centuries ago, who often placed the marketplace close to their palace in recognition of the importance of trading in the economic strength (wealth) and more important the military might of the empire and kingdom. The document needs to link relevant identified development interests to improvements within the environment of urban marketplace institution, as it is a significant part of the corner-stone of the economy in African urban areas. Equally important, it fails to recognize the strategic role of the institution in addressing inequity and inequality that characterize African urban economic structure. Mean-while, the same document enthusiastically and wisely supports sectors and activities that link the continent to global and intercontinental institu-tions, even though the marketplace is known to have linkages to local and global formal and informal economies. Ordinarily, an Africa-centric development document would hold in high regard its foremost indige-nous urban economic institution, the one that continues to demonstrate its ability to create jobs and grow and sustain the urban economy by contributing to reduce urban income inequality in a long-range policy document focused on African development. Highlighting the prominence of the marketplace institution is warranted, given the continent's export strategy that does not even encourage local processing of tea leaves before export, even as the continent still holds 30% of world's mineral resources. A useful intercontinental linkage would insist on a reformed and repurposed twenty-first century-type export strategy that encourages local processing of strategic raw materials which will form a backbone for a return to universal increased employment in the formal economy to help African cities to open their doors to the world, to paraphrase World Bank experts. The agglomeration and spillover effects will lead to the creation of related jobs in research and jumpstart technological advancement. In its absence, we argue that the flagship African urban economic institu-tion should have been properly meshed into the *Agenda 2063* cloud and promoted as a contemporary resource and an engine of indigenous urban economic development that deserves to be encouraged, supported, and strengthened because it is sustainable. It is arguable, but we will demur, if some observers suggest that strengthening financial institutions and empowering women, as stated in the document, indirectly recognizes the institution in albeit subtle way. Policy-wise, highlighting the institution in such a strategic global document will reassure the (international) develop-ment community that Africa values its own economic heritage, especially as the informal economy is beginning to show progress in supporting lives and livelihoods in a world that is slowly but surely mulling the need for economic and social justice.

After reviewing almost four decades of studies in the informal sector, Onyebueke and Geyer (2011) document the necessity for more substan-tive academic research work on the informal economy. They recommend that future works provide less theoretically fragmented, but more empirically persuasive analysis of the dynamics within the sector, and not an aggregate study of the informal economy that tends to reconstitute existing knowledge. This is consistent with the comment by Suzanne Friedberg (1997: 40) in reviewing *African market women and economic power: the role of women in African economic development*, that what is needed "is more attention to differentiation and stratification between and within groups of traders." We agree that the differentiation and analysis of dynamics within the strata should embody the need to methodically document and clarify the character and structure of participants within identified economic segments or strata differentiated by relevant traits within the group. Such a deep dive will reveal useful dynamics that planners will use in their work to build better (West) African cities of tomorrow. To contribute to address the challenge posed by these authors, not only are we providing empirical information on the group dynamics of a specific non-formal economy group—traders—we extend the contribution through differentiation by evaluating how the activity of stall traders, a stratum, within the group impact the urban transport system that they depend on for economic success. Subsequently, we are developing the argument regarding the sustainability of the group's spatial operational boundary around facts generated from the strata's group dynamism. We will show that carefully integrating these facts into urban development planning and design will produce mutually beneficial urban development outcomes. This will add some weight to the admonition to "plan for economic informality" that was suggested by Kinyanjui (2014) for accommodating Taveta Road female traders in the Central Business District of Nairobi, Kenya. Despite the fact that the formal sector is secondary to the informal sector in these areas, it still appears to attract the interests of urbanologists who tend to dismiss the prominence and needs of informal sector actors by minimizing the magnitude of their activities and any associated impacts, and in the current context, on the urban transport system. Because most of the data points establishing the linkage are empirically malleable, they can be adjusted to influence the dynamism within the marketplace institution to allow for the creation and implementation of strategies to institutionalize a harmonious co-existence of the marketplace institution and urban transport, that is, address the paradox of the marketplace in (West) African urban development. In the end, the economic survivability of the institution still depends on enhanced (urban) accessibility.

BASIS FOR MARKETPLACE SUSTAINABILITY

We can safely state that the operation and management processes relied on by traders in Onitsha Marketplace (and elsewhere) combine to induce essential business contacts that inadvertently but significantly impact the urban mobility system. In general, the lack of enforceable urban development policies and regulations has resulted in sprouting of marketplaces in many African countries. Often governments have built marketplaces and provided stalls for traders, but the number of spaces provided often fails to match the demand by current and aspiring traders because there is no data-centric planning for these projects. Very often, an elected official 'just decides' to build a marketplace for his constituents to earn bragging rights in anticipation of the next election. Even for those who can afford them, the available stall space is often insufficient to safely lock up their merchandise. In addition to security problems, failure to have sufficient stock in the shed means that at the beginning/ending of each business day, and in-between, traders are forced to make trips to pick-up or deliver goods, bring goods to the marketplace, or take them home. In other words, these markets create unintended consequences on the urban environment. Meanwhile, there is the fear of mysterious market fires (Popoola et al., 2016) that often provide the opportunity, it is alleged, for developers to replace traditional (West) African market with Western-style shopping centers—a subtle de-marketization of Africa? Displacing and dislocating more traders from existing marketplaces, when modern malls and shopping centers replace existing traditional marketplaces with even fewer affordable stalls, is inimical to the ability of marketplaces to contribute to economic development. Given the other reasons why stall traders leave the business allows that the foundational basis for minimizing such out-of-stall contacts lies in creating disincentives for making those trips—and therein lies the usefulness of empirically malleable data such as those identified in this work. Implementing and maintaining wise disincentives will be better achieved by first institutionalizing necessary planning standards into the development and design of urban marketplaces. Recognizing and properly managing the daily activities of marketplace stall traders through integrated urban development process will produce immediate and tangible changes to how traders interact and intersect with another major land use—(urban) transportation. Furthermore, there are those cultural obligations—visiting business associates, the bereaved or colleagues in the hospitals—collectively categorized as socializing that take entrepreneurs outside the shed during business hours. These culturally-induced contacts contribute to explain why the differently structured social characteristics in these areas justify differently structured approaches to transport planning. Such contacts, for example, strengthen marketplace interrelationships and build social cohesiveness within the institution. These culturally-induced trips may appear to be beyond the realm of traditional land use-transport planning consideration, but in these areas, they do constitute a serious trip purpose. Ordinarily, meaning in Western societies, they will make up a prominent portion of discretionary weekend trips; therefore, we will argue that by minimizing other non-culturally contaminated but universally-accepted or legitimate business contacts, planners can begin to address these wicked marketplace-transport problems. But, by misjudging and therefore mislabeling such contacts as frivolous could serve as a justification to postpone the need to revisit existing urban transportation planning processes for these areas and play into the hands of those who may want to delay the necessary professional adjudication of a planning bias based on ethnocentrism of alleged cultural backwardness that produces the preponderance of informal sector actors in the Global South, even though sociologists remind us that no culture is better than the other.

To better understand the argument on sustainability of the marketplace, we will outline what we know about marketplaces that some critics could present to show that the marketplace institution is not sustainable. They may suggest that a better option will be to formalize and demarketize the marketplace by breaking it up into several modern shopping malls and shopping centers to dilute its effects, the collateral damage to the teeming shopping poor notwithstanding. This dominant traditional African urban economic institution is characterized by the following:

1. Contrary to prevailing orthodoxy market-stall traders in large urban marketplaces make out-of-stall daily contacts or trips as a result of the style of their business practice.
2. These irregular or nonroutine contacts occur during business hours and outside of routine commute times; therefore, the marketplace has a direct linkage with urban transport and also affects its character.

3. As these contacts have their destination outside of the geographically defined marketplace, they have unintended but unexplored consequences on the urban mobility system.
4. Location which is a fixed input in traders' service production process is a significant factor in total trips produced by a market stall.
5. Stalls that have a means of personal transportation produce a greater number of contacts than stalls where none exist.
6. Even more importantly, the greater the number of automobiles available to a stall, the greater the number of out-of-stall contacts produced by the stall.
7. There is a linear relationship between the size of the stall and the number of contacts produced by the stall. The most substantial increase in the number of trips produced by a stall occurs when the size of the stall increases from two (2) to three (3) occupants and ;
8. Large (4⁺ occupants) stalls tend to produce a greater number of trips than small (1–3) stalls, and stalls exclusively occupied by males generate a greater number of trips than stalls exclusively occupied by females; although, the number of contacts produced by stalls exclusively occupied by both males and females is not statistically significant.

The alternative—marketplaces are not sustainable—that could be suggested by those critics raises important issues but our findings establish some theoretically important facts. Sustaining marketplace trade is congruent with the on-going international efforts to recognize and upgrade the urban non-formal economy as a viable sector in the economic ecosystem of African cities. Of noteworthy is that the factors that bolster the arguments for non-sustainability are manageable through thoughtful urban planning processes that will allow marketplaces to keep pace with the rate of city growth, to borrow from Joan Clos, UN-Habitat director. With international recognition of the sector, the stage is set for (West) African governments to deliberately support and strengthen the capabilities and resourcefulness of the unique entrepreneurs who practice their profession in the marketplace. The support will include trader education and continuous collaboration in planning, designing, and building new or modernizing existing markets while concurrently placing an eye on access issues. The public–private partnership will reduce alienation of traders in addressing urban development concerns that benefit their livelihood. It also provides an opportunity to discourage traders from perceiving local urban development as the responsibility of government and indigenes. Traders should learn that they are important stakeholders in the condition of the urban economic space that allows them to accumulate wealth that they often use in developing their places of origin. Invited and treated as co-owners, marketplace traders could be persuaded to emotionally invest in improving the quality of life in the city where they live and work which will assist in sustaining the marketplace.

Evaluating the model for location, we obtained results that are contrary to expectations, and they result from events outside the control of the trader—inertia or habit of shoppers. To many local and non-local consumers, the Onitsha Main Market is synonymous with Onitsha Market as the commercial town is known throughout West Africa—a one-stop shopping district. Coupled with the human-scale open mall character of the Main Market that shelters shoppers (partially) and sellers (fully) from the elements, more shoppers tend to be attracted to it than the relatively new and very open (non-open mall type) markets in the periphery. Traders in the Main Market also stock relatively more variety of goods. The assumption is that with that type of convenience, and availability of (non)household goods at one location, CBD market traders are predisposed to make relatively more sales with the attendant need to restock the shed as they cater to the needs of customers. Consequently, CBD traders make relatively more out-of-stall contacts over and beyond those of similar stalls along the express road, but that does not make these marketplaces unsustainable. Supporting the revenue stream of traders by choosing supportive market location will be a proven method of sustaining marketplace trade. The building of a marketplace could be a political and policy decision but scoping the appropriate location should be a professional process not guided by the first village to donate a piece of land for the new market, or the preferences of the individual with the largest project donation. The process will, for example, also allow planners to evaluate access for potential visitors to the location.

There is also the location of wholesale distributors and the character of the adjacent land use. The CBD is the site of early European trading and distribution houses. The tradition has survived into this century. Understandably, a significant proportion of distributors, including importers, who consume relatively larger business spaces outside the geographic market boundary, are found close to this traditional (colonial) downtown. The arrival of new merchandise would trigger successive trips by traders and because of the proximity, CBD stall traders appear to ordinarily maintain regular contacts with suppliers. The more regular face-to-face contact gives CBD traders an unwritten right of first refusal when new merchandise arrives. For relationship-building, it is reasonable to assume that stall traders could run an errand to distributors' shops to merely 'check out' the latest styles and hot-selling items, place orders, or just discuss business. The combined effect of these decision choices is that they contribute to increase the propensity of contacts by downtown traders. Traders were asked to identify the number of sheds another trader in their line of business would require to meet adequate storage and business space. Without realizing that they were revealing their own preferences, 61.4% responded that just one more shed would meet their needs, and cumulatively 92% of traders suggested a maximum of 2 (two) more sheds to meet their space business need. This finding is instructive. It provides guidance to planners on space design and allocation. Based on existing stall size, this is equivalent to requesting additional 48–96 square feet of space (4.5–8.9 sq. meters) which would potentially reduce daily urban trips made by market-stall traders by 20–40%. The expectation is that spending more time in the shed would contribute to traders' ability to consummate more sale and improve the rate of capital accumulation not just for the stall but perhaps for an adjacent shed that the trader may be compelled to babysit. The amount of space requested suggests that traders are reasonable entrepreneurs who have clear but measurable goal of how a revised marketplace development design standard could support and strengthen urban market trade. The ability of planners to meet the space demand of traders is a demonstration that despite their impacts, marketplace trade is actually sustainable with adjustments at the edges. This means that the scoping process for location should include the availability of sufficient land area that will offer traders the opportunity for larger stalls. Squeezing in a new market on that small piece of land before that national or local election will deny the input of land-use planners, designers, and beneficiaries for a sustainable marketplace. This will run counter to the advice of Joan Clos, executive director of UN-Habitat, regarding planning vis-à-vis the maturity of political systems. "In a weak system," according to Clos, "sometimes the way they do planning is by authoritarian means, without taking into account the rights of the people, (Harsch, Africa Renewal, April 2012)." In refurbishing existing markets, developers should not be allowed to lead and control the process in order to manage the temptation of built-in profit motives that places the needs of investors above the needs of beneficiaries.

Does the location of other urban institutions such as churches, government offices, medical facilities, schools, and financial houses play a role in the sustainability of marketplace trade? Tanimowo (2017) has evaluated land-use mix and intra-urban travel in Ogbomoso, Nigeria and found that tracts with high land-use mix generate and attract relatively large number of trips while low land-use mixes attract and generate fewer trips. But, in a review of studies on the impact of the built environment on travel behavior in US cities, Hong, Nasri, and Rafiq (2012) report statistical significance of the built environment in some of the studies but several other empirical studies showed no insignificant correlations. This is another example why sole reliance on imported data for indigenous planning in (West) Africa is suspect because quite often they lack applicability as a result of associated structural differences in socio-cultural and economic frameworks. Anyway, elsewhere, to better understand the impacts of changing land uses on transportation demand in Dhaka, Bangladesh, Ahmed et al. (2020) reviewed 20 establishments with six different land-use categories. They found that trip generation depends on factors such as surrounding land uses rather than a single factor inherent to the given land use—a finding that is close to Tanimowo. The relevance of these studies is that they support a suggestion that given the intensity and variety of surrounding land uses near the Main Market, a condition that is outside the control of traders, those traders have shown a higher propensity to engage in a greater number of stall-based contacts than those in periphery markets. So, the concentration of urban facilities and institutions (different land use categories) within the historical Onitsha CBD tend to serve as strong trip attractors or trip destinations. The high concentration of these nodal points near the downtown also creates the opportunity for traders to fulfill pressing familial and personal responsibilities while away from home in addition to separately completing necessary business tasks. In other words, CBD traders appear to be presented with relatively more intervening opportunities than their counterparts located in periphery markets, and nothing more, and that will not make us believe that marketplaces are therefore not sustainable. Because traders can take advantage of various urban amenities and services provided by other social institutions while at work, it suggests that participating in those contacts contributes to healthy social consciousness as it helps to maintain that balance between family and work. Does it then make any cultural sense to eliminate the institution when it contributes to the positive well-being of its workers?

Another reason to sustain the marketplace institution is related to the plight of apprentices who are supported by the institution. The traditional educational system established within the institution may have to be turned over to local schools and/or the national educational systems, if marketplaces are not sustained. Splintering urban marketplaces by removing apprentices from the institution would truncate the cumulative benefits of the program. The apprenticeship system serves as a job training, internship, and employment program, depending on where participants are in the different stages within the elongated program. Of those who identified their status (371 out of 513 traders interviewed), almost 40% are recorded as traders-in-training or assistants. Repurposing the apprenticeship program outside of the institution requires providing new infrastructures, that is, finding land at adequate locations and building the buildings, recruiting willing (ex)practicing traders as instructors, or hiring and training instructional staff, funding the program, and, here is the biggest challenge—situating newly minted traders or graduates in the market post-apprenticeship that requires stocking new sheds with adequate goods—an expenditure that is currently absorbed by traders in the institution without government funding or outside financial assistance. The traditional apprentice program should be retained within the institution, as it serves a seamless process for reproducing labor and generating new entrepreneurs in the urban marketplace who are capable of managing their own business. The proximity of ex-masters within the marketplace also increases access to counseling for new independent traders upon separation from their masters. As a comparison, this is not like US Small Business Administration's SCORE Program that provides (often fleeting) guidance to existing or budding entrepreneurs on how to overcome business pitfalls or address impending business problems. It is not compatible with extended services provided through the apprenticeship program in (West) African urban markets or those provided by other artisans. Typically, SCORE provides retired and experienced entrepreneurs with volunteer opportunity to advise and mentor newly formed or struggling small businesses who want to take advantage of their free advice, typically for short periods in the lifecycle of the business. The apprenticeship program, on the other hand, can last between

5–10 years under the supervision of one actively practicing master-trader. The continuity provides a fertile ground for imparting values.

For those who select the transit mode, the difference in street layout and traffic character between the CBD and the periphery markets affects the frequency of mode choice. The Main Market is bounded by two local, pedestrian-friendly streets served by transit. The express road lacks this quality, although the express road markets are served by road-side "intermodal" intercity surface stations for bus, taxi, and motorbike transport. These stations primarily serve as transfer destinations for inter-city transport services with residual travel opportunities for intra-urban transit/transport services. At the CBD market with slower traffic speeds, there are also secluded on-street opportunities for loading and unloading of passengers and goods that are more convenient for passengers and safer for intra-urban bus operators. At the express road markets, not only are operators harassed by traffic police for impeding express traffic flow, there are also no comparable sheltered areas for passenger interactions. Dropping off/picking-up passengers along the express road is dangerous and unsafe because of the high traffic speed, and, therefore, the self-imposed dwell time is quite short in order to promote traffic flow and safety. Moreover, the traffic mix near the express road markets also includes trailers, big intercity buses, and other goods-carrying vehicles (lorries) which undermines safety for transit users. So, while the wait time along the express road may be shorter, boarding a transit vehicle is more challenging which might affect the proclivity, and hence mean transit mode trip rates of stalls located along the express road. As a result, CBD traders are more likely to utilize transit services more often than express road markets. We know that transit mode can assist in improving access to urban markets, especially for poor customers. In order to sustain marketplaces, planners should strive to place markets where the use of transit is safe, and pedestrians have secluded space for safe access to the mode and the marketplace. Increasing and improving pedestrian (*read* customer) access will contribute to sustain the institution and maintain its economic viability.

According to the OECD (1998: 25), the accumulated urban capital in West African urban areas was estimated to be about $300 billion in public infrastructure, roads, markets, and housing. As a sunken cost, it will be outright recklessness to simply eliminate these marketplaces and wipe out the value of associated invested capital. These markets should be retained to reproduce further urban investments but should be modernized to attract additional economic activity, irrespective of sub-Saharan Africa having relatively low urbanization rate and GDP per capita, when compared to other regions, according to a World Bank report (Lall et al., 2017). The bank data recognize that the region is urbanizing while poor, Table 7.1. Notice that in 2013, the region was worse off than Latin America and the Caribbean in 1950 and East Asia and the Pacific in 1964, in terms of GDP per person. Given these conditions and characteristics, there should be no debate about the need to retain and sustain the marketplace as a destination source for sustenance for urban dwellers while serving as an avenue for employment and income enhancement institution.

Elsewhere, we introduced the term 'formal informal' to describe upper-tier traders whose activities in the marketplace also intersect with the urban transport space. We arrived at the term by examining the descriptive criteria provided by the International Labour Organization for defining the informal economy. According to the document *Women and men in the informal economy* (2018), if the business is registered to relevant national institutions, then the economic unit or the business is part of the formal sector; therefore, because registration of the economic unit, the market stall, is a requirement under state/national legislation, we can define a stall business as a formal economy business. Our traders are required to register and pay an annual rent to the state. Size of unit, measured by number of workers, is another criterion. If the entity has more than five workers and is in a fixed visible premise, then the economic unit is part of the formal economy but, if there are five or fewer workers or, if the entity is not in a fixed premise, then the economic unit is part

Table 7.1 Urbanization Rate and GDP Comparison

	Latin America and the Caribbean, 1950	Middle East and North Africa, 1968	Asia and the Pacific, 1994	sub-Saharan Africa, 2013
Urbanization Rate (%)	41%	41%	37%	37%
GDP per capita (2005 dollars)	$1,860	$1,806	$3,617	$1,018

Source S.V. Lall, J. V. Henderson, & A. J. Venables, World Bank, 2017: 17

of the informal sector. Since, all market-stall traders have fixed premises and when differentiated by size (also measured by number of employees), some have fewer occupants than the others, then Onitsha market-stall traders concurrently fall within and outside of ILO criterion for size. As a result, we have a hybrid of businesses in the marketplace. Taken together, we conclude that there is a formal–informal economic activity mix, based solely on ILO criteria. This reconfirms the concept of spectrum within the two sectors and the absence of a clear dichotomy. As marketplace-trading activity is arguably maturing and becoming part of the formal economy and, as the marketplace and traders have established recognizable linkages with the formal economy, it is inconceivable that African urban governments will hesitate to provide conditions that will contribute to sustain the burgeoning sector, as many traders are becoming part of the new urban middle class. Besides, the services that traders provide permeate the entire consumption world of rural and urban African dwellers, and it is predicted to continue as more consumers rely on the distributive capacity of urban marketplace institution to meet their daily downstream and upstream household consumption and transaction needs. Consequently, this is an institution worth preserving for future of the African society.

Empirical evidence shows that total mean daily trips produced by Onitsha markets would increase from about 25,700 to 38,100 trips, should the number of stall occupants increase from two (2) to three (3) occupants); or, there would be an increase of about 48.3% in total mean daily trips produced by market-stall traders. To sustain the institution, this finding creates an opportunity for policy makers, planners, and traders to agree to reduce the potential effect of the institution on the transport system by proactively controlling the number of occupants in the stall. This could be paired with encouraging co-habitation of market stalls. The institution can be sustained and the quality of transport concurrently enhanced by merely capping stall occupancy to two (2) individuals to take advantage of the linear relationship between stall size and trip production. Furthermore, stalls could be required to pay an impact fee if the occupancy exceeds two individuals. In practice, stall size interrelationship with transport and potential imposition of an impact fee is information and knowledge that should be shared with traders and their leadership about how their innocent operational staffing practice is interfering with the quality of urban transport and threatens the sustainability of the marketplace institution. This will minimize resentments, should attempts be made to regulate stall size without proper justification. But to reduce controversy and make this policy work better, efforts should also be made to provide additional market stalls, in conjunction with managing the number of individuals in a stall. If government (and traders) can manage stall size, the argument about sustaining the marketplace will be substantially muted.

Where stall occupants have available to them a personal means of transportation during business hours, those stalls tend to generate a greater number of trips than stalls where none exist. There is also empirical evidence that shows that the greater the number of a personal means of mobility, the greater the propensity to make business contacts. The act of bringing personal automobile to work, for the few who have access to it, has a disproportionate effect on the transport system. The effect of having a personal means of transportation and the linear increase in contacts, as a function of increases on the number of a personal means of transportation may not surprise many planners, but to the average trader whose business success is symbolized by ownership of a car in a cash-and-carry economy, it may be confusing why an individual cannot use their automobile during the day, just because they are in the marketplace. Traders are certainly unaware that driving during work hours have such deleterious effect on the community and presents an existential threat to the general city to make it to reconsider accommodating this unofficial city whose community members contribute to the challenging traffic conditions. That such a rational choice could cost the society additional resources in the up-keep of the transport system is a fact that Onitsha traders and other traders in (West) African need to appreciate. Traders need to be persuaded to contemplate how their behavior is part of the ecosystem of urban transport problems. But the traders who we are asking to modify their behavior are those who are already middle income and; therefore, will be expected to vocalize their concern about the implied shaming and will likely engage in a pushback. They are also most likely to belong to the leadership cadre within the trader organization. These are not the individuals that the state wants to antagonize with a proposal to not sustain their livelihoods or the marketplace institution. Instead, collectively, governments need to incorporate and collaborate with traders' leadership in the planning, implementation, and maintenance of projects and programs that promote marketplace trade. Evidentiary information should be useful in explaining how traders can sustain their business by making different stall operational and management choices that affect out-of-stall business contacts. For example, by building public or public–private fee-charging auto parking structures near markets, government can modify trader behavior with appropriate parking fees or surcharges without appearing to lean on middle-class traders about their driving habits.

It appears that the urban environment of traders does not constrain their propensity to engage in and complete stall-based contacts. In other words, to our small-scale operators, no matter the severity of intra-urban travel constraints imposed upon them, such constraints are considered trivial since their economic survival is at stake. This is particularly significant because in terms of Western business standards, a small business operator who faces similar environmental constraints would readily seek alternative means of movement or else reduce their propensity to make stall-based contacts to sustain their business. But the economic and social worldviews in these areas do not allow the luxury of cutting back on contacts because it could spell economic doom for the family, as there are no official social security or government-sponsored financial assistance for unemployed workers and their families. According to Saghir and Santaro (2018), urban planning has been identified as a missing link in the ability of cities in developing countries to be resilient. The authors implore city planners to advise policy makers on balancing investments in services and infrastructure with growing demand and they amplify the potential threats of any failure to act. This will mean investing in those services that take the trader out from outside the boundaries of the marketplace and in transport infrastructure to ease the pain and reduce the cost of intra-urban movement when traders engage in business contacts. Indigenous empirical data would assist planners in proposing additional investments in projects to accommodate growing demand by presenting reasoned and intelligent advice on improving services within the marketplace. For planning purposes, the empirical evidence provided here is instructive, should planners become sensitized to issues related to urban market-stall traders and commit to maintaining optimal stall operation as the marketplace continues to provide dependable social security and employment benefits for traders, their families and other relatives—another justification to sustain the institution to support improvements in urban income inequality.

In Chapters 2 and 3, the discussion focused on the poor transportation infrastructure in Onitsha. It is confounding that it does not appear that urban market-stall traders, who are directly affected by bad roads and inadequate transportation infrastructure care enough to band together to seek redress or openly complain and demand action from the state. This is reminiscent of a Houston study (Mladenka, 1977) of residents' propensity to contact the government about unacceptable municipal services where it was found that blacks are less likely to bother to complain, no matter how unacceptable the quality of service. Accordingly, some planners will remind us that based on our findings, the condition of the urban transportation infrastructure (see UN-Habitat, 2012: 27–30) has not been a deterrent to the propensity of our "blacks" or traders to make out-of-stall contacts, as they continue to muddle through the system; therefore, there is no need to invest in any additional marketplace improvements. There is a more persuasive counter-argument: If traders are surviving under these conditions and stall traders are becoming members of the middle class, imagine what they can achieve if (West) African countries refocused attention on their needs and improved conditions for trading activities? Improvements to existing conditions are a better route to strengthen the urban economy. Moreover, Tonelli and Dalglish (2012) have shown that microenterprises in developing economies incur high cost of inefficient transport facility system. True, and African urban market traders are taking action: In Kenya, traders have organized to convert Taveta Road Market shops (in Nairobi) to stalls that ultimately have become predominantly owned by indigenous women traders; in Ghana (Techiman Market), traders advocated for marketplace improvements such as toilets, market stalls, water, and electricity to improve their quality of life and have demonstrated a willingness to financially contribute to make it happen, and in South Africa, traders, with the help of a non-profit organization, Asiye eTafulani, refurbished the Durban Warwick Junction Market to accommodate the needs of various sellers in the new market. Marketplaces are being sustained in Africa and these serve as role models for traders in Onitsha and elsewhere and as catalysts for sustaining the marketplace.

Some of the same critics may suggest that traders are inwardly focused, while others will argue that they are merely self-interested business people. Either way, it may appear on the surface that traders are more interested in actions that directly benefit their accumulation of capital, and not necessarily interested in public social welfare projects, such as enhancing overall transport system. The question is then how is this behavior assisting to improve urban living conditions to warrant sustaining urban marketplaces? Lyon (2003) has examined associations of urban food traders in

Ghana and describes how traders have sustained their internal associational cooperation for many years in contrast to other forms of outside collaborations. It was found that a strong leadership and more importantly, the benefits of continued internal social relations that allow traders to gain information and access to informal credit and secure contract supplies have greater value than maintaining outside or non-market relationships—self-interested citizens or capitalistic entrepreneurial actors. Often traders feel that those outside relationships are not inherently useful for business prosperity. In Onitsha, it is widely known and reported that the statewide trader organization, Amalgamated Market Traders Association of Anambra State, AMATAS, has a wide support of and enduring relationship with the state government, but the primary interest of AMATAS is in rebuilding damaged markets and/or building new markets for different sellers—actions that will ingratiate the leadership to its dues-paying members. Those facilities will directly contribute to improve overall capital accumulation but undoubtedly worsen the state of the transport system. These are illustrative examples of self-interested traders who are focused just on advancing their own business success and may not necessarily demonstrate a deliberate attempt to ignore out overall urban societal problem. After all traders quite understand that transport is the vein through which their capital accumulation and business success flow, when it is available in the community where they reside and conduct business. Either way traders may not be willing to act as innocent bystanders when there are discussions that the marketplace is not sustainable because any attempts to whittle down or diminish the economic gains made through the marketplace institution will certainly be unacceptable to these business city occupants. They will be expected to mobilize in opposition.

We can therefore certainly suggest that there is plentiful justification to support the sustainability of the marketplace institution despite its impact on the transport system. The underlying argument is for all stakeholders to recognize and appreciate the yin-and-yang interrelationship that exists between investing in the marketplace institution and the direct positive effect it has on improving the character of urban transport. The linkage between the marketplace and transport has always been a missing but unrecognized link in sustainable development of (West) African urban economic space. Institutionalizing the need to invest to intelligently manage the linkage is a fundamental issue facing all stakeholders interested in organized and continuous economic growth in these areas. Continuing to deny or downplay the existence of the linkage does not in any way eliminate the continuing threat posed by unintended consequences of the institution on urban transport. Emphasizing the mutual benefits of enhancing the marketplace is not a call to diminish urban transport investment; rather, it provides justification to elevate overall community interest, and preserve, broaden and strengthen the role of the marketplace in (West) African economic architecture. After all, the OECD (2016) has projected that by 2050, about 56% of Africans are expected to live in cities. For (West) African urban market-stall traders who substitute labor for capital, if increased population leads to increases participation in marketplace employment, and as stall managers concurrently add more occupants to the stall, then there will be observable increases in trips produced by the marketplace institution with associated direct negative effects on the transport system, and this is not an exaggeration. Assuming that the urban transportation system is not upgraded or enhanced in tandem to absorb the impacts of increased travel demand by traders, there will be further deterioration in the traffic system which will hurt the economic activity of the same traders, and eventually the overall urban economy. The marketplace is certainly sustainable, despite these impacts. What is needed is planned and managed co-existence with the urban transport system. For Onitsha that the Oxford Business Group (2012) describes as arguably one of the largest commercial nerve centers in Africa, not sustaining the marketplace will substantially diminish the significance of the nerve center. Continued inaction will also impede further growth in the urban economy of the proposed ONA (Onitsha-Nnewi-Awka) commercial-industrial corridor identified by the UN-Habitat for Humanity-Nigeria government report, as a key development axis. Certainly, similar development axes must exist in other (West) African countries.

MARKETPLACE AS A CITY WITHIN A CITY

The magnitude of trips generated by Onitsha market-stall traders is equivalent to those of a US city with population between 7,760 and 11,190 residents in a country where 84% of all incorporated places have less than 10,000 residents. The number of stall traders found in daily urban markets such as Makola (One and Two) in Accra, Ghana, Dantokpa (North and South) in Cotonu, Benin exceeds the population of many towns and large villages in Africa and elsewhere. Therefore, as a social unit, should a large urban marketplace be considered a 'city within a city,' as marketplaces continue to play a prominent role in (West) African urban economy? We posit that a large urban marketplace functions as a city within a city and deserves the designation of a city. If that premise is accepted, then marketplaces deserve commensurate infrastructures like those available to a city to allow them to properly function to sustain the urban economy. This transformation will allow planners and other stakeholders to seriously examine the inner workings, quirks, and needs of its residents. Besides, providing relevant infrastructures will contribute to confine a significant proportion of out-of-stall business contacts within the marketplace perimeter. This is like confining growth within an urban growth boundary to control sprawl and reduce the cost of urban infrastructure and services for municipalities.

As any other city, a large (West) African urban marketplace temporary city also has numerous visitors, this time known as customers that inflate the daily population of the marketplace city. As an efficient information gathering and distribution nerve center, various ethnic groups that inhabit the marketplace city use the marketplace to disseminate information and, it also serves as a place of gathering to discuss improvement problems in their communities of origin, just as (non)trader members of the larger urban community organize and meet for similar reasons. For example, you will find in the marketplace city women's solidarity associations that get 'the sisterhood' together for financial support or offer of assistance in sourcing goods for sale, just as similar women's groups within the larger community promote infant and children's welfare or religious beliefs such as Christian Women's Association or Federation of Moslems Women's Association. The inference is not that equal number of organizations exist in both the temporary marketplace city and the general city. We are merely demonstrating the existence of social organization in the two communities. Moreover, there is no suggestion that similar organizations do not exist at other workplaces, but the key difference is the absence of similarly-sized critical mass of individuals within a single geo-fenced work space daily as is present in large urban marketplaces.

Visiting a typical (West) African city, you will observe a few homesteaders in the periphery or the equivalence of suburban and peri-urban parts of town, and their poorly constructed homes announce your impending arrival to town. Very soon you may observe a roadside sign that welcomes you to town. For the marketplace, those poor homesteaders are equivalent to our pavement capitalists and other hawkers that you find on the periphery of large urban marketplaces because they cannot afford a stall in the marketplace just as our poor peripheral home-steaders cannot afford better housing inside town. This is the common duality of employment that also characterizes urban marketplace trade so much so that it tempts many researchers to lump all sellers together with these hawkers and dismiss all sellers as poor urban vendors. Just as you encounter numerous upscale homes as you enter the city so will you encounter better-off marketplace traders who own and operate market stalls as you get inside the market, and who live out their business lives from those stalls. Many traders will tell you that they have been in busi-ness for several years and often at the same market and perhaps in the same stall, just as our homeowners in town. It is most likely that it will be the same stall, a sign of relative financial fitness, because relocating to another stall will result in loss of customers, cooperating stall neighbors, and livelihood (even if temporarily), especially when governments rarely expand market infrastructure by adding stalls at the same marketplace.

While in the city, upon closer inspection, you will realize that resi-dences typically require utilities such as water, power, and sewer services for healthy living. Residents also need sanitary and clean environment or they will complain to government, if these services are lacking in quality and/or quantity. Meanwhile, houses are being constructed within the city with materials often purchased from traders. House construction needs carpenters, masons or bricklayers, electricians and painters who arrive from their homes every day to practice their skills at various work sites. Unlike traders, in order to earn a living, these artisans tend to spread out in the entire city where the job is or where they can find work while all traders daily congregate at one location. But like homeowners, traders also need running water, power, and other utilities in their community and often are willing to pay for them, like taxes paid by home owners for such urban services. Like homes in the community, these amenities also should be made available in any new/refurbished marketplace as part of the site plan approval. Moreover, it has been demonstrated that traders own a large proportion of real estate in the city where they reside so they understand the usefulness of these amenities in the household for its occupants. So, what we have is how most city residents spread out daily to make a living by providing services to community residents while traders congregate daily in the marketplace city to make their own living servicing customers by providing saleable goods that add value to the life of the customer. In other words, employment in the city is varied for its residents, but in the marketplace, everyone is in the same type of employment and profession—urban market trading. Because the general community residents have scattered work locations their numerical strength at each employment location rarely matches the number of traders in that large urban marketplace city, not the self-employed at any given workplace, employees in different government offices or even longshoremen at the large marine dock. In the marketplace city, entrepreneur traders are also self-employed or are (technically) employees as traders-in-training and apprentices. Very often, the goals and aspirations of employees in the general city do not align properly with those of their employers, but in the marketplace city, the socialization is quite different—there is complete alignment of goals and aspirations between employers and employees, and that is profit maximization. Another unique feature is that it is not common to find cooperation among different employers in the general city where competition is so severe that some businesses may want to buy out or squash their competitors. In the marketplace city, there is maximum cooperative competition that, on the one hand, allows traders to pool resources to place large orders in order to reduce cost and increase the rate of capital accumulation while on the other hand, there exists a fierce competition over pricing and sales tactics. There are other situations where traders, based on the sociology of complex marketplace interrelationships, have developed solidarity over long periods of time for sourcing goods for sale. Moreover, marketplace socialization and cultural tradition encourage and allow traders to leave their business to visit bereaved colleagues or others who have situations, just as many general city residents do but typically perform such rites after work (for those in the formal sector) or during the weekend. The strong institutional relationships and social ties in the marketplace force traders to engage in these necessary contacts from their workplace, a non-marketplace workplace behavior that will typically lead to discipline or dismissal by other employers in the general city (except for the self-employed). These similarities and differences exist albeit at varying scales within general and marketplace cities, but they nonetheless demonstrate the existence of 'community' in the two cities—individuals with shared values, interests, and experiences with individuals inside and outside the acting community. In both communities, the elected leadership, for example, constitutes those inside the acting community. Acting community members are those who make things happen.

Let us examine politics and organizing in the two cities. City residents are voluntarily organized into groups for the betterment of the community or may be involved in politics to elect their preferred candidates into office. The groups that organize to elect a preferred candidate become insiders of the acting community for a temporary time while those who organize for the betterment of the community are permanent members inside the acting community. In the city, there are elected officials who manage the affairs of the community but there are also individuals who are not elected but do wield power. It is also the same in the marketplace where you will find a vocal and well-placed trader(s) who may not be members of the union leadership but are influential. These individuals are outside the acting community because their opinions carry a lot of weight and affect actions in the community. Community members contact their leaders to make demand for community services. In the marketplace city, not only do traders have their own leadership and government through the traders' union or organization, but as we stated earlier, in Onitsha, the one litmus test for a leadership position is the ownership of a stall in the market that the trader wishes to represent, equivalent to residency requirements in a city in order to run for political office. It will be difficult to imagine street vendors, other non-anchored pavement capitalists, with similar level of collective voice, despite their numerical strength. These pavement capitalists are 'restricted' from entering the acting community. In addition, their spatial dispersion and diffusion are militating factors against developing and owning a voice in urban politics to improve the welfare of group members. But for stall traders, their internal government, the Union, provides leadership and is also the governing body that settles conflicts and enforces marketplace rules and regulations outlined in the byelaw. It metes out punishment, according to union byelaws and imposes fines on offenders. Requiring that the leadership own and operate stalls at representative locations ensures that the representative fully understands the opportunities and business constraints in that marketplace. Union leadership and members have one common goal, and that is self-interested residents agitating for improvements in the marketplace to improve profit. In urban politics, elected leaders and activists exhibit similar traits for general city residents and elected leaders have established government institutions to help them to enforce rules and city regulations. They have city hall, staffs, and administration buildings where they meet to conduct city business. Such infrastructure eludes leaders in the marketplace city but traders would appreciate similar amenities within or adjacent to new or redesigned marketplaces. The provision of meeting facilities will disallow traders from traveling outside the confines of their city, the marketplace, to hold meetings or to vote on internal matters. The facility could also house the offices of the Market Master whose staff manages the market for the benefit of traders, similar to the functions of a mayor, city manager, or council chairperson. Encouraging these government representatives to live out their bureaucratic lives by working within the future market is like community policing where members typically live in the community where they police or maintain the peace. They get to know each other and that reduces mistrust between police and residents and, it increases cooperation and understanding, and in this case, between government and traders, as the Office of the Market Master conducts city business from among its beneficiaries. Providing the services and amenities will also contribute to reduce the demand traders place on the urban transport system. Empirical evidence shows that traders leave the stall for purposes such as socializing, eating a meal, and visiting the bank or government offices, just like general city residents except that they are spatially distributed and that colors or masks their impact on the system. Placing those opportunities in the marketplace together with traders' administration building will directly reduce transport investment due to reduced impacts by traders; or, at least, improve the travel experience for other road users, including shoppers.

What about taxation in our two cities? People in the city pay taxes, and residents in the marketplace city pay a monthly tax disguised as rent for government-allocated stalls, sometimes in addition to a monthly business surcharge. These taxes support government to provide or maintain whatever meagre urban service to city residents and marketplace-city residents. In fact, it will be reasonable to deploy taxes collected in the marketplace city to improve internal amenities and services in a same way that government taxes are used to enhance community-wide urban services. This will serve as a method to develop rapport, collaboration, respect, and sense of community.

Lastly, zoning provides another similarity that supports the concept of designating a large urban marketplace a city within a city. One distinguishing feature of (West) African urban markets is the zoning or segregation of traders by product or the type of good sold. Mbisso (2017) reports that in Tanzania's Temeke Stereo Market, gates are named after the type of goods sold nearby such as *geti la mihogo* (cassava gate) or *geti la nazi* (coconut gate). It reduces the search cost for shoppers but intensifies the eyeball-to-eyeball competition to sell that last merchandise at cut throat price with narrow margin. This is one of the reasons why traders will band together to acquire saleable goods at the lowest price. It works because of the level of trust among traders and a demonstration of the understanding of benefits associated with such cooperation. In the absence of that traders may resort to other schemes such as bait and switch to counterfeiting products to improve margin. This contributes to explain why customers expect to haggle over price because the power struggle between buyer and seller forces an equilibrium price. This is an endearing feature of the marketplace city. Attaining proficiency in haggling is one of the reasons why apprentices are retained for such a long period of time in the program to master the skills of extracting the highest price from a customer through skilful negotiation. In several (West) African cities, vestigial land-use zoning rights (see details in Lamond et al., 2015) and privileges allow the wealthy to live in GRAs (government reserved areas) originally developed and reserved for former and post-colonial administrators while the rest of the citizens are excluded from these special zones. The existence of GRAs in post-colonial (West) Africa is a demonstration that some semblance of land-use enforcement still exists in many countries (Coquery-Vidrovitch, 2012). There are other areas zoned for residences, although mixed use is typically the norm. In the marketplace city, not only are traders segregated (zoned) by product type, but poor traders who cannot afford market stalls suffer from additional segregation—economic zoning where they are relegated to the periphery of the market or onto roadsides and sidewalks near the market. Due to marketplace zoning, you will not find a stall that sells foodstuffs intermingled with sellers of provision goods or vice-versa, just as uses are separated from each other in a city where the zoning code is a functioning regulatory tool. So zoning or legal segregation based on universally accepted and defined set of criteria is a common feature of our two cities.

What we have is a resilient and vibrant enclave with its own socio-political and economic character that replicates what is observable and characteristic of the larger urban community. Until now, this disguised city has been simply labeled a marketplace but all along it is an unrecognized economically powerful urban community that should have been considered and included in any responsible and responsive urban development plans and land use policies. It functions as any other city while retaining its distinct business peculiarities. The one global uniqueness is that the only business within this city is business, and profit maximization is the unitary motivation for all residents. It also serves as the center of capitalism for the entire urban community with a subculture of cooperative competition borne out of self-interest to uphold the integrity of the institution. Some critics may suggest that the profit-oriented, self-interested motivation may have contributed to blind traders to the deleterious effects of their operational methods on the transport system, and equally a disinterest to contribute to its improvement; therefore, fact-based trader education will engender collaboration and cooperation for developing mutually beneficial solutions, as traders are also members of the wider community through their own after-hour residences. With this conviction, planners and policy makers should unfasten themselves from ignoring the linkage of the institution to urban transport and use evidentiary facts to persuade themselves and then traders to modify their behavior. Next, we will discuss how the urban transportation planning process could be repurposed to assist that transformation, as it will reflect and address the differently structured socio-cultural and economic features in these areas that continue to produce different travel behavior structure and characteristics observed in cities with large urban marketplaces, that is, a dominant informal sector.

Reimagined Urban Transport Planning Process

We have established the existence of a unique business operational regime indigenous to residents within the marketplace city. With an understanding of the existence of an economically-dominant center of capitalism Marketplace City within a General City, we must accept the argument that different approaches are appropriate and necessary for any meaningful urban transport planning and associated development polices in these areas. In the Global South. this is an overdue introspection that will contribute in revising existing processes embedded in universal transportation planning framework to recognize and accept the marketplace institution and traders as major actors in a meaningful urban development planning discourse. The glaringly different economic and social structures in (West) African urban societies suggest that continued reliance on a familiar framework based on routine home-based work and school trip that is routine in the Global North is a poor substitute in areas where controlling trip-makers value and rely on non-home-based, non-peak hour travels over home-based trips to support their economic activities.

Their travel behavior has proven beneficial based on their ensuing dominance of the urban economy. Because of the persistent non-formal (others may refer to it as informal) structure of the economy, unlike in the Global North that is dominated by a formal economy, it is certainly acceptable to suggest that community residents of large (West) African urban marketplaces, the Marketplace City, be considered the most important unit in transportation planning data for combined Marketplace and General City transport planning processes. Their travel history during business hours should provide the core source of origin–destination data inventory for defensible urban transportation planning, supplemented by home-based household data, as appropriate. This proposal should be considered only if the (West) African General City has any interest in sustaining its urban economy. Subsequently, for advocacy planners, development practitioners and policy makers, thought should be given to developing and implementing interconnected policies and development alternatives that address the unique infrastructure needs of businesses in the Marketplace City that, at the same time, will contribute to address attendant urban transport problems in associated (West) African General City. Because of the interrelationship between the dyadic land uses, transport and marketplace, their common problem should therefore be solved together. Adopting this progressive urban development framework to benefit the most important and succeeding African indigenous economic institution will tantamount to introducing and maintaining a continuous targeted development aid program for traders thereby confirming that useful urban problem-solving techniques should always be localized. In return, the purported new aid program will continuously produce economic benefits for residents in both the Market City and the General City.

In several circles within the Global South, there is the belief that the different existing socio-economic urban structure deserves a different but appropriate approach to urban transportation planning to signal a planning break from societies dominated by the formal economy. Planners should question the validity of deploying European and American planning models that rely on household travel behavior in the Global South where an unregimented non-formal economy and indigenous social structure impinge on and determine societal travel behavior. Transport planners and researchers appear to propagate this dissonance as they stubbornly continue to aspire to conform to the narrative of planning standards solely based on drivers and automobile travels to work and school, based on numerous published transport planning studies. This is continuing even as the non-formal economy and urban marketplaces are winning the power struggle with the formal economy, even though not long ago, the non-formal economy was separate and considered a sub-par economic sector. The label was used to define and globally segregate, and some will argue undermine the vast economy in the developing areas relative to conditions in the developed West. In Africa, for example, at least eighty percent of urban employment is in the non-formal economy—a demonstration that irrespective of the label capitalism and competition are well and alive in the continent. Transport planning and development should not all be about engineering, it should also include considerations of the social and economic dimension of the end users. Commenting on transport planning in sub-Saharan Africa, Porter (2007: 251) writes, "transport planning also requires a detailed understanding of the economic, social and political environments in which transport takes place and interventions are made." That is a re-emphasis on localizing transportation planning processes by considering the environment within which beneficiaries derive their livelihoods. The characteristics of that environment should complement engineering machinations of transport planning for that society to derive meaningful results. Voices in the Global South appear to be succeeding in their argument that the informal sector should be considered 'productive,' recognized, and integrated into the accounting of Gross National Product of countries. We extend the argument by proposing that the travel behavior of the key economic groups in the same informal economy be front and center in formulating urban transport planning processes and development measures to reflect the change. An appeal, therefore, to re-examine the neglect of the importance of the marketplace institution in transportation planning and urban development regimes is proper, timely, and long overdue. At another level, it is quite inexplicable that current processes fail to rely on the travel behavior of individuals 'residing' within the dominant urban economic entity for transport planning data and information when their travel behavior keeps the urban economy robust, similar to the function performed by work and school commute trips generated by households in the West. Consequently, the proposal requires the reimagining of the traditional and widely adopted but appropriate planning orthodoxy in the West where urban transportation planning process primarily relies on trips generated by those households in residential neighborhoods. The residential neighborhood is so vital in the process that it constitutes the starting point from where the roadway hierarchy or classification system starts, a classification that ends with the highway at the top of the access pyramid for efficiently ferrying automobile users to work and school. This criticism and suggested modification are designed to challenge unintentional biases held by those in academia and raise the consciousness of experts in development institutions that influence Third World policy making. Individuals and institutions are challenged to confront and are encouraged to conduct appropriate introspection of long-held convictions[1] to assist the process to willingly veer away from 'established and normal' planning practices for these areas. You see, the established and normal planning practice has so far failed to recognize the relevance and significance of the vast informal economic structure in the character of urban travel, therefore it was easily dismissed with the wave of the hand, and the place of the marketplace in re-defined and proper area-specific or localized urban development plans. This is theoretically relevant given that the linkage between marketplaces and urban transport is so far largely unknown, globally unexplored, and professionally ignored. To make the proposed leap or transition, leadership and support from the Global North are essential, and with globalization of actions to address embedded social injustice, it will also be timely. In the interim, it is expected that at least these observations will initiate the conversation. We believe that integrating the travel behavior of the predominant informal economy trip-makers into the urban transportation planning process properly aligns with current efforts by bodies such as the International Labour Organization, ILO, to raise the status and significance of non-formal economy entrepreneurs in the (urban) economy of developing areas. After all, in a democracy, if you have the majority of votes, your party controls the political discourse through dominance of policy-making processes, and similarly, if you control the majority of shares you command substantial voice in a company; but, in the developing areas, if an urban economic

---

[1] As the manuscript was being prepared, it was reported (Williams, Cohen & Herb, June 25, 2021) that "the US government finally appears to be taking seriously what has for so long been considered a fringe issue," and that is that the Pentagon now is interested in accepting to formalize the study of Unidentified Aerial Phenomenon (UAP), known to many as UFO (Unidentified Flying Objects). People who believed in UFO for the past several decades were often ridiculed and stigmatized. Not anymore as more data and information on the frequency of occurrences (144 sightings) have compelled the Pentagon, the center of military power in the world as we all know, to a change of heart. Williams, K. B., Cohen, Z & et al. (2021). *US intelligence community release long-awaited UFO Report*. CNN Politics. June 25.

institution and associated activities dominate the urban economy, just as home/work/school trifecta in the West, planners and other practitioners have simply ignored the institution and its attributes in planning and managing accessibility, the vein through which economic prosperity and vibrancy flow in all communities worldwide—and that is at the core of the paradox of the marketplace in (West) African urban development.

The Urban Transportation Planning (UTP) process started as early as 1925 in the United States to organize the planning and specifically systematic planning for the impending highway system. It provided for continuous planning that uses data to project behavior of urban motorists. The process has undergone numerous criticisms in the literature and in professional practice, it has evolved to meet the needs of the time in the West. This work is another step in the evolutionary life of the urban transportation planning process, even though it is not clear that most planners in the developing areas are yet sensitive to or are willing to advocate for such transformation, as a significant amount of their research is still interested in studying households and urban commuting behavior. This is based on a long-standing tradition. It was in the 1970s' that the transport planning model was exported to several prominent cities in (the developed and) developing areas such as Sao Paulo, Bogota, Lagos, Nairobi, and Madras (Dimitriou, Working Paper 26, 1987). The process typically involves establishing a relationship between (current and projected future) land use and traffic, and traffic generation is mostly attributed to automobile drivers. Presently, Africa has a low motorization level of 2% per capita car ownership compared to 50% in Europe and 70% in the US, but some planners and other researchers continue to rely on a planning process that focuses on what drivers do after they leave home to access different land uses in the urban economy in areas in Global South in solidarity with their Western cohorts. Road users in developed and developing areas generally exist in opposite ends of the urban economic and land-use continuum, one in mostly formal—mainly drivers—and the other is mostly non-formal where users mainly consist of pedestrians, some transit and IMT (intermediate means of transport) users such as ox-carts and bicycles, and of course some drivers. The resulting differences in the land use-transport dichotomy that are produced by differing socio-economic characteristics are manifested in the preponderance of non-home-based travels in places such as Onitsha and many other urban centers in the Global South where the informal economy predominates. The preponderance of those trips is an outgrowth from an economic system marked by dominating economic activities such as the marketplace where trip-makers place higher value on non-home-based trips, even when those trips contribute to diurnal off-peak traffic problems at levels that are not quite understood, recognized, or considered relevant by planners steeled in a transportation planning process where off-peak trips are routinely discounted because they are minimal and are easily accommodated on roadways constructed to accommodate peak-hour travels.

The transportation planning model principally uses socio-economic characteristics of (home-based) travelers superimposed upon existing transport facilities to simulate, quantify, and project future travel demand. Despite the spatially different social and economic structures, the continued and exceptional influence of Western consultants (training) and international development establishments (training and funding) in developing countries appear to be a major obstacle to differentiate the urban transport planning process in the Third World from the existing internationally adopted process. With this universal process, experts can easily deploy themselves in any new contract worldwide which is quite cost-effective but bad for locals. As a result, the process has no self-interest in reforming itself and recognizing the differences and, the existence of a flagship economic institution in areas such as (West) Africa where the strength of the urban economy resides in the ability of marketplace traders to non-routinely access supplies, maintain traditional marketplace relationships, and service customers in order to serve as the backbone for continued urban economic vitality. Work rules and expectations in societies dominated by formal economic structures dissuade significant intra-urban travel outside of morning and evening peak commute hours which contribute to explain why many Westerners often describe as 'chaotic' (as in unorganized) the traffic conditions in many African and other cities in the Global South. The traffic pattern is merely reflecting the travel behavior produced by a culturally different, a vastly different economic system, and an expansively different social structure. This should constitute the appropriate lens through which to view the un-patterned travel behavior of traders because it merely reflects the un-patterned (non-formal) economic and societal organization in motion. In visual terminology, observers often dismissively describe this phenomenon as an ordinary all-day traffic 'chaos.' To illustrate this point about mislabeling, have you wondered why Western forays into areas such as Vietnam and Afghanistan have not yielded decisive victories similar to World War

II that was mainly fought in Europe with similar socio-economic characteristics and culture? One of the biggest interpretations is that the West failed to understand the different cultures, peoples, and socio-economic relationships in those areas as they tried to remake the locals into mini-Westerners and transported and applied Western perspectives to the war, and those war frameworks did not quite fit or respond to local conditions to decisively defeat the enemy. This will contribute to explain why despite vast capital investments in transportation by governments and foreign donors, (urban) transportation problems appear to be getting worse in many developing countries. This is because in the developing areas, it appears that planners have not understood the intricacies of local culture and socio-economic relationships and (in)formal frameworks before developing transportation planning models which then fail to take indigenous factors into account in order to proffer commensurate and responsive solutions. Planners should distance themselves from the familiar—they should consider reimagining and repurposing the current transportation planning process to reflect, reinterpret, and underscore the marriage between the major economic institution in the economy represented by marketplace trade and urban traffic conditions, and understand that if we control and manage the marketplace institution, we will begin to meaningfully manage and control the urban traffic conditions. In this new world view, they will not just look at urban traffic as chaotic but examine the real source of the 'chaos,' especially in cities with large urban marketplaces. An argument could be made that the existing (household-based) transport planning model might work best in rural Africa where you will observe a distinct AM-PM peak travel split when school-age children go to school and adults either go to the farm or attend local periodic markets in the morning, and in the late afternoon, there is a reverse commute. In those areas, internal roadways and pathways within and connecting adjoining communities are relatively quiet and deserted during that off-peak travel time. That was why in the olden days, slave raiders used the off-peak travel time to conduct their nefarious activities in (West) African communities.

Mind you the key modification or reimagining is primarily in repurposing the data collection step of the UTP process so that a large urban marketplace forms the source of data from a defined geographic data collection area or the cordon for the inventory phase of the UTP process in a given urban area. The data collection step lays the groundwork for the process, therefore defining the cordon boundary as co-terminus with the boundary of the marketplace establishes acceptance of current proposal. It will also demonstrate that the most expensive and major work in the process recognizes the importance of the marketplace institution in the planning process. Because the marketplace often occupies a geographically defined area, establishing a cordon will not be difficult for planners: instead of accosting individuals and traders leaving or entering the cordon with a survey material, planners will collect the necessary data from traders while they are in the stall, their unofficial residence; otherwise, how will planners identify who is or who is not a trader at the cordon boundary? In the West, distributing survey material to drivers within the cordon is quite simple—all drivers leaving a cordon typically receive travel survey material in a typical transportation planning study. To reinforce and elevate the position and usefulness of traders in future planning, data could be collected on sales volumes and revenue to assess, for example, which market location rewards entrepreneurs the most. (Remember—traders will be asked to estimate the information for other traders in the same line of business). Concurrently, the process could evaluate whether locations with highest sales volumes (and income) also produce the greatest number of intra-urban contacts. Such information will be useful in assessing potential sites for new markets to balance travel demand against stall management. An urban transport planning process that uses trader-level Origin-Destination (O-D) data, like individual-level household data, to understand trip destination and detailed trip purpose will inform future marketplace-land use relationships regarding trip production (from the marketplace zone) and attraction (to other zones in the general city). Ultimately, this data will be useful in simulating and estimating or modeling future travel behavior of marketplace traders. Clearly, understanding the characteristics of traders' travel behavior will be germane in managing their travel demand and future capital investments to benefit the roadway and marketplaces. In other words, the paradigm shift will assist planners and practitioners to contain traders within the marketplace and allow for improved access opportunities for members of the public and shoppers who will patronize traders for a stronger urban economy when (West) African cities reduce traffic congestion, especially near large urban marketplaces. Moreover, addressing trader needs will discourage cities from attempting to build their way out of traffic problems, as they have so far failed to understand that the traffic pattern is the product of the persistent non-formal economic structure anchored by large urban marketplaces.

A generalized guidelines for transportation planning for capacity building developed by the US Federal Highway Administration and Federal Transit Administration (2020) allows for several steps in the process—engage the public and stakeholders, monitor existing conditions, forecast future population and employment growth, identify current and projected transport needs, analyze various transportation improvement strategies, develop long-range plans and short-range programs, estimate outcomes, and develop a financial plan. As you know, placing the development of financial plan at the end avoids stifling of useful ideas during the preceding discussion phases. For a reimagined and repurposed urban transportation planning process, it is the forecasting and identification phases that the proposed change would mostly affect, as analyzing and implementing fact-based marketplace improvements will contribute to address mobility issues related to marketplace-urban transport linkage as traders' origin–destination travel data will be collected from individuals at the stall level. For transportation engineers and planners, the repurposing means that upon completing travel and land-use inventory steps, the urban transportation planning process that involves modeling trip generation, trip distribution, modal split, and network assignments will result in developing long-range plans and short-range program options that are suitable for large (West) African urban markets in order to minimize their impact on the transport system. If stakeholders understand the inner workings of the marketplace, planners can use that expert knowledge to process and concurrently develop a better transport system that will be shielded from inadvertent and large impact by the travel behavior of traders which addresses overall transport problems based on Marketplace-oriented Development Strategy, MODEST. Area-wide and corridor planning studies, affecting large urban marketplaces, should also incorporate the suggested repurposed planning process. In other words, planners and policy makers should use any and every planning opportunity to highlight the inextricable nexus between large marketplaces, where they exist, and urban transport. Not only will proper location, design, and management of the needs of inhabitants of the Marketplace City minimize trader impact on the transport system, it will also maximize the benefits of smart transport investment for the General City.

Traders have been stereotyped for the longest time as a docile group of informal economy actors operating on the fringes of the urban economy, while spending the entire business day in the stall. As a result, they have not been accounted for in the overall urban development process. This has contributed to a misguided or incomplete assignment of traffic congestion problems to all appropriate offenders. With a revised and properly updated assignment matrix, it will be useful and critical, for example, for planners to seriously and justifiably consider different design standards for marketplaces to de-incentivize out-of-stall trip making. The UTP process should, therefore, strive to understand the social and economic conditions in which the major users interact with urban transport in order to formulate meaningful marketplace-transport reinforcing solutions. A long time ago, a World Bank Staff Working Paper (1984: 35) warns that for improved transportation planning in the developing areas, it is particularly important to obtain data that are adequate for their purpose. A generous and perhaps useful interpretation of the words "adequate" and "purpose" would imply planning that relies, for our purposes, on data from the marketplace institution that will assist traders in contributing to reduce urban unemployment and income inequality, when purposefully applied. To support our interpretation, the word "adequate" means "sufficient for a specific need or requirement" according to Merriam-Webster. Therefore, can planners justifiably continue to fasten themselves to the current practice of ignoring out those in the Marketplace City who occupy the critical command post of (West) African urban economy while promoting and solely relying on the travel behavior of households in the General City for urban transport planning processes and expect any meaningful changes in traffic problems and economic mobility in these areas? The same question applies, as appropriate, to policy makers and development institutions, alike. Suppose that this argument is in the other direction somewhere in the West—planners in the 21st Century are finally being collectively and explicitly urged to rely on household decision units that generate all the work and school trips in conducting urban transportation planning studies? Puzzled critics would rather want to understand why planners have not already realized the location of the household unit in the urban travel space, especially in the AM and PM travel times on residential and other roadways and developed methods to meet their travel needs. To address this gap, in preparing students for planning in Africa, Bolay (2015: 418) observes that the formation of the Association of African Planning Schools in 2008 will allow the 43 institutions (now 51 institutions in 18 countries) in the consortium to reform planning education on the continent. It is anticipated that the reform will allow students to question some of the accepted planning dogmas that fail to consider and incorporate the character of African urbanization, the social-cultural structure and economic frameworks in addressing land use and transportation issues that reflect local human conditions. Collecting and analyzing data from large urban marketplaces are intelligent starting points for the inclusion and participation by those most affected by and whose roles significantly affect urban transport conditions. This will constitute a premier form of urban economic-oriented cum citizen-centered planning approach that has eluded cities with large urban marketplaces. The symbolic acknowledgment and recognition will be beneficial and futuristic as an increasing number of traders are becoming visible middle-income earners, the non-formal economy is becoming more resilient in promoting economic development and growth, and as more urbanites may engage in distributive trade as a lucrative profession.

In conclusion, we expect some pushback to the proposal to reimagine and repurpose the UTP process to effectively incorporate the marketplace institution in urban development discourse because change is difficult, but acceptable as long as nobody is worse off, and nobody will be in this instance, but no matter what, the institution's direct impacts on the state of the urban transport system in (West) Africa persists, nonetheless. Critics could argue about the potential cost increases in a revamped data collection arrangement without offering data to support the extent of the increases, if any. We acknowledge the potential for increased data collection cost due to the minor paradigm shift or a small tweak to the process, but we believe that the benefits of sustained economic growth in (West) African countries, due to the change, will outweigh any associated incremental data collection and modeling costs. Modifying and adopting the change to the process to benefit the mass of informal economy participants in regions with known disparate economic and social frameworks is a small price to pay for expected continuous and expanded urban economic benefits.

References

African Union. (2013). *Agenda 2063: The Africa we want*. Addis Ababa.

Ahmed, T., Mitra, S. K., & Rafiq, R. (2020). Trip generation rates of land uses in a developing country city, Transportation Research Record: *Journal of the Transportation Board, 2674*(9), 412–525.

Bolay, J. C. (2015). Urban planning in Africa: Which alternative for poor cities? The case of Koudougou in Burkina Faso. *Current Urban Studies, 3*, 413–431.

Retrieved May 28, 2021, from http://www.scirp.org/journal/cus; https:// doi.org/10.4236/cus.2015.34033.

Coquery-Vidrovitch, C. (2012). Racial and social zoning in African cities from colonization to post-independence. In E. Bogaerts, & R. Raben (Eds.), *Beyond empire and nation: The decolonization of African and Asian societies, 1930s–1970s* (pp. 267–286). Brill. Retrieved May 26, 2021, from http://www.jstor.org/stable/10.1163/j.ctt1w8h2zm.14.

Dimitriou, H. T. (1987). *The urban transport planning process and its derivatives: A critical review of their evolution and appropriateness to Third World Cities.* Working Paper 26, The University of Hong Kong.

Friedberg, S. (1997). *African market women and economic power: The role of women in African economic development,* B. House-Midamba, & F. K. Ekechi (Eds). Review Article, *Journal of Political Ecology, 4,* 40–42.

Gantner, G. (2009). The urban market: Social and spatial configuration in the African city. Conference Paper, *African Perspectives.*

Harsch, E. (2012, April). *For sustainable cities, Africa needs planning.* Africa Renewal.

Hong, J., Nasri, A., & Zhang., L, & Shen, Q. (2012). How built environment affects travel behavior: A comparative analysis of the connection between land use and vehicles miles traveled in US Cities. *Journal of Transport and Land Use, 5(3),* 40–52.

International Labour Organization. (2018). *Women and men in the informal economy: A statistical picture.*

Kinyanjui, M. (2014). *Women and the informal economy.* Zed Books, London.

Lall, S. V., Vernon, H. J., Venables, & Anthony J. (2017). *Africa's cities: Opening doors to the world.* World Bank, © World Bank. https://openknowledge.wor ldbank.org/handle/10986/25896 License: CC BY 3.0 IGO.

Lamond J., Awuah B. K., Lewis E., Bloch R., & Falade B. J. (2015). *Urban Land, Planning and Governance Systems in Nigeria.* Urbanisation Research Nigeria (URN) Research Report. London: ICF International. Creative Commons Attribution-Non-Commercial-Share Alike CC BY-NC-SA.

Lyon, F. (2003). Trader associations and urban food systems in Ghana: Institutionalist approaches to understanding urban collective actions. *International Journal of Urban and Regional Research, 27(1),* 11–23.

Mbisso, D. A. (2017). Spatial character of urban petty trading marketplaces in Dar es Salaam, Tanzania: Space form, configuration, and use. *International Journal of Recent Scientific Research, 8(4),* 16724–16731.

Mladenka, K. R. (1977). Citizen demand and bureaucratic response. Direct dialing democracy in a major American city. *Urban Affairs Quarterly, 12,* 273–274.

Nchinto, W. (2006). *A city of divided shopping: An analysis of the location of markets in Lusaka, Zambia*. Paper presented at 42nd International Society of City and Regional Planners' Congress, 14–18 September.

OECD. (1998). *Preparing for the future: A vision of West Africa in the year 2020*. OECD.

OECD. (2016). Where can cities take Africa? 307 (Q 3) *OECD Observer*.

Onyebueke, V., & Geyer, M. (2011). The informal sector in urban Nigeria: Reflections from almost four decades of research. *Town and Regional Planning, 59*, 65–75.

Popoola, A., Adekalu, O. B., & Audu, A. A. (2016). Analysis of causes and characteristics of market fires in Lagos State, Nigeria. *International Journal of Agriculture and Rural Development, 19*(1), 2407–2421.

Porter, G. (2007). Transport planning in sub-Saharan Africa. *Progress in Development Studies, 7*(3), 251–257.

Romanik, C. T. (2008). *An urban-rural focus on food markets in Africa*. The Urban Institute.

Sanghir, J., & Santaro, J. (2018, April 12). *Urbanization in Sub-Saharan Africa*, Center for Strategic and International Studies.

Tanimowo, N. B. (2017). Land use mix and intra-urban travel pattern in Ogbomoso, a Nigerian medium sized town. *Journal of Human Ecology, 20*(3), 207–214.

The Urban Institute. (2008). *An urban-rural focus on food markets in Africa*. The Urban Institute.

Tonelli, M., & Dalglish, C. L. (2012). The role of transport infrastructure in facilitating the survival and growth of micro-enterprises in developing economies. In *The Joint ACERE-DIANA International Entrepreneurship Conference 31 January – 3 February 2012*, University of Notre Dame.

UN Habitat. (2012). *Nigeria: Onitsha Urban Profile*.

US Federal Highway Administration & Federal Transit Administration. (2020). *The Transportation Planning Process Briefing Book*.

World Bank. (1984). *Towards better urban transport planning in developing countries*. World Bank.

CHAPTER 8

Strategies for Improving Urban Development: Addressing the Paradox

Improved development strategies for (West) African urban areas to address the linkage of the marketplace to urban transport are predicated on providing enhancements within the marketplace institution that will produce positive spillover effects on urban transport system, otherwise known as MODEST. This will contribute to maximize the benefit of resources directed at the betterment of the urban transport infrastructure. Therefore, the following discussion is based on the following premises:

- A temporary Marketplace City (MC) exists in (West) African urban areas and functions within the official General City. It has the characteristics of a city and, therefore, deserves similar attention from urbanologists.
- The impacts of traders in the non-contested MC on the character and condition of urban traffic have not been properly assigned by planners and traffic engineers, even as traders traditionally interpret it as a sign of efficient stall operation to maximize profit.
- The urban economic structure is dominated by the non-formal economy and itself dominated by the marketplace institution with dominant intra-urban travels that are hitherto unrecognized by planners. The resultant trifecta of marketplace-trader activities-urban transport travel character is a major factor that has molded the character of the urban travel space, and

K. Ochia, *Marketplace Trade and West African Urban Development*, https://doi.org/10.1007/978-3-030-87556-5_8

- The traditional UTP process has so far failed to incorporate the trifecta into urban development planning in the Global South, including (West) Africa.

To achieve the proposed transformation through MODEST in the urban development realm, large urban marketplaces are presented here as urban growth poles that are infused with a powerful trip-making centrifugal force. Designating marketplaces as growth poles will re-focus the attention of local and international stakeholders and persuade them to re-direct resources to address the internal operational problems of the marketplace to advantage local urban traffic and transport problems.

Francois Perroux developed the Growth Pole Theory in mid-twentieth century, upon realization that the concept of equilibrium in economic growth was no more tenable as firms were innovating and shifting the ability to produce and grow. There was a realization that different economies exist—those that are internal to the firm and external to firm, but internal to industry, and therefore external to industry but internal to the urban area—that affect the production process, and then of course price. The theory was originally developed for groups of related industries in an input–output linkage where the product from one becomes a raw material input for the other to stimulate economic growth and development through linkages with those secondary industries and businesses downstream. The concept was created to identify and understand a manufacturing sector where the dominant firm in an industry forms a core or growth pole because several reasons make it difficult for similar growth at other locations. The growth pole idea is now shifting to global supply chain as there are linkages between the core industry and production activities elsewhere and sometimes far away, the effects of which led to delays in delivery of goods manufactured overseas during the COVID-19 pandemic. Extending the application, the concept was deployed by countries such as Mali and Kenya (in the 1970s) in their national development plans to disperse economic development to poles (other cities) to reduce rural–urban migration to the national capital and primate city. We then extend the argument as we consider large urban marketplaces that have grown to dominate economic activity within an urban or metropolitan area or a defined geographic area. Others have argued that next in hierarchy are growth centers (akin to non-large urban marketplaces) which have less influence than growth poles but a tad higher than growth points (like large non-urban marketplaces) with much limited zone of influence and the amount people affected. In other words, there are also other scalable marketplaces in the shadow of large urban marketplaces in any selected region and geographic areas.

In (West) Africa, there are numerous marketplaces within metropolitan urban areas and within geographically defined regions, together with large marketplaces spatially distributed within the region or even within the urban area. But what you notice is that for some reason, in a very large urban area with several markets, there are just a few marketplaces or just one marketplace of economic and regional consequence, and the same applies to marketplaces in a geographic region. In other words, just as a manufacturing firm dominates the industry and forms a growth pole, or a primate (capital) city dominates other cities in a (developing) country, there are also large urban marketplaces that become prominent and dominate the others. Like a firm in an industry, growth also is not uniform among all marketplaces, but there is consolidation within a few marketplaces, or growth is limited to a single marketplace or marketplace town. We are not advocating the creation or elevation of any existing urban marketplaces to a growth pole or growth center status but we are arguing that known existing large urban marketplaces be treated as recognizable and equally situated growth poles. They are poles in the universe of marketplaces, and having achieved the economic prominence, should be sustained to support the non-formal economy and prosperity in the said urban economy where the marketplace acts as a shield at attempts to slow down increases in urban employment and as a catalyst in promoting equality in urban income distribution. Large urban marketplaces or marketplace towns, for example, benefit from their scale and agglomeration economies in inter-urban transport services and availability of supplies that have created the imbalance with other marketplaces in the first place. Transport can serve and has served as an agglomeration economy because the construction of the (River) Niger Bridge in Onitsha and the completion of connecting highways to Lagos in the west and other cities to the east, for example, pushed Onitsha to become a prime regional commercial or marketplace city. This river port city ultimately possesses all the transport advantages it needed to become a preeminent marketplace and one of the largest in West Africa. Because of the centrifugal force that they generate, marketplaces that serve as growth poles tend to attract more traders, more goods and more buyers and the competition leads to lower prices for consumers and Onitsha markets are known for low product prices. Traders have also innovated (just like firms) to stay afloat with improving selling tactics and (collectively) sourcing goods (directly from local, national, and international manufacturers) and buying bulk produce (from farmers even before harvest) to maintain and/or improve profit margins. Applying the growth pole concept, therefore, is appropriate to these economic powerhouses and they appropriately deserve attention within urban planning and development spaces. The Built Environment journal (Janssens & Sezer, eds., 2013) produced a special edition devoted to *Marketplaces as an Urban Development Strategy*. Incidentally, the essays are mainly based on stories from Europe and China. Moreover, discussions are focused on addressing how to facilitate interaction among people and groups from different backgrounds who conduct their businesses in or patronize these open marketplaces that are often operated by immigrants and sometimes characterized by city officials as a problem and an eyesore that should not be sustained. In any case, the editors are also interested in the general role of marketplaces in the city.

With their controlling economic role in (West) African urban centers, the following discussion on delivering urban development for and centered around growth poles is divided into three areas—role of governments, role of institutions, and role of marketplace organizations. Segregating the strategies is useful in organizing our thoughts, as the achievement of these non-mutually exclusive goals requires the continuous collaboration and cooperation of all the three stakeholder groups. We must emphasize that in practice, the implementation of any or all these strategies should not minimize or affect interest in deployment of resources in additionally and separately striving to enhance the urban transport infrastructure.

Role of Government

Marketplaces as Cities, Growth Poles and MODEST Goal

(West) African governments should recognize large urban marketplace as (business) cities within (general and official) cities and place them in Urban Marketplace Development Districts designated as Growth Poles. The effective zone of the growth pole shall include areas within a ¼ mile radius from the official boundary of the marketplace, except when constrained by topography. Urban developments plans should also adopt the MODEST goal, that is the Marketplace-oriented Development Strategy. This is similar to urban mixed use developments that force residents to use transit by limiting the use of automobiles (by disallowing parking), providing wide sidewalks for pedestrians, and issuing low or reduced transit passes. The developments are known as Transit Oriented Developments, TOD, and they are effective transit use-inducing urban real estate development projects. By focusing on marketplace needs, the MODEST concept allows the marketplace to become a tool for reducing (off-peak) urban traffic problems. It is also a modest goal. Moreover, like a Special Economic Zone, with the designation as a growth pole, policy makers, planners, and development practitioners will be empowered to re-direct and pay attention to the marketplace as a separate and prominent entity in the urban economic architecture. This long-running economic entity that has been functioning as a traditional SEZ should have the necessary infrastructure and improved amenities that are aligned with the local development strategy of the general and official city wherein they are located (see Fruman and Zeng, World Bank Blog, July 27, 2015). Designated as a city within a city, government will begin to understand that the business city deserves certain facilities and amenities to allow it to properly function. Concurrently, as a growth pole in a scalable economic zone, government could redouble its efforts to support and strengthen the ability of stall traders to continue to play their role in the urban economy. There is nothing inherently bad in allowing a particular type of economic activity—tourism, chip manufacturing, the movie industry—to prosper and dominate the economy of an urban area as domination does not tantamount to elimination of others and allow it to generate necessary agglomeration effects for individuals and other sectors within its impact area. If traders break bulk in large marketplaces, then shoppers—urban, rural, and regional—get goods at better prices, and the transport sector is another beneficiary as reduced transport cost encourages increased use of transport services. This is why intercity transport operators are already benefitting from buyers who visit Onitsha and similar large urban (West) African commercial centers from within the region and other countries. The designation will send a symbolic signal to international agencies and organizations that (West) African governments are serious about consolidating the contributions of large urban marketplaces as key agents in increasing urban economic mobility in the region. As a growth pole it will also allow the center to clarify and position it to play the role of the new core source of O-D trip data points for enhanced transportation planning. Equally important, it demonstrates the pivoting of interest in addressing the vexing problem related to marketplace-transport linkage in the development process.

Create Department of Marketplaces and Traders, DMaT

Apart from designating large urban marketplaces as new urban growth poles, governments can do more. In response to international outcry against gender discrimination and a demand to recognize structural discrimination and associated subjugation of women, Africans now have a Ministry of Women Affairs and Social Development in Nigeria, 1989; Ministry of Social Welfare, Gender and Children's Affairs in Sierra Leone, 2002; Ministry of Gender in Zambia, 2012; Ministry of Gender, Children and Social Protection in Ghana, 2013, and State Department of Gender in Kenya, 2015. These cabinet-level ministries were all created by African governments in the last two decades, in response to national and international outcry to empower women. The ministries are charged with providing equality to and protection for women and children, as African governments finally realized that they were neglecting to use over 50% of its human resource capacity by perpetuating unconscionable and indefensible structural discrimination against women. The emergence of these ministries has substantially elevated the role of women in political and economic development in African countries. Collectively, the existence of the ministries has contributed to mainstream gender equality in national development. This success story is instructive.

Since, governments established the ministries to focus on women's issues today, a lot of progress has been made in incorporating gender issues into everyday development discourse. There is a glaring similarity begging for attention in the neglect of the urban marketplace in the histography of (West) African urban economy, as we now realize that it is wise for government to pursue gender equality while enforcing the rights of children (and senior citizens) under the umbrella of a government ministry dedicated to celebrate the importance of women in society. The ministries have done a good job in advocating for improvements in gender rights. All these is an illustration of how making an issue politically-visible is a catalyst in drawing public-policy attention to that issue. This is why it is of critical socio-economic importance to create a Department of Marketplaces and Traders, DMaT, to elevate the position of the marketplace institution in (West) African urban economy. The analogy rests with the understanding that presently women's issues are addressed through an apex government ministry with demonstrable societal benefits. A DMaT will allow government to better take advantage of the marketplace as a resource in urban economic development. Elevating the issue facing women and children with an authoritative voice in public policy making has contributed to achieving stated gender goals and objectives, and we draw a parallel for traders and the marketplace institution. A similar authoritative voice should be extended to the marketplace institution to demonstrate that (West) African society, its leaders and other stakeholders have a vested interest in promoting this indigenous capitalistic institution, as it is winning the power struggle with the formal economy. Continuing to ignore the importance of the marketplace institution in urban development planning is affecting the propensity of (West) African governments to improve urban transport, and focusing on large urban marketplaces (think MODEST) will also yield dividends for the transport system.

Minimize Development Leakages

This is another area of interest. Leakages in African development programs have been widely represented in the literature (JKA Ogata Sadako Research Institute, May 2013). It is mostly through negative inclusion and positive exclusion—layering departments and agencies (negative inclusion) with numerous decision points in planning and implementation of programs/projects that minimizes or eliminates (positive exclusion) the input and involvement of beneficiaries. Due to layering, information and resources are lost, wasted, or invented, and non-relevant inquiries, requests, delays and obfuscation are deployed to extract illegal favors. Meanwhile, beneficiaries whose input and buy-in are required and necessary to establish the project/program and ensure ownership thereafter are excluded to the detriment of society and donors. Oni (1999), for example, has provided a comprehensive framework for organizing and managing multi-modal transportation planning, administration, and financing in Nigeria at federal, state, and local government levels that identifies every mode and their interrelationships with the other modes to enhance integrated transportation service delivery in Nigeria. To guard against loss of project/program that will benefit traders and the marketplace, DMaT is proposed to be the single department responsible for coordinating and implementing programs and policies affecting traders and marketplaces, in consultation with relevant agencies and stake-holders. This will define and instill accountability in contracting, the key source of waste and abandonment of projects and programs in many countries in the developing areas, as contracting responsibilities will be distributed among finance and budget, and risk management offices in DMaT. With the diffusion of responsibilities strengthened by mandated coordination, inspections and annual audits within the department, the streamlining will reduce collusion that leads to fraud and waste.

Consider that the proposed institutional structure for implementing the UN Habitat-Nigeria government Onitsha-Nnewi and Awka development plan (2009) has about 20 agencies, departments and groups involved at local and state levels. The multiplicity of agencies starting from the office of the governor to local town planning authorities and eight technical working groups, TWG, including education and environment, appears to be an overkill for participatory planning. The multiplicity of authorities creates a potential source of delays in project implementation, as decisions are dragged out at each level of the decision units, even though this is reflecting the culture and diversity of power centers in the society where personal enrichment has overshadowed civic responsibility. Consulting with key individuals/groups, that is those in the acting community, is encouraged but government should not cede planning responsibilities to non-professionals with narrower community views. We are not, however, advocating complete corporatization or privatization of marketplace issues because that might replace societal benefits with corporate profits. DMaT, for example, will ensure that traders and their leadership are involved in the selection, location, and design of marketplaces, that traders are not forcibly relocated or displaced without proper rehabilitation, and that stalls are plentiful and rents affordable. The department, working with traders' representatives, will work out conditionalities for issues such as revenue collection and expenditure, facility maintenance, and security regimes at marketplaces. Such transparency will establish clear roles and responsibilities, and most important, accountability as a single agency is responsible for coordinating and maintaining policies and programs affecting large urban marketplaces. The segregation of marketplace issues and development into a distinct government department will send a strong and clear signal to traders and local and international agencies that the institution is a dependable co-equal as an engine of urban economic development.

Maintain Collaborative Development Planning

Because their key goal is to preserve the financial well-being of the family and business, encouraging traders to collaborate with public agencies/officials who they believe have not been helpful in the past could be challenging, except if they are confronted with data on how their current behavior contributes to the character of urban transport and traffic conditions, and explain how they could benefit from improved conditions. Thirty percent of stalls have a personal means of transportation but they generate a disproportionate number of trips (11,880 mean trips daily or about 4.2 million trips annually in Onitsha), demonstrating the implications of driving during work hours. Collaborating with authorities in implementing urban policies should constitute part of the exchange for an economic-oriented cum citizen-centered planning approaches for Marketplace Growth Poles. Government understands the need to involve citizens in development planning but sometimes chooses to ignore them for expediency because of unequal power relationships. This runs the gamut of widening a roadway where roadside traders and residences are affected to (re)locating and designing new urban marketplaces where developers and financial institutions and government are often leading the charge without input from traders. The alienation of citizen beneficiaries leads to citizen apathy in the upkeep of the facility upon completion or the sabotage of the project and/or process. Allowing citizens into the process from the planning stage through implementation creates pride and a sense of ownership; otherwise, after the 'government crowd' leaves, the neglected but affected citizen-beneficiaries who now have no stake in the project could resort to proverbial removing doors and windows from the structure until it falls into disrepair. As equal partners and mutual beneficiaries, government will be in a better position to discuss options for reducing trader impacts. Urban Marketplace Development District projects, integrated into the city's economic development plan, should involve representatives from marketplace leadership, the Office of the Market Master, local land use planning office, local/state DMaT and transportation departments, and outside consultants as necessary, as a core group for planning and renovation of existing marketplace or locating, designing, and constructing a new marketplace because in the end, traders will be the occupants of the facility and, therefore, they should have a voice in the process. Folks may have opinions but government has both opinion and facts in the form of empirical data. With continuous and comprehensive dialog over short- and long-range marketplace-transport linkage issues, it is conceivable that traders could reconsider and adopt the city that supports their business and provides their livelihoods as their own. Government should be playing with a team made up of all urban development players (stakeholders) and not just the captain (top state or provincial leaders) and the goal-keeper (top local elected government officials).

Upgrade Land use and Land Development Plans

A search of city and state land use zoning documents for Nigeria-yielded rates for ground rents and fees for certificate of occupancy. Perhaps, vestiges of colonial secrecy laws that made it a punishable offense for public servants to "reveal" government (public) information (that is, make it available to the public) still discourage the generous distribution of public documents. Perhaps, due to centralized planning, a similar search for Accra shows a *Zoning Guidelines and Planning Standards* published in 2011 for Ghana, but the City of Nairobi, Kenya has *A Guide of Nairobi City Development Ordinances and Zones*, with an uplifting slogan that states "in pursuit of excellence in local planning." A zoning ordinance codifies land regulations and ensures that every type of property (land) identified in the comprehensive land use plan receives the highest and best use. There are vagaries in land use control authorities and institutions in different (West) African countries, but most urban residents may not be aware of the existence of a zoning ordinance, but planners and practitioners are fully aware of the process and the existence of this implementing document. Universal access to such documents, including site plans and design requirements, will contribute to improve project delivery. To this end, local and state land use regulations should institutionalize marketplace development design standards that require the provision of necessary facilities and accommodating amenities that meet market stall operational needs to minimize urban transport problems emanating from marketplace operation. Martin Wachs, a one-time Research and Development Coordinator with the US Army Weapon Systems Laboratory conducted a survey of Chicago residents, mean family income of $14,800/year, on the effectiveness of planning and the best method for making decisions about where, when, and how to build transport facilities (see Highway Research Record, No 229, 1968). Out of six methods respondents ranked "Leave the decisions to the planners, but have them work closely with leading group of citizens before, during, and after the time when the decisions are made." The lowest ranked choice was "Give our elected officials complete power to decide which of the planners' proposals should be accepted." The desire of and prerequisite for citizens to have a say in the provision of facilities or projects is not a new idea, but it has increased over the years, as demonstrated by Thondoo, Marquet & et al. (2020) in their review of transport planning in small and big cities in the developing areas. Using Port Louis, Mauritius, they found that citizen-centered approaches provide a unique opportunity to reform urban transport planning policies in developing countries. Valuing citizen preferences through their input provides mutually assured advancement and support of policies and projects. With the input of traders, marketplaces will be designed and built at human-scale, with overhead shelters as rains are becoming more incessant and temperatures increasing due to climate change, with stalls that provide security but not enclosed within walls that will hem-in traders. The openness will reflect familiar and traditional open marketplace layout and ambiance that also are friendly to shoppers. Familiar experiences, such as zoning of goods, should be encouraged to reduce search cost for goods, relatives, and friends and an open market ambiance that invites customers into the marketplace. Planners and architects should be sensitive to the sense of scale, temerity, and navigational skills of, especially shoppers from the hinterland. And access within the ¼ mile of the marketplace urban development zone should be a development priority, recognizing that areas beyond that (arbitrary) boundary are typically subject to the effects of distance decay function.

Role of Institutions

Legitimize the Non-Formal Economy

To many, the term "informal" may connote inferior, subpar, and perhaps to some critics, illegal, but the stigmatization has stuck and has propagated the wholesale economic discrimination of activities majorly found in the Global South, and to pile on, it is acceptable that several activities in the underground economy are aptly described as and lumped in as part of the informal economy. One method of segregating illegal underground economic activities from legal socially acceptable economic activities is to apply the term non-formal to activities such as marketplace trade to differentiate it from the formal economy, as an opposite but equal and legitimate form of economic activity. The International Labour Organization has recently suggested the use of the term informal economy, instead of the previous term informal sector. The organization is also working to promote and elevate the importance of informal activities, therefore, we suggest another transition—apply the term "non-formal" to describe those activities previously mixed in together with other activities in the informal economy basket. The re-tagging will further demonstrate legitimization of marketplace trade and other activities and remove the stigma of perceived economic inferiority and backwardness unintentionally and unconsciously ascribed to it, especially when is not even clear why the existing 'informal' label was assigned to the vast economic activity that incidentally is most prevalent in the Global South,[1] any justifications in the literature notwithstanding.

Trips made by traders sustain the vibrancy of the urban economy, and we do not expect their trip character to undergo any rapid changes; therefore, what is needed is introspection, more so during the ongoing global yearning for social justice, to borrow from Werner Sengenberger at ILO. With value introspection—in academia, policy making arena, and development institutions—the suggestion to legitimize the sector with a more professionally-responsible and equitable label will become more acceptable and adoptable and, like the famous son of a lion in a popular movie, the non-formal economy and marketplace trade will regain its rightful place in Pride Lands known as linkages to urban transport and relationships to urban development, and create benefits that, as a strategic position, will become self-evident. Some critics would suggest that the bias is partly responsible for why we have not invested to explore the contributory power of marketplaces as sources of unrelenting traffic problems in these areas and a missing link in integrated urban development. The Global North should again serve as a catalyst for this overdue introspection. Understanding and integrating the travel behavior

---

[1] In the 1999–2002 World Happiness Report, the happiest countries were found in the periphery—Nigeria, Mexico, Venezuela, and El Salvador, despite their high levels of poverty when respondents were simply asked to rate how happy they were in their lives. Thereafter, it became a quality-of-life question where such qualifiers such as levels of GDP, trust, and corruption, life expectancy were added and suddenly, as a predictable design change, the happiest countries shifted to the center that is populated by countries with high-income levels—Finland, Denmark, Switzerland, and Iceland—quite a clever modification.

of non-formal economy actors in those high activity centers into the transportation planning process and urban development will begin to support future improvements of overall urban economic conditions in (West) Africa.

The OECD has projected that by 2050, about half the population of Africa will be living in cities, more properly population centers, given the absence of adequate urban services (roads, water, and electricity) available to those residents. Alarm bells are also being sounded by experts at the World Bank that African cities need to open their doors to manufacturing to ensure that economic growth keeps pace with population growth. When paired with local processing of major raw materials for export, necessary urban improvements can occur in (West) African countries. The agglomeration effects will contribute to reduce unemployment and underemployment, as it expands formal employment; otherwise, the marketplace non-formal economy traders will continue to maintain their grip on (West) African urban economy with attendant un-patterned urban travel profiles.

Support for Differentiation of Non-Manufacturing Sector Actors

A different role is reserved for researchers who act as influencers. As mentioned earlier, there is a tendency to group different non-manufacturing activities together into that all-encompassing non-formal economy category, with differentiation often reserved only for farm activities. With that typology, pavement capitalists and other peddlers are often mixed in with established traders and described as petty traders. Most studies on informal economy or micro-entrepreneurs have also tended to focus on small-scale manufacturing firms. It gives the impression that small-scale non-manufacturing non-formal economy entrepreneurs are not contributing or are not usefully present in the economy. The bias continues even though when growth in employment is measured for West African countries, commerce (wholesale, retail, hotel, and restaurants) has a comparatively high score as other sectors such as Transport, or Finance (World Bank, 2018: 32–33), but when productivity is the focus, commerce of course quickly falls out of favor. It is perhaps difficult to quantify the value of say the happiness or satisfaction in out-haggling the trader (seller) and accomplishment derived by that buyer who found a good pair of shoes and fabric for her traditional wedding at a good price. As a result, trading tends to have low or no productivity index that economists tend to discount to help them to undervalue the non-formal sector. For example, does the multiplier effect of money spent by shoppers add value to that currency or the economy? As an illustration, Rafael La Porta of Tuck School of Business at Dartmouth and Andrei Shleifer of Harvard University (2014), in their work on informality and development in developing economies, appear dismissive of non-firm entrepreneurs when they describe them as "proverbial sellers of flowers and vegetables." They provide extensive data and comparative analysis in such areas as efficiency, productivity, and value-added to demonstrate the superiority of even informal manufacturers over informal "self-employed sellers and peddlers living at near-subsistence levels." Manufacturing has always been promoted as the engine of economic development and growth since it powered the industrial revolution and shunted its way to the front of human economic activity in Europe back in the 18th Century and gradually displaced other activities as the rightful economic development activity. There have been changes in technology and diversification in economic activities but that has not widened that cone of vision that still justifies the promotion and preference for small-scale, even low-level, non-formal manufacturers over entrepreneurs in other non-formal areas of human endeavors, irrespective of the similarity in size of business, for example. The personal but widely accepted convictions of Tuck and Shleifer notwithstanding, we have established that some of these self-employed sellers are key players in the urban economy of (West) African countries and should be celebrated as shining examples of capitalism at work and presented as assets, and not lumped together with pavement capitalists and quickly disposed of in the literature to leap into extolling only the benefits of even low-level manufacturing in the same Global South.

A World Bank publication (2003) reminds readers that being an African reduces the chance of an individual being in the manufacturing sector by 95%, suggesting that the African (urban) economy after all is not dominated by manufacturing, formal, or informal. The universal misconception of the irrelevance of non-formal economy entrepreneurs encourages researchers to often not disaggregate sellers and conveniently categorize all sellers as subsistence workers. The non-differentiation makes it easy for other researchers and planners to not pay attention to groups such as marketplace-stall traders who are embedded within the strata. Neglecting their worth in the economic fabric of society, for example, is discouraging the flow of targeted and trader-centric financial support to participants to allow growth. Elsewhere, a World Bank publication (2017) talks about drawing manufacturing firms and skilled workers to a livable urban African environment as a method of making African cities "economically dense." Very true, but as we have pointed out, trading has been an indigenous economic activity that even sustained large (West) African empires and today's urban economies. Market-stall traders in large urban markets in (West) African countries should be studied and differentiated from sellers of flowers and other street peddlers. They are contributing to increase the rate of income distribution and economic mobility. Research institutions can also assist in minimizing the unequal treatment meted out to small-scale non-manufacturing entrepreneurs engaged in distributive trade to jettison their consideration in local urban development discourse and universe.

Create an Enabling Environment

From legitimization to differentiation, and next is how institutions can enable indigenous marketplace-stall traders in their quest to make the marketplace institution a part of the urban development agenda. The World Bank, UN-Habitat for Humanity, the OECD, the International Labor Organization, and Brookings, to name a few organizations that are interested in development in the Global South, have independently or in collaboration with several African institutions, such as the African Development Bank and governments produced reports and plans for development projects and programs to benefit countries, regions, and selected cities. Apart from the other areas of interest, these reports routinely address issues also related to the non-formal economy and provide generalized and individualized recommendations. We are suggesting that they go further—openly and specifically recognize the marketplace institution and elevate and focus on it as a major economic development institution in (West) Africa. This would stimulate additional discussions of that elusive concept of marketplace-urban transport dyad that forms the foundation for MODEST, as we earlier discussed.

Jean-Claude Bolay (2015) has evaluated alternative urban planning processes that would benefit the African poor. The author notes that cities of the South are almost always considered less "modern" than Western cities, but the same cities, at an extremely rapid pace, are being inserted into the world of economic globalization. The author is concerned that this is leading to growing tensions between urban authorities and their local interests, and formal and non-formal entrepreneurs, and their constituent supporters we will add. These constituents are individuals, organizations, agencies, and institutions who are promoting their favorite causes or priorities. Bolay argues that urban planning that does not promote megaprojects and cause further marginalization in employment, and land use deterioration, as in contributing to global warming, will promote the welfare of the poor. Africa has become a battleground for megaprojects funded by international interests. Simply put, as part of the insertion into economic globalization, there appears to be another Scramble for Africa but this time to construct infrastructures to connect regions and produce African transformation in power generation, transport, and telecommunication (OECD/ACET, 2020) that will position the continent in the supply chain for a global economy and benefit the same foreign investors. In a report *Quality Infrastructure in 21st Century Africa*, the OECD Development Center and the African Center for Economic Transformation are concerned that the Chinese are front and center to serve Africa's projected population that will be one-quarter of the world's total population by 2050, and in sub-Saharan Africa, where the population will be double by above 1 billion in 30 years. The report observes, for example, that "Africa still needs significant infrastructure investments to boost universal access to digital infrastructure." As a result, it has developed an Infrastructure Business Model 2.0 to counter and replace the rather less inclusive and flawed Chinese investments processes, even as the document recognizes that China "currently commits more infrastructure finance to Africa than all other external sources combined," mainly meaning Europe and America. This new frame work is quite impressive and progressive as it will "Apply structure and time frames to the upstream processes for project and programme development, integrating quality issues – environmental, social and governance (ESG) – economic linkages and job creation, social returns, community consultations and financial modelling" in project implementation that is quite suitable for the modern times. Integrating those areas of human livability and conditions into project development will be an upgrade and achievement for the continent, as the most important infrastructure are people. One important point is that these megaprojects are likely to overburden African governments with loans that will further impinge on the level of poverty on the continent, some critics would argue is precisely the purpose of such policy in order to burden Africa and maintain long range economic dominance. It is refreshing, however, that the revised delivery process for these projects includes employing local African labor, than imported labor and material, because that will add value to people's lives, the human infrastructure, as these are some of the same people whose governments will be paying back the project loans for a long time. The first Scramble for Africa brought a religious belief that taught Africans to offer the other cheek when they are hit by an adversary while those who preached the religion were armed to the teeth to preserve their investments and access to appropriate local resources. This time around, while increased access to power, communication and transport will enhance the business of marketplace traders, investing in marketplace needs, a people-centered strategy, with similar vigor, for example, by modernizing existing marketplaces will provide meaningful community benefits and contribute to real economic transformation for Africans who are engaged in distributive trade, the doyens of the urban economy, to establish a fairer power relationships between Africans and these new investors. Ultimately, as many Africans intersect with the marketplace on a daily basis, they will immediately feel the uplift at this major urban economic space. Perhaps, these infrastructure projects should be linked to enhancing marketplaces, as part of a separate Infrastructure Business Model 3.0 to create an enabling environment for marketplace traders and the institution. Very often, the institution falls outside the radar of purveyors of development projects on the African continent, despite its strategic position in the economy. Some may argue that taxes paid by operators of these telecommunications and power services, for example, should be used to build and/or upgrade local projects, but the same individuals should be reminded about the rate at which public funds tend to disappear in public hands in many of these countries. The work of Stephanie Hanson (2019), Council on Foreign Relations, is illustrative of the corruption levels in Africa, mainly because existing weak institutions are incapable of combating the problem. In any case, the linkage will remind entities who will benefit from the African infrastructure market (market = people who will consume the services and generate returns for investors) that outside of the much familiar and celebrated pavement capitalists, there are presently marketplace-stall entrepreneurs who are unknowingly addressing current urban job market issues and improving income distribution, and bearing the burden of sustaining the urban economy. Owners of infrastructure development projects in Africa should enter into a social contract with the people, and also advocate for and/or provide direct resources to upgrade internal marketplace-stall operation because it will benefit all users found in the universe of the African urban economic space. Carving out spheres of interest for infrastructure investment purveyors as part of the Scramble for Africa 2.0 is reminiscent of the 1884–1885 Berlin Conference that regulated and formalized colonization for a different type of purveyors and carved up Africa for European trading interests whose detrimental effects are still felt on the continent today. This time there should be efforts at the people's-first principle by creating linkages that would promote and support the interests of locals, such as technology transfer (for formal manufacturers) and improving the welfare of entrepreneurs who are currently holding up (West) African urban economy. Some critics might argue that it is plausible that with improved and assured power and communication supplies, coming right behind will be large international business conglomerates who will muscle their way into local distributive trade and replace marketplaces and traders, as they import and directly retail to locals.

At another level, these infrastructure development promoters and supporting institutions could consider funding studies and pilot projects for a better understanding of the dynamics of large (West) African urban markets and show how practitioners could accommodate the activities of large marketplace-stall traders in urban development. The need for such vigorous and serious evaluations are long overdue to strengthen that major (West) African urban economic engine. It is expected that a capital project that upgrades an existing large urban market and improves access roads within ¼ mile perimeter or constructs a new or modern urban market will attract additional private sector investment, in addition to increasing sales, profits, and income in the local economy. The acceptance of this challenge will be transformative in overall economy of (West) African countries. On the other hand, de-marketizing (West) African urban areas by continuously emphasizing small-scale manufacturers and ignoring out those in successful distributive trade or constructing large shopping malls/plazas to "modernize" African urban shopping landscape are anathema to what is needed in these areas. This is, especially discouraged, given the history of sub-urban malls in the West where they are now out-of-sync with emerging smart growth principles, shopping habits, and concerns over global warming. A modern open marketplace with necessary amenities will be a breath of fresh air because of the ambiance, easy accessibility, and user-friendliness.

ROLE OF MARKETPLACE TRADERS

Support Education of Traders

For the strategies to manage marketplace-transport linkage through enhanced urban development processes to succeed, or for the concept of MODEST to succeed, part of it requires that traders change their attitude, a behavioral change that could be effectively achieved through supportive education. Consider this. Assuming there are five (5) occupants in each stall, Onitsha market traders would dump about 17.4 million trips annually on the transport system; three (3) occupants per stall would yield 13.4 million mean trips while two (2) occupants would result in 9.0 million out-of-stall contacts that the transport system would have to accommodate every year. Ordinarily, this would attract the attention of development experts and planners, but first there must be a recognition and acceptance that this phenomenon is even taking place daily in real-world economic life of humans in (West) Africa. There should also be a parallel change in the attitude of researchers and other stakeholders who are urged to better understand the interrelationship between large marketplaces and urban transport.

Regarding those who have a personal means of transportation available to the stall: the attribute has a disproportionate impact on urban traffic. For stalls without a personal means of transportation, at 95% CI (confidence interval for the mean), they produce 1.7 to 2.3 trips, but for those who have just one (1) means of personal transportation, the numbers jump to between 3.7 and 4.9 trips. It will be surprising to traders to learn that those who have up to two means of personal transportation available to the stall produce the most impact on urban traffic—with 5.6 mean daily trips/stall and ranging between 3.2 and 8.0 trips, when there are no means of personal transportation available to about 70% of stalls. When this type of fact is shared with traders, it will resonate because it is a true representation of their daily business experience. They may be intrigued because there has never been an opportunity accorded them through participation to discuss research results and initiate them into the nuances of the development planning process, despite their critical mass. Discouraging the use of personal means of transportation must be tempered with increasing other travel options.

When confronted with facts, different people react differently but consciously most tend to admit error and are willing to enter a meaningful discussion about how to address the problem. If the issue is related to the number of occupants in the stall, government should not decree a reduction in stall size without providing sufficient supplementary stall spaces when traders learn that the third occupant is the worst offender in contributing to marketplace-transport linkage problems. By providing additional stall space appropriate for different sellers, government will be improving the character of urban traffic in cities with large marketplaces. We acknowledge other contributors to road traffic problems such as narrow roads, the mixing of traffic, absence of intersection and traffic controls but additional information regarding how traders exacerbate those problems should be a part of the discussion. If the road is narrow and you have fewer users, road traffic problem jumps into another scale. Traders should also be a part of deliberations related to planning and implementation of urban development projects. Understanding, contributing, collaborating, and exercising participatory management are elements that will engender buy-in from market-stall traders regarding developments within the proposed Urban Marketplace Development Districts currently occupied by traders.

Consider Financial Support for Marketplace Infrastructure

We know that the longer a market-stall trader spends in the stall, the better for the urban transport system and perhaps their pocketbooks, and providing amenities within the confines of the marketplace will contribute to make that happen. As studies in Ghana (Nezic & Carr, 1996) show traders are willing to contribute money to improve marketplace conditions such as transport, health, and safety services. Similarly, the International Labour Organization (2002: 76) has found that informal sector workers are often willing to pay for access to water, sanitation, and waste disposal at their work sites in South, Southeast, and East Asian cities. It is certainly plausible that Onitsha and other (West) African traders will be willing to consider financial contribution to improve conditions in the marketplace. But then there is the issue of trust. If government unilaterally built a new market and decided the rent for stall space, some well-heeled individuals will rent several spaces and sublet those spaces to several sellers, and that will defeat the purpose of reducing marketplace impact on transport by building a new market with additional stalls. However, should traders, government, international development agencies, and private developers collaboratively plan and build such a facility, traders will provide input for minimizing stall allocation problems because they have a financial and reputational stake in the project. In other words, allowing traders to contribute financial and moral support in providing market facilities will go a long way to elevate and deepen the interest of traders in addressing local traffic problems. The collaboration will contribute to develop that elusive mutual trust between government and traders. In several urban and semi-urban, and perhaps large rural communities, there are structures labeled marketplaces that are constructed by government and communities that merely consist of a roof propped up by four poles holding the corrugated zinc roof. The floor space and walkways between the row of shelters are not graded or paved. Often what you find is that traders or sellers will string out along the roadway adjacent to the same corrugated zinc and pole-designated new marketplace to sell their wares to the detriment and disappointment of the entity responsible for erecting the structure. One of the reasons is that the beneficiaries never participated in the planning and design of the facility and in the absence of meeting their needs the disengagement forces petty traders to shun the structure in favor of the open roadside to display and hawk their goods.

Studies, for example, have shown that traders have not benefitted from micro-finance loan programs to allow them to grow their business, and programs such as 'Tradermoni' or *mali kauli* practice in Dar es Salaam that are so small to effect any changes. A cynic might wonder whether the lack of national and international financial support for urban market traders is a deliberate strategy to force traders to stay small to allow formal manufacturing to take over as the mainstay of the urban economy. This is a fair debate to be had as part of (West) African urban development discourse in the twenty-first century. Urban market-stall traders deserve public policy-based and structured financial support to grow and prosper.

Empanel and Empower an Urban Marketplace Development District Committee (UMDDC)

A recurring problem in some (West) African cities is the mysterious fire accidents that destroy existing marketplaces. Shopping plazas often replace the previous traditional market, and these modern plazas tend to have fewer shops and command higher floor space rent. As members of the UMDDC marketplace traders should participate in regeneration planning to replace open markets that were destroyed by fire with a modern version that protects sellers and buyers from the elements. It will give members of the UMDDC—union representatives, local and state government representatives such as transportation, economic development and land use, and citizen groups—the opportunity to collaboratively identify and provide appropriate replacement structure and associated amenities to delink marketplaces from urban transport to minimize their impact. This is where interested international development agencies could also play a role—sponsor urban development loans to assist in arresting the de-marketization trend in urban (West) Africa—by refocusing attention on upgrading and modernizing indigenous urban marketplaces. Such unique urban renewal opportunity will demonstrate that the quad—government, traders' representatives, developers, and international development agencies/institutions—recognizes the equally relevant and significant economic contribution of non-manufacturing activities of the marketplace institution.

Finally, the Sub-Saharan Africa Transport (Policy) Program (SSATP), Africa's leading transport policy forum that is an international partnership of 40 African countries, 8 regional economic communities, and two African institutions, is working to provide sustainable and safe transport in Africa, in collaboration with the World Bank. It has developed forward-looking proposals for sustainable accessibility and mobility for African urban areas (Stucki, 2015). It is anticipated that perhaps governments would adopt the EASI (Enable, Avoid, Shift, Improve) conceptual framework developed by SSATP as a robust guide for public action that is designed to achieve sustainable accessibility and mobility in urban areas of Africa. The actions will improve urban transport, hasten, and contribute to maximize benefits for marketplace traders, if paired with marketplace improvements. Their recommendations, summarized by EASI, include creating preconditions for continued participation by civil society in development of transport systems, providing adequate human and financial resources, reducing opportunities for individual-ized motorized travel through adequate land use-transport planning and management, and increasing modal share for public transport and non-motorized mode while improving efficiency and safety (Improve). On the whole, the framework promotes improved efficiencies in governance, land use, use of public transport, walking, bicycling, and the use of road space. Marketplace stall traders who produce so much urban traffic can reduce road space use by spending less time interacting with the road system. This is where the need for adequate land use-transport planning and management becomes critical because the marketplace has a key role to play when it is considered a major land use that interfaces with urban transport, hence the MODEST concept. Suppose a parking structure (or even a parking lot) were a part of remodeling and modernization of an existing large urban marketplace, traders' representatives should be a part of the committee that determines surcharges for traders to park their automobiles in the structure to dissuade single-occupant vehicle drivers from using the structure, an idea that the EASI framework supports, together with encouraging a civil society participation. The same UMDDC members will also participate in providing oversight for contract award and monitoring construction to ensure project completion and accountability. In collaboration with DMaT staff, they could serve as a voice in securing financial support for traders. Members will be expected to participate in setting up maintenance and security services for marketplaces to deter future fires and burglaries. The Public–Private-Partnership, P3, so created, another EASI recommendation on improving efficiency in governance, will increase trust and strengthen marketplace institution-government relationships. Members can be encouraged to promote and sponsor an Adopt-a-Street (to the marketplace) program and contribute to the maintenance and upkeep of selected roadways within the Urban Marketplace Development District. Such roads should be upgraded to have shoulders, pedestrian walkways or sidewalks, road signs, and street lights to announce entry into the district that houses the marketplace and the Urban Marketplace Development District, an urban area's economic activity center.

Conclusions

This is an attempt to differentiate the traveling salesmen/pavement capitalists' petty traders from marketplace-stall traders who have permanent business locations and are climbing into the middle-income class. Petty traders are often found in (West) African rural and urban marketplaces and they tend to occupy the interest of most researchers, policy makers, and the international community interested in addressing poverty issues in (West) Africa. The strategic position of marketplace stall traders in the urban economy has allowed them the opportunity to provide employment and reduce urban income inequality, but their contributions to the (West) African urban economy have often gone un-noticed.

However, their management and operational styles have created travel characteristics that suggest the presence of a linkage between large urban marketplaces and transport, also an un-noticed impact and contribution to the state of urban transport structure. Accepting the existence of this relationship is the first step in elevating and then addressing problems related to marketplace-transport dyad. Despite these observable impacts, development experts and policy makers have not incorporated marketplaces into urban development policies through a Marketplace-oriented Development Strategy and plans and, that is the source of the paradox. The majorly un-patterned economic structure (non-formal economy) in (West) Africa and other developing areas in the Global South is reflected in an un-patterned traffic structure resulting from the differently structured socio-economic frameworks. To survive the cut-throat competition embedded in this un-patterned capitalistic non-formal economic system, traders have developed complex socio-economic relationships within the marketplace institution. These complex socio-economic relationships serve as a centrifugal force that generates all-day stall-based (irregular) trips that result in what some Westerners may label as "chaotic" traffic system. Designing new marketplaces or modernizing existing marketplaces as part of an urban development process and placing marketplaces at appropriate locations will contribute to improve urban traffic and the urban transport system. This can be achieved by institutionalizing marketplace planning and design standards into the urban land development process. A large urban marketplace occupies a strategic command post as an indigenous economic powerhouse that will continue to contribute to reduce urban employment and income inequality for a long time; therefore, addressing the internal marketplace needs of traders will produce positive externality on the urban transport system. It is up to planners, researchers, development experts, practitioners, and policy makers to reimagine the location of the marketplace in (West) African development space to effectively address the paradox of the marketplace in urban development.

Planners, development experts, and policy makers cannot achieve this goal alone. But planners must first repurpose the existing urban transportation planning process to rely on residents in the un-official Marketplace City to serve as the core data source for appropriate transportation planning in (West) Africa. The re-purposing and re-integration is long overdue, given that a large proportion of employment in these areas is in the non-formal economy led by those in distributive trade who value non-home-based trips over home-to-work trips. Trader education, collaboration, and support are also essential for continued vitality of the urban economy. International agencies and institutions, who are interested in (West) African infrastructure development are encouraged to lend their academic, social, and financial capital in elevating the significance of urban market-stall traders in urban development to complement the work efforts of the International Labour Organization in that context. There are no reasons to believe that the findings and recommendation for improved urban development outlined herein to benefit marketplace traders and the institution in Onitsha, Nigeria should not be applicable, adaptable and useful to other (West) African countries with large urban marketplaces.

REFERENCES

Bolay, J. C. (2015, December). Urban planning in Africa: Which alternative for poor cities? The case of Koudougou in Burkina Faso. *Current Urban Studies, 3*, 413–432. https://doi.org/10.4236/cus.2015.34033

Fields, G. S., & Pfeffermann. G. (Eds.). (2003). *Pathways Out of Poverty: Private Firms and Economic Mobility in Developing Countries*. The World Bank/Kluwer Academic Publishers. © World Bank. https://openknowledge. worldbank.org/handle/10986/25896 License: CC BY 3.0 IGO.

Fruman, C., & Zeng, D. Z. (2015, July 27). *How to make zones work better.* World Bank Private Sector Development Blog.

Haile, F. H. (2018). *Structural change in West Africa: A tale of gain and loss. Policy Research Working Paper; No. 8336.* © World Bank. https://openkn owledge.worldbank.org/handle/10986/29370 License: CC BY 3.0 IGO.

Hanson, S. (2019, August 6). *Corruption in Sub-Saharan Africa*, Foreign Affairs, Council on Foreign Relations.

International Labour Organization. (2002). *The informal sector in Asia from the decent work perspective.* ILO.

Janssens, F., & Sezer, C. (2013). Marketplaces as an urban Development strategy. *Built Environment, 39*(2), Special Issue.

JKA Ogata Sadako Research Institute for Peace and Development. (2013, May). *Development challenges in Africa Towards 2020,* Fifth Tokyo International Conference on Africa Development.

Lall, S. V., Vernon, H. J., Venables, & Anthony, J. (2017). *Africa's cities: Opening doors to the world.* © World Bank. https://openknowledge.worldb ank.org/handle/10986/25896 License: CC BY 3.0 IGO.

Nezic, T., & Kerr, W. A. (1996). A market community development in West Africa. *Community Development Journal, 31*(1), 1–12.

OECD/ACET. (2020). *Quality infrastructure in 21st Century Africa. Prioritising, accelerating and scaling up in the context of PIDA (2021–30).*

Oni, S. I. (1999*). Urban transportation at state and local government levels.* Paper presented at the Sixth International Conference on Competition and Ownership in Land Passenger Transport.

Porta, R. L., & Shleifer, A. (2014). Informality and development. *Journal of Economic Perspectives, 23*(3), 109–126.

Stucki, M. S. (2015). *Policies for sustainable accessibility and mobility in urban areas of Africa.* Sub-Saharan Africa Transport Policy Program (SSATP); Working Paper No. 106. © World Bank. https://openknowledge.worldbank. org/handle/10986/24089 License: CC BY 3.0 IGO.

Thondoo, O., Marquet, S., Márquez, S., & Nieuwenhuijsen, M. J. (2020). Small cities, big needs: Urban transport planning in cities of developing countries. *Journal of Transport & Health, 19*,. https://doi.org/10.1016/j.jth.2020. 100944

Wachs, M. (1968). A survey of citizens' opinions of the effectiveness, needs, and techniques of urban transportation planning. In Highway Research Record, *Transportation system planning and current census: Techniques for planning, 229,* 65–76.

Appendix

Correlation Matrix Tables

Location: CBD

	Y	X_1	X_2	X_3	X_4	X_5	X_6
TOTRPS	1.00	.53	.51	.04	−.11	−.06	−.09
VEHAVA		1.00	.28	−.06	−.24	.01	.01
NEMP			1.00	−.01	−.15	.25	−.10
TEXTI				1.00	−.23	−.28	−.28
FOODS					1.00	−.20	−.20
READY						1.00	−.26
HARD							1.00

Location: Express Road

	Y	X_1	X_2	X_3	X_4	X_5	X_6
TOTRPS	1.00	.37	.33	−.24	−.09	−.04	.25
VEHAVA		1.00	.43	−.15	−.15	−.18	−.18
NEMP			1.00	−.12	−.24	−.17	.09
TEXTI				1.00	−.22	−.19	−.21
FOODS					1.00	−.28	−.22
READY						1.00	−.26
HARD							1.00

© The Editor(s) (if applicable) and The Author(s), under exclusive
license to Springer Nature Switzerland AG 2022
K. Ochia, *Marketplace Trade and West African Urban Development*,
https://doi.org/10.1007/978-3-030-87556-5

NEMP

	Υ	X_1	X_2	X_3	X_4	X_5	X_6	X_7
TOTRPS	1.00	−.12	−.04	.11	−.06	−.37	.48	.48
FOODS		1.00	−.25	−.25	−.22	.10	−.23	−.23
READY			1.00	−.25	−.22	−.00	−.10	−.10
HARD				1.00	−.23	.00	.01	.10
TEXTI					1.00	−.13	−.02	−.08
LOC						1.00	−.36	−.23
NEMP							1.00	.43
VEHAVA								1.00

PETRPS

	Υ	X_1	X_2	X_3	X_4	X_5	X_6	X_7	X_8	X_9
TOTRPS	1.00	−.12	−.04	.11	−.06	−.37	.48	.00	.26	.20
FOODS		1.00	−.25	−.25	−.22	.10	−.27	.41	−.34	−.14
READY			1.00	−.25	−.22	−.00	−.09	−.09	−.03	.05
HARD				1.00	−.23	.00	.16	−.17	.07	.06
TEXTI					1.00	−.13	−.09	.14	−.07	−.05
LOC						1.00	−.27	.00	−.14	−.24
PETRPS							1.00	−.31	.44	.27
NMALES								1.00	.46	−.16
NFEMS									1.00	−.28
MAFEMS										1.00

MAFEMS

	Υ	X_1	X_2	X_3	X_4	X_5	X_6	X_7
TOTRPS	1.00	−.13	−.04	.11	−.06	−.37	.48	.20
FOODS		1.00	−.26	−.26	−.23	.10	−.24	−.14
READY			1.00	−.26	−.23	−.00	−.11	−.06
HARD				1.00	−.23	.00	.11	.06
TEXTI					1.00	−.13	−.08	−.05
LOC						1.00	−.23	.24
VEHAVA							1.00	.20
MAFEMS								1.00

NMALES

	Υ	X_1	X_2	X_3	X_4	X_5	X_6	X_7
TOTRPS	1.00	−.09	.45	.13	−.06	−.35	.03	−.03
FOODS		1.00	−.22	−.26	−.24	.06	.40	−.26
VEHAVA			1.00	.09	−.06	−.20	−.30	−.13
HARD				1.00	−.22	−.00	−.17	−.24
TEXTI					1.00	−.15	.13	−.23
LOC						1.00	−.03	.03
NMALES							1.00	−.10
READY								1.00

NFEMS

	Υ	X_1	X_2	X_3	X_4	X_5	X_6	X_7
TOTRPS	1.00	−.09	.45	.36	.13	−.06	.36	−.03
FOODS		1.00	−.22	−.41	−.26	−.24	−.06	−.26
VEHAVA			1.00	.56	.09	−.06	−.20	−.13
NFEMS				1.00	.13	−.09	−.24	−.02
HARD					1.00	−.22	−.00	−.24
TEXTI						1.00	−.15	−.23
LOC							1.00	.03
READY								1.00

INDEX

Lightning Source UK Ltd.
Milton Keynes UK
UKHW010729271222
414464UK00001B/173

9 783030 875589